T5-ARI-881

The author: Cyril Greenland is Professor
Emeritus, McMaster University, Hamilton, Ontario.

PREVENTING CAN DEATHS

PREVENTING
CAN
DEATHS

*An international study of deaths
due to child abuse and neglect*

CYRIL GREENLAND

TAVISTOCK PUBLICATIONS
LONDON AND NEW YORK

First published in 1987 by
Tavistock Publications Ltd
11 New Fetter Lane, London EC4P 4EE

Published in the USA by
Tavistock Publications
in association with Methuen, Inc.
29 West 35th Street, New York NY 10001

© 1987 Cyril Greenland

Typeset by Boldface Typesetters, London EC1
Printed in Great Britain

British Library Cataloguing in Publication Data

Greenland, Cyril.
  Preventing CAN deaths: an international   HV
  study of deaths due to child abuse and   6626.5
  neglect.
  1. Child abuse   .G74
  I. Title   1987
  362.7'044   HV715

ISBN 0–422–61210–3

Library of Congress Cataloging in Publication Data

Greenland, Cyril.
  Preventing CAN deaths.

Bibliography: p.
Includes index.
  1. Child abuse – Cross-cultural studies. 2. Abused
children – Mortality – Cross-Cultural studies. 3. Child
abuse – Prevention. I. Title. [DNLM: 1. Child abuse –
prevention & control. 2. Mortality. WA 320 G814p]
  HV6626.5.G74 1987   362.7'046   87–17983
ISBN 0–422–61210–3

A package containing details of the sources of data used in this study, a
register of cases and a list of reports of inquiries into child-abuse and
neglect deaths is available, post free, at a cost of £5.00 ($10.00) from the
author Dr C. Greenland, c/o Tavistock Publications Ltd, 11 New Fetter
Lane, London EC4P 4EE.

For Jane,
our children,
grandchildren
and
for the love of children
everywhere.

Contents

List of tables

Preface

The decision to study child-abuse deaths was fortuitous. Initially my aim was to demonstrate the efficacy of a high-risk check list developed in an earlier study of lethal family situations (Greenland 1980a). However, for reasons which are no longer important, it proved impossible to gain access to case records in Canada or in the UK, or to the necessary research funds. So, in order to continue this line of research, it was necessary to proceed in another direction. The opportunity to do so occurred when Professor Rolf Olsen invited me to submit a proposal for a Ph.D thesis to be undertaken in the Department of Social Administration at the University of Birmingham. My thesis, lugubriously titled, 'Deaths due to child abuse and neglect in the UK, USA and Canada: the identification and management of lethal family situations', was designed to answer three main questions:

1   Can high-risk situations be identified in advance in order to prevent the tragedy of child-abuse deaths?
2   Is it possible to identify concepts or strategies which might enable social workers, nurses, and physicians to protect vulnerable children without increasing the risk of disrupting the lives of families and children who are unlikely to suffer severe injury or death?
3   Do existing guidelines, regulations, or legislation enable the relevant professionals to intervene effectively and selectively in order to protect high-risk children?

Since the doctoral thesis, completed in 1984, was approved by the external examiners, Dr Margaret A. Lynch, Senior Lecturer in Community Paediatrics, Guy's Hospital, London, and Dr Selwyn Smith, Professor of Psychiatry, University of Ottawa, both distinguished specialists in the field of child abuse, it can be assumed that they were not entirely dissatisfied with my answers. Perhaps it was for this reason that Professor Rolf Olsen encouraged me to transform the thesis into a book.

While the study of child-abuse deaths was not entirely trouble free, it had many advantages. Most obvious was the consensus that they were indeed high-risk cases. Also, by virtue of the inquests, inquiries, criminal trials, the records of these tragedies, being in the public realm, were available for research purposes. Once the research was under way, colleagues, especially the Chief Coroner of Ontario, and the pathologists, paediatricians, police, and social workers, were extraordinarily generous in providing supplementary information. Having completed the research, I also had the good fortune of being invited to share my conclusions with colleagues in many interdisciplinary seminars and workshops in the UK and Canada. This experience renewed my resepct and admiration for the front-line workers, their supervisors and managers. They all share the awesome responsibility of handling child-abuse cases with exceedingly meagre resources. Their pressing need for practical information and useful concepts was high on my list of priorities in writing this book. However, in responding to them, I am conscious of disappointing some of my academic colleagues who, quite properly, place a higher value on theoretical discourse than on the blood and guts of professional practice.

Although this topic will be considered later, it is necessary to mention the highly selective public response to reports of child-abuse deaths. Particularly puzzling is the explosion of concern when a child in the care of or under the supervision of a child-welfare agency is seriously injured or killed. Amplified by the attention of the news media, this concern is quickly transformed into public outrage. The result is a transfer of hostility from the assailant who struck the fatal blow to the social workers who failed to protect the child from harm. In essence, this is what happened following the deaths of Maria Colwell in 1973, Kim Anne Popen in 1976, and Jasmine Beckford in 1984. In Canada, as well as in the UK, the public censure resulting from these deaths had an extremely damaging effect on the practice of social work. As with the practice of defensive medicine, defensive social work leads to unthinking adherence to procedures designed to protect the staff and their employers rather than to promote the client's best interest.

It can, of course, be argued that by projecting the blame for child-abuse deaths on to the social workers rather than on to an inequitable social system, the news industry serves its class interests by sabotaging a particularly vulnerable part of the welfare state. But apart from the traditional muck-raking role of the press, it seems naïve to underestimate the public consternation and outrage which erupts following the violent death of children. These phenomena are conceptualized by Rutstein, Berenberg, Chalmers, *et al.* (1976), as 'sentinel' events which are 'preventable and signal a failure in the health care system'. Kotelchuck (1984: 114) adds that ' "Sentinel" events are countable events (numerators) that do not require the calculation of population-based rates (denominators) to judge their importance.' Since child-abuse and neglect (CAN) deaths are relatively infrequent, cause great public alarm, and signify a failure in the social-welfare system, they seem well qualified to be treated as 'sentinel' events and to be dealt with accordingly.

Examining the phenomenon of child abuse in the late 1980s, future historians of childhood may well be perplexed by the erratic cycles of concern about this ancient problem. Since child abuse was 'rediscovered' in the 1960s by the late Dr Henry Kempe and his distinguished colleagues (Kempe, Silverman, Steele, Droegmueller, and Silver 1962) a huge socio-medical industry has been developed, with branch plants throughout the western world. It is mainly concerned with crippling injuries and deaths due to child battering. Much less attention is paid to the higher incidence of morbidity and mortality associated with neglect and impoverishment. Following its 'discovery' by Dr Henry Kempe (1978) as a 'hidden pediatric problem and neglected area', sexual abuse is fast becoming a dominant concern of the child-welfare field. Overwhelmed by this baffling problem, many child-protection agencies have little or no interest in the equally pernicious mischief caused to children by poverty and neglect. The challenge for the child-welfare field in the next decade must surely to be deploy its resources, moral as well as economic and political, to promote the welfare of all children. Treating emotionally, physically, and sexually abused children who come to public attention is most important – but it is not enough.

Since the completion of this book brings to an end twenty years of research in the field of criminal violence, my final remarks are addressed to the new generation of researchers and especially to the decision makers in the funding agencies. Next to the prevention of abuse and neglect, one of the most urgent tasks is to reduce the lasting harm which, in so many cases, they cause to children. Finding ways of helping children to overcome the profound psychological trauma associated with parental violence should have the highest priority. Particular attention must also be paid to the close relationship between CAN and, for example, cerebral palsy and mental retardation. Since physically and mentally handicapped children are at high risk from abuse and neglect, they obviously need a high degree of protection. In respect to the mental handicaps, this point was made by Buchanan and Oliver in

1977. More recently, in relation to cerebral palsy, Diamond and Jaudes (1983: 73) report that, in 9 per cent of their cases, cerebral palsy was caused by child abuse. They concluded that: 'children with cerebral palsy must be seen as being at special risk for child abuse, as a cause for and a response to the handicapping condition'. This finding should provide a starting point for a series of challenging and most urgent interdisciplinary studies on both sides of the Atlantic.

Acknowledgements

This book was completed at the Centre of Criminology, University of Toronto, where I have the good fortune to be a Visiting Fellow. I am greatly indebted to the Director, Professor A.N. Doob, to members of the faculty, the support staff, and to the students of criminology, for their hospitality and intellectual stimulation. Special thanks are due to the librarians at the Centre for Criminology. Their skill, dedication, and imperturbability, in the face of many importunate demands, were always impressive. I am similarly indebted to the librarians at the Robarts Research Library and the Science and Medicine Library, University of Toronto, to the Toronto Academy of Medicine, and to the Queen Street Mental Health Centre librarians.

It is, of course, impossible to undertake a work of this magnitude without incurring many debts which can never be repaid. In this respect I am particularly conscious of the forbearance of my family, especially of my wife Jane Donald Greenland, our children, and of our friends and colleagues. Their understanding and loving support, over many years, is still a source of wonder. Much more difficult to acknowledge is my debt to the research subjects and especially to the dead infants who provided the *raison d'être* for this study. I can, at least, thank some of the offenders, residing in prisons and mental hospitals, who trusted me, a stranger, with their confidences. They have, in unique ways, contributed enormously to my growth as a person and to my understanding of the antecedents of murderous encounters.

Finally, it is a great pleasure to express my gratitude to Professor Rolf Olsen for recommending the publication of this book, to Monica Sandor and Joseph Benderavage, who commanded the word-processor to produce perfect copy, and to John Robert Colombo and Mary Jackson who helped me cut a huge manuscript down to an acceptable size. These good friends and colleagues will, I'm sure, join me in dedicating this work to people all over the world who love and care for children.

Cyril Greenland
Toronto, February 1987

1

CAN deaths in the 1980s –
an overview

The health of children is important in itself because of the importance of children for the future of society. It is also important
because the vulnerability of children makes them a good indicator
of the health conditions in the population as a whole. Just as the
miner's canary gave warning by its death of the presence of noxious
gases in the mine, infant mortality has served as an indicator of dangerous conditions which may affect the entire population.

(Reed 1984: 123)

Despite the phenomenal decline in the rate of infant mortality and
the corresponding increase in life expectancy over the past twenty
to thirty years, concern about child deaths has never been greater,
at least in the western world. This paradox deserves close attention. This is why we must start with the warning contained in the
quotation which heads this chapter. It seems reasonable to assume
that our concern about the fate of children in the 1980s may well
reflect an even greater anxiety about the escalation of global violence which threatens human survival. This, in turn, may explain
the declining birthrate (Teitelbaum and Winter 1985: 158–9)[1]
which makes the lives of children even more precious. At the
same time, technological advances in medicine have, for example,
provided the means for saving the lives of pre-term infants who,
only a decade earlier, would not have been 'salvageable'. For-
tunately the rapid growth of intensive neonatal-care programmes
in this period has drastically reduced the perinatal mortality rate
of low-birthweight babies.[2] In addition, the extent to which the
growth of medical technology drives social policy should not be
ignored. As in the case of *in vitro* fertilization and organ trans-
plantation, once the technology exists for prolonging life, policy
makers, in order to resist the onerous responsibility of 'playing God', have little choice except to sanction its use regardless
of cost or the long-term consequences. Concern about child-
abuse and neglect (CAN) deaths should be considered in this
broad context.

The aim of this opening chapter, in essence a literature review presented in eight parts, is to frame and supplement the succeeding

chapters. Part 1 is concerned with the politics of child abuse. Part 2 considers some of the problems involved in defining and estimating the incidence of CAN deaths. Part 3 provides additional information on socio-economic factors associated with child abuse. Part 4 touches briefly on the 'multi-problem' families. Part 5 examines the relationship between pregnancy and CAN deaths. Part 6 introduces the concept of warning signals and help-seeking behaviour. Part 7 considers some of the problems arising in response to the inquiries into CAN deaths. My conclusions are summarized in Part 8.

1 The politics of child abuse

The discovery of child abuse, or more accurately its rediscovery (Lynch 1985: 7–15), dates from 1962, when the term 'battered child syndrome' was coined by Henry Kempe and his colleagues. Their objective, to arouse public indignation and to attract professional interest in the plight of abused and neglected children, was successfully achieved. Twenty-five years later, with the addition of sexual abuse rediscovered in about 1978, the general topic of child abuse still attracts banner headlines, TV programmes, scholarly articles, and books.

Ten years after the term 'battered child syndrome' was coined, Kempe and Helfer (1972: xi) recognized its limitations.

> For some, this term means only the child who has been the victim of the most severe form of physical punishment, i.e. that child who represents the far end of the child-abuse spectrum. For others, the term implies the total spectrum of child abuse, beginning with the parents (or future parents) who have the potential to abuse their small children and ending with the severely beaten or killed child. This lack of clarity has led to moderate confusion, both in the literature and in the minds of those wishing to help these children and their families.

Despite this confusion, Kempe and Helfer (1972: xii) elected to preserve the term 'the battered child' for two main reasons, first because ' . . . our total understanding of the problem of abnormal rearing is still inadequate and, second, the need to provide a continuous impact on the problem of physical abuse to small children remains.' They did, however, provide a more succinct definition of the battered child as 'any child receiving non-accidental physical injury (or injuries) as a result of acts (or omissions) on the part of his parents or guardians'.

The term 'the battered child' was eventually abandoned by Helfer and Kempe (1976: xix). They felt that enough progress had been made to move on to a more inclusive phrase, 'child abuse and neglect'.

The problem is clearly not just one of *physical* battering. Save for the children who are killed or endure permanent brain damage (and these remain a prime concern), the most devastating aspect of abuse and neglect is the permanent adverse effects on the developmental process and the child's emotional well-being.

Stimulated by Kempe and Helfer's (1972) modified definition and alarmed by the increase (real or detected) in severe injuries and fatalities due to child abuse in the UK, the Tunbridge Wells Study Group adopted the term 'non-accidental injury' (NAI) (Franklin 1973). Recognizing that the rehabilitation of the family may be more important to society than its punishment, the Group hoped that the ambiguous expression NAI would increase professional objectivity and be less threatening to abusive or potentially abusive parents who, in this way, would be encouraged to seek professional help.

Although widely accepted and used in the professional literature, the term NAI, as a euphemism for child abuse, has obvious limitations. It lacks precision, it is limited to physical trauma, and by definition it excludes neglect, failure to thrive, and severe emotional and sexual abuse. It is also important to recognize that in practice the distinction between accidental and non-accidental injuries is often difficult to determine. The difficulty is magnified when legal decisions have to be made about terminating parental rights and prosecuting offenders.

In looking back over the past twenty-five years, it can be seen that medicine, especially paediatrics and radiology, has made an outstanding contribution to the diagnosis, treatment, and pevention of child abuse. But the process of 'medicalizing' child abuse has been a mixed blessing. In addition to their diagnostic skills and ability to repair broken bones and comfort damaged children, physicians were able to exert considerable influence on the press and on legislators. As a result, in less than a decade all the American states and Canadian provinces adopted legislation concerned with reporting, treating, and preventing child abuse and neglect. In this way child abuse was conceptualized as a disease to be treated by doctors in much the same way as other diseases. The introduction of mandatory reporting, which is reminiscent of the reporting of infectious diseases, serves to confirm the disease model.

The critics of the disease model argue that the social basis of child abuse, which is mainly rooted in poverty and economic inequality, is ignored and neglected by the legislators. This view is vigorously stated by Pelton (1978: 608–17) in his landmark paper on the myth of classlessness. After noting that child abuse and neglect are mainly associated with poverty and are not, as it were, democratically distributed throughout society, Pelton writes:

> The belief in the classlessness of child abuse and neglect has taken hold with such tenacity among professionals and the public, despite evidence and logic to the contrary, [it] suggests that it serves important functions for those who accept it. Maintenance of the myth permits many professionals to view child abuse and neglect as a psycho-dynamic problem, in the context of the medical model of 'disease', 'treatment', and 'cure', rather than as predominantly sociological and poverty-related problems. Moreover, like the popular conception of an epidemic disease, afflicting families without regard to social or economic standing, the myth allows the problems of abuse and neglect to be portrayed as broader than they actually are; indeed as occurring in 'epidemic' proportions.

Similar, although somewhat more peevish, critiques of the 'diseases' model of child abuse have been presented by Pfohl (1977) and Antler (1981). Pfohl (1977), for example, argues that the medical discovery of child abuse enabled the relatively 'low-status' paediatric radiologists to form an alliance with the 'more prestigious segments within organised medicine'. Antler (1981), like Pelton (1978), also complains that the disease model of abuse places stress on the physical aspects of child abuse, 'while locating the cause of the disease in the personality of the abusing parent'. However, unlike Pelton and the other critics, Antler (1981: 52) exhorts social workers to reclaim the turf of child abuse.

These and related theoretical issues are addressed, at a somewhat higher level of sophistication, by Parton (1985). In a chapter on the discovery of the 'battered baby' (1985: 60–1), he describes the role of the National Society for the Prevention of Cruelty to Children (NSPCC), founded in 1895, in importing the 'battered child syndrome' into the UK in 1964. This resulted in the establishment in 1968 of the NSPCC Battered Child Research Unit, modelled on Kempe's National Center for the Treatment and Prevention of Child Abuse and Neglect in Denver, Colorado (now the Henry Kempe Center). In 1972, the NSPCC, in co-operation with the Manchester University Department of Pediatrics and the City of Manchester Social Services Department, established a special unit to deal with the battered baby syndrome. Since then, the NSPCC has opened ten special units based on the Manchester model. The register of cases dealt with by the special units provides the foundation for a valuable series of research reports on child abuse in England and Wales. A recent epidemiological study of 6,532 abused and neglected children, dealt with by the special units from 1977 to 1982 (Creighton 1984: 441–8), confirms Parton's (1985: 61) impression that the NSPCC continues to conceptualize child abuse as a 'medico-social' problem.

With the exception of Newberger and Bourne (1978), a paediatrician and a lawyer respectively, the critics of the 'disease' model of child abuse fail to appreciate that this problem is best resolved by broadening the conceptual basis of medicine rather than by eliminating its influence. That the process of changing medicine from a disease to a social-health orientation is slow and painful cannot be denied. On the other hand, few would deny that some small measure of progress has been made since the early 1900s, when Bernard Shaw described the current medical services as a 'murderous absurdity' and the physician as a 'credulous impostor, petulant scientific coxcomb, and a parasite on disease'.[3] Shaw, who no doubt would have had something to say about the medicalization of child abuse, would also be pleasantly surprised to discover the extent to which some of his wild ideas have influenced current medical thinking, if not its practice. This is illustrated by two quotations which serve also to reveal a growing consensus on both sides of the Atlantic. S.D.M. Court, Emeritus Professor of Child Health, University of Newcastle upon Tyne, in his foreword to *Child Health in the Community* (Mitchell 1980: v) wrote: 'Health is determined by the interaction between the child, his environment and the society in which he lives, and is not a measurable quantity independent of this relationship.' Much more directly related to our immediate concern about CAN deaths are the sentiments expressed in the report of the Select Panel for the Promotion of Child Health, to the United States Congress and the Secretary of Health and Human Services (US Department of Health and Human Services 1981c, IV: 27).

> Most childhood deaths are environmental in origin and most environments are subject to ameliorative changes. Inadequate socioeconomic and medical environments that affect neonatal deaths, mechanical, thermal and other forms of energy that kill by injury; teratogens and carcinogens that cause birth defects and malignant neoplasms all can be controlled.

With a characteristic national passion for contradiciton, the same US Select Panel for the Promotion of Child Health (1981b, I: 109–10) reached quite opposite conclusions in respect to child abuse and neglect:

It is now known that abusive and neglectful parents are found at all socio-economic levels, and that no educational, racial or religious group is exempted altogether. It is also known that about 90 per cent can respond to various new and successful forms of therapy. Usually child abuse is the result of a family crisis or series of crises, with some triggering event. Its remedy almost always involves counselling for the entire family, not just the abusive person. Likewise, treatment generally requires a team effort involving numerous professionals, including nurses, pediatricians, child psychiatrists, psychologists, social workers, educational specialists, attorneys, and child care workers.

Since this kind of treatment is likely to be very expensive, the Panel recognizes the need for prevention programmes, 'based on early assessment of family risk'. Because there is no mention of poverty, poor housing, or the need to change the environments and social conditions in which child abuse and neglect is endemic, it is tempting to assume that Pelton's fear of a medical conspiracy to perpetuate the 'disease' model of child abuse is not entirely without foundation.

2 Defining CAN deaths

The definition of abuse and neglect is not what the doctor thinks it should be, or what the social worker thinks it is, but it is actually what the Court says it is. The Court is, of course, influenced by the public, and its definitions will change from time to time and may be different in differing localities, based on the emotional climate of the cities in that area.
H. Kempe in Tunbridge Wells Study Group (Franklin 1973: 1)

Since death is the most extreme consequence of child abuse and neglect, the phenomenon can only be understood in relation to child abuse and neglect defined at a particular time, place, and legal context. This is why Kempe's 1973 observation on the relative nature of the definition is so useful. At the outset it must be admitted that the lack of a consistent definition of child abuse and neglect (CAN) and the virtual absence of uniform reporting procedures for bringing these cases to public attention provide a treacherous foundation for research in this field (Kadushin and Martin 1981; Lynch and Roberts 1982). In relation to deaths due to CAN, the problem is magnified. Because of the absence of witnesses, current legal standards require levels of evidence and proof that are rarely attainable. What can be said with certainty is that the incidence of serious, that is life-threatening, child abuse and CAN fatalities are underreported by official statistics. In addition to underreporting, investigators such as Jason *et al.* (1982) have demonstrated substantial bias errors in reporting. Based on an analysis of 'confirmed' and 'ruled out' cases in Georgia, USA, Jason and her colleagues report that teenage mothers are much more likely than older mothers to be included among the 'confirmed' cases.[4]

The absence of external signs of injury in some of the children who die as a result of abuse also explains the low level of reliability of the official statistics. Commenting on this in a letter to the *British Medical Journal* (12 July 1980), Creighton (1980a) made three points: '1 NAI [non-accidental injury] occurs almost exclusively in the home in the absence of independent witnesses. 2 Injuries sustained may not be the immediate cause of death. 3 Some deaths due to NAI get misdiagnosed.'

Creighton and Owtram (1977) point out that only two of the nine deaths of children placed on the child-abuse register in 1975 were medically attributed to non-accidental injury. 'The remaining seven required additional social and legal evidence before a decision could be made about the contribution of NAI to death.' One child, whose death was officially recorded as being due to broncho-pneumonia, had over one hundred bruises on her body.

Hall (1975) also comments on the need for social investigations in order to confirm the diagnosis of death due to NAI. Similar concerns are expressed by Downing (1978) from Nebraska. In her study of child mortality, Downing described a 15-month-old infant who, following hospitalization for 'failure to thrive', was returned to an impoverished home. The infant, *in extremis*, was readmitted to hospital suffering from 'pneumonia, starvation, severe dehydration and a 107.6 degree temperature'. The death certificate listed the immediate cause of death as 'pulmonary congestion and oedema, aetiology unknown'. The fact that the infant's death was precipitated by neglect as well as abuse did not, apparently, concern the pathologist. Since the failure to identify the true cause of death may have profound consequences for other children in the same family, Downing proposed the establishment of a child death evaluation team. Such a team has already been established in Los Angeles County (1982) under the auspices of the Department of Health Services.

Although these brief observations do less than justice to the work of Creighton and Owtram (1977), Downing (1978) and Hall (1975), the point has been made that terms such as 'battered child', 'child abuse' and 'NAI' lack diagnostic precision. The problem is compounded by the fact that some clinicians and pathologists ignore or neglect to obtain the social evidence that is essential to the diagnosis of 'death due to child abuse or neglect'. On this basis, it seems reasonable to assume that an unknown proportion of infant deaths, currently attributed to accidents, sudden infant death syndrome or pneumonia, could more accurately be reported as due to abuse, neglect, or some combination of the two.

The latest available US reports (US Department of Health and Human Services 1981a) indicate that somewhere between 652,000 (10.5 per 1,000 population of children under 18 years) and 1,000,000 children per year are abused or neglected. The same study, estimating the number of CAN deaths at 1,000 per year, suggests that fatalities from this cause are less common than was previously assumed. This opinion is confirmed by the American Humane Association (1983) study indicating that 850,980 reports were processed by child-protective service agencies in 1981. However, almost half (48 per cent) of the cases were closed after the initial investigation. Data from 25 of the 54 jurisdictions revealed 585 fatalities. Neglect, or deprivation of the necessities of life, was the cause of death in 56 per cent of cases. Of the remainder, 34 per cent died as a result of physical injury. The reverse was true for the estimated 1,000 deaths in the US Department of Health and Human Services (1981a) study which reported that 72 per cent of deaths were due to physical assault, and 28 per cent neglect. However, a different picture emerges in *Highlights of Official Child Neglect and Abuse Reporting, 1984*, the most recent report of the American Association for Protecting Children[5] (1986), and *Official Child Neglect and Abuse Reporting, 1984*, based on 500 fatalities reported from twenty-three jurisdictions. Major physical injuries accounted for 47 per cent of the fatalities, 'deprivation of necessities' for 44 per cent. The balance consisted of a mixture of minor injuries and neglect. These somewhat inconsistent and inconclusive findings illustrate the hazards of drawing conclusions from single studies.

Despite the limitations imposed by underreporting and biased reporting, there is substantial agreement among researchers about the epidemiology of child-abuse deaths and the nature of the phenomenon. For example, there is a growing consensus that child abuse is best understood as a continuum ranging from parental incompetence to homicide, rather than as a result of any specific pathological traits associated with the perpetrators or victims. It is also agreed that the majority of victims of life-threatening CAN, excluding sexual abuse, are very young children, usually under the ages of 5 or 6. The parents, especially abusive mothers, tend to be younger than the average. Many of them started child-bearing as teenagers. Single-parent families, low incomes, poor housing, and social isolation combine to cause situational stress which is frequently reported in the literature of child-abuse deaths.

3 Socio-economic factors

The central theme of the pioneering research by Gil (1978) on child abuse is that violence in families is rooted in societal violence, and therefore can be neither understood nor overcome apart from it. The importance of Gil's approach lies in the recognition that violence to children and adults takes place on several discrete but interrelated levels. In addition to the interpersonal violence, which can do psychological as well as physical harm, Gil identifies institutional violence and, of course, societal violence. By legitimizing poverty, discrimination, unemployment, and slum dwelling, society not only provokes interpersonal and institutional violence, but also inhibits the full growth of its victims, especially children. In respect to child abuse, similar points are made, albeit in a much more limited way, by Pelton (1978). The contributions of Gil (1970) and others remind us of the tendency in our society to rediscover, at least in every decade, the extent to which poverty is a blight on the lives of children. More than forty years ago in the UK, Titmuss (1943) demonstrated that the infant-mortality rate is an exceedingly sensitive indicator of society's economic and social well-being. Although, in general, the infant-mortality rate has declined in the western world, the inequalities between rich and poor children, noted by Titmuss, have not diminished.

Studies of the relationship between social classes and child mortality (Black 1980; Pharoah and Macfarlane 1982) in England and Wales confirm that the death rate among children in social class V was more than twice that of social class I. This class gradient, applying to morbidity as well as mortality, was steepest for accidents, respiratory diseases, measles, and meningococcal infections.

Although equivalent data are not available in Canada, several studies indicate that the social-class gradient relating to child deaths is not unique to the UK or the USA. For example, a study of deaths due to accidents, poisoning, and violence (Nicholls and Davies, 1980) revealed that male mortality, at all ages, was 88 per cent higher in the lower- compared to the higher-income groups. However, for females the difference in mortality rates for low- and high-income levels was less than 50 per cent.

The role of race as well as poverty, in relation to infant deaths in Chicago in 1964, was discussed by Lerner (1976). After showing that post-neonatal deaths accounted for about 30 per cent of all infant deaths, Lerner pointed out that the rates for the poverty areas, 12.9 per 1,000 live births, was more than double the comparable rate of 5.2 for residents of non-poverty areas. However, in relation to the non-White population living in the poverty area, the infant mortality rate at 15.5 was double that of the White population living in the same area. Even more important is the finding that the non-White infant death rate in the poor areas was double that of the non-Whites in the non-poverty areas. This means that the excess of deaths was most likely attributable to environmental rather than racial or genetic influence.

Official data relating to the impact of social class and income levels on the health status of Americans, particularly children, are scarce. For this reason the publication by the Maine Department of Human Services of *Children's Deaths in Maine* (1983) is doubly welcome. A unique feature of this study was the question: 'Is the mortality rate among Maine's Low-Income Children, ages 8 days to 17 years, higher than among *Other* children, and if so is the difference statistically significant?' 'Low-income children' were defined conservatively as those children and their families who received services from the Department's income security (AFDC Food Stamps and Medicaid Programs). This group, including all the 'poor and near poor' children, represented 21 per cent of Maine's population. The analysis revealed that for 'all causes' of death, the ratio of *poor* to *other* children was 3 to 1. In descending order of frequency, the other ratios were: homicide, 5 to 1; fire, 4.9 to 1; drowning, 4 to 1; congenital anomalies, 3.1 to 1; other disease-related conditions, 3.6 to 1. Commenting on these data, Human Services Commisioner Petit (Maine, 1983: [5]) wrote:

> A difference between the death rates of children according to family income levels may not be surprising to most people who work in human services. What is surprising – and alarming – is the magnitude of that disparity – a ratio of more than 3 to 1. We believe this finding has serious implications for current policy concerning children.

The New York City Mayor's Task Force study (1983) provided a wealth of information on the relationship between poverty and death due to CAN. It was found that 80 per cent of the adults involved as *cases*, when classified by occupation, were unskilled or unemployed, compared to 54 per cent of the *possible cases*, and 44 per cent of the *non-cases*. In respect to Medicaid or Public

Assistance status, 90 per cent of the *case* families had such contact, compared to 67 per cent of the *possible cases*, and 36 per cent of the *non-cases*. Similarly in regard to the mother's education, it was found that *case* mothers had a lower grade level, 9.7, compared to 11.4 for *possible cases*, and 11.5 for *non-cases*. Taking all these factors into account the authors of the New York City Mayor's Task Force (1983: 19) study concluded:

> The data on child and family characteristics indicates that the children came from multi-problem families; some suffered from severe pathology or severe dysfunctions. These data provide a crucial context for understanding and interpreting the findings in this report. The difficulty of treating these families partially explains what happened, or did not happen, when these families came into contact with various human services and health programs before and after the death of the child.

In case there are any lingering doubts about the relationship between poverty and/or pathology and the incidence of infant mortality and especially CAN deaths, relevant quotations from various major studies are presented in chronological order. These quotations will also serve to introduce a brief examination of the 'multi-problem family' issue.

Creighton, S.J. (1980b: 11), NSPCC, *Child Victims of Physical Abuse, 1976*.

> the parents of the injured children are mainly in semi-skilled and unskilled occupations and large percentages of them are unemployed and receiving supplementary benefit.

American Humane Association (1983: 23), *Annual Report, 1981*, 'Highlights of official child neglect and abuse reporting'.

> over 40 per cent of all reported families are headed by a single female caretaker who depends on public assistance. This supports the notion that there is a strong association between the stresses of poverty and the inability to adequately care for children. The problem is that the Child Protection Services (CPS) are neither equipped nor intended to alleviate poverty.

Texas Department of Human Resources (1981: 68) on child deaths in Texas (1975–77).

> we are dealing with severely troubled and multi-problem families, who through desperation, inadequate parenting skills, or social alienation, have engaged in abuseful or neglectful behavior leading to the death of their children.

US Department of Health and Human Services (1981a), *National Study of the Incidence and Severity of Child Abuse and Neglect*.

What is new in this study is the finding that, while low-income families predominate among those receiving protective services, they
also predominate among the much larger numbers of maltreated
children who are *not* receiving such assistance.

4 Multi-problem families

The difficulty with cross-national research is the uncertainty
about the meaning of words used in the US and UK studies. The
expression 'multi-problem family' is an example of this difficulty.
Does it mean, literally, a family with many problems? Or does it
refer to that pathological entity frequently encountered in the
British literature, 'the problem family' (Blacker 1952; Philp and
Timms 1957)? In reading, as it were, between the lines, it becomes
clear that Oliver (1983), in his paper on dead children from
problem families, is concerned with highly pathological family
situations. His 'hard-core' families include those with abuse and
neglect in at least two generations and the recipients of multi-
agency support.

It seems reasonable to assume that the expression 'multi-problem
family', used in the Texas (1981) and the New York City (1983)
studies, implies substantial pathology aggravated by an abun-
dance of social problems, including poverty. This suggests that
the reduction of poverty, if this were possible, would not of itself
lead to a decline in the incidence of CAN. In terms of developing
rational strategies for intervention, designed to save the lives and
protect the health of vulnerable infants, these complex issues
are of considerable theoretical interest as well as of practical
importance.

There is, of course, substantial evidence (Jason *et al.* 1982)
to support the criticism that the high incidence of poverty
and multi-problem families among 'reported' cases is merely
an artefact of the reporting system. Those responsible for
reporting are less likely to take chances with single, poor,
isolated, ill-educated, non-White mothers who are suspected
of neglect or abuse. Another more subtle explanation might
be the tendency for 'problem families', in the face of stress,
to exhibit behaviours that cause the rest of society to become
anxious. Querido (1946) (quoted by Philp and Timms 1957: 3)
expressed this succinctly: 'Whatever is the prevailing social
problem these (social problem) families express it in its most
acute form.'

5 Pregnancy and post-partum depression

While it has not gone unnoticed, the role of pregnancy and post-partum depression, as a precipitant of child abuse, has not been sufficiently recognized. Quoting Deutsch's *Psychology of Women* (1945), Bakan (1971: 97) recognized that, after a very painful and exhausting delivery, the young mother's anxiety and aggression are intensified.

> If she is aggressive two options are open. She can direct the aggression to the husband, the first cause, or to the child, the second. Needing the babying herself and fearing the aggression of the male and sometimes feeling also her loss of sexual attractiveness, she may divert the aggression toward the child.

This kind of psychoanalytical interpretation of post-partum aggression is attractive but superficial. In practice, the background and motivation for attacks on infants are much more complex. This much is confirmed by Resnick (1969), Rodenburg (1971a and b), Asch and Rubin (1974), Kaplun and Reich (1976), in their studies of child murder. In relation to child abuse, the hazards of pregnancy and the post-partum period have been noted by Schloesser (1964), Elmer (1967), Skinner and Castle (1969), Baldwin and Oliver (1975), and Greenland (1978).

Elmer's (1967) findings are particularly illuminating. She reported that of the twenty abusive mothers in her study, 'nine were pregnant at the time of the abused child's admission to hospital, one abusive mother had miscarried just before the time of her admission, and two others had an infant other than the patient during the year previous to admission.' Only one mother in the control group had experienced such an event. 'These data', wrote Elmer (1967), 'show a clear connection between the phenomenon of child abuse and the burdens intimately related to pregnancy and children.'

An additional complication, relating to the role of parturition in child abuse, is the high frequency of prematurity and low-birthwieght babies in this population. Smith (1975), for example, reported 'The prevalence of low birth weight among the battered sample born in hospital was four times greater than the national average.' Confirming this finding, Creighton (1980b) reported that the ' "low birthweight" babies in her population tended to be injured at a younger age.' 'This', wrote Creighton, 'accord[s] with the hypothesis of mother–child bonding failure caused by prematurity, suggested by Klaus and Kennell (1970).'

Describing the difficulties parents have in becoming attached to their premature infants, Marshall Klaus is reputed to have said (Gray *et al.* 1976), 'You can't love a dish rag.' Since then, considerable progress has been made in preventing bonding failures that might lead to child abuse and neglect. This problem has been energetically tackled in the USA by Hunter and her colleagues (1978, 1979) from the University of North Carolina School of Medicine and Department of Social Work, and most eloquently in the UK by Ounsted and his colleagues (1982) at the Park Hospital for Children in Oxford.

6 Warning signals and help-seeking behaviour

Since simple solutions are unlikely to effect a reduction in the overall incidence of CAN, the problem of protecting the lives of known high-risk children is of vital importance. Accepting that the crude response – the removal of all high-risk children to a safe place – is neither desirable nor practicable, what are the options? The literature on this topic, which is scarce, anecdotal, and inconsistent, makes this a particularly difficult field for research. This is especially so because evidence of help-seeking and warning behaviour is usually obtained, with the wisdom of hindsight, after the occurrence of the tragedy. It is also virtually impossible to determine in how many cases warning signals were observed and responded to appropriately. Yet there is no doubt that, in a substantial proportion of cases, the child at risk has previously been identified and brought to the attention of the relevant child protection agency. Greenland (1973) showed that at least 10 per cent of all abused children had been previously abused. Examining a smaller population of severely abused children, requiring hospital admission, he reported that 20 per cent had been previously abused. Ten per cent also had brothers and sisters who had been abused in previous incidents.

Similar data are provided by Creighton (1980b) in the UK. She reported a previous injury rate of 35.2 per cent and a postregistration injury rate of 10 per cent. The Texas (1981) study, providing data on 267 CAN deaths, shows that 64 (23.9 per cent) had experienced child-protective services before the abuse or neglect incident resulting in the child's death. Comparable data come from the New York City (1983) study. This shows that almost half (49 per cent) of the 45 *cases* had been previously reported, and 24 per cent were under the supervision of a child-protection agency at the time of the fatality.

Premonitory, warning, or help-seeking behaviour has been

reported in many studies of violent crimes associated with mental disorder (Greenland 1971a). In their paper, 'The battered child syndrome', Bennie and Sclare (1969) observed, 'Of particular significance in the context of evaluating dangerousness is that five of the ten patients had seen a doctor immediately preceding the crime, in some cases to complain about the child's behaviour and to seek help in management.' Scott (1973b) in his study of twenty-nine fatal battered-baby cases, said that 'three-quarters of the men gave unmistakable warning of their subsequent actions.'

The importance of recognizing 'open warnings' as a means of protecting children 'at risk' has been a major concern of Ounsted and Lynch (1976), and Lynch and Roberts (1977a). Lynch and Roberts (1982: 119) provide a typical example of such warning behaviour.

> Two weeks before a ten-week-old girl arrived in hospital, moribund with bilateral subdural haematomata, her mother had caused a minor bruising to the baby's buttocks during a feeding battle. She had demonstrated the injury to the family doctor who, not realizing the significance of this 'open warning', reassured the mother that she had done no serious damage and prescribed a tranquillizer to calm her down.

The notion of a 'critical path' leading to the tragedy of a severe injury or death, Ounsted and Lynch (1976), has considerable heuristic as well as practical value. However, in highlighting the features frequently found in the critical-path analysis, there is danger in using these items as elements in a high-risk check list, rather than as a means of assisting distressed families. Lynch and Roberts (1977a) warn against this. Despite these warnings, numerous attempts have been made to develop check lists to enable professionals to identify high-risk parents. For example, on the basis of ten questions, Kempe and Kempe (1978) claim to have 'made 76.5 per cent correct predictions'. This and other such claims have been vigorously disputed by Montgomery (1982) in his review of problems in the perinatal prediction of child abuse. His critique is, in part, based on data obtained from a 1980 study of an early warning register in Dundee, Scotland. In regard to testing the validity of high-risk screening procedures, Montgomery estimated that a prospective study of all children born in Ninewells Hospital, Dundee, over a period of two years would yield only about twenty index cases. This would hardly justify the enormous labour and cost of such research, so, for the time being, it must be assumed that the effectiveness of high-risk check lists and of other such predictive devices has yet to be proved.

7 Inquiries into CAN deaths

The temptation to discuss inquiries into CAN deaths as an aspect of the politics of child abuse was resisted because to do so might have been interpreted as cynical or frivolous. On the other hand, it would be inept and certainly misleading to deny that powerful political forces are involved in the decisions to hold public inquiries into child-abuse deaths. Experience in Canada with the judicial inquiry into the death of Kim Anne Popen (Allen 1982) and in the UK with the inquiries into the deaths of Maria Colwell (DHSS 1974) and Jasmine Beckford (Brent 1985), confirms that the news media, which tend to treat the social services with hostility, use these occasions to attack vulnerable social workers. Their vulnerability stems from the fact that, according to the press, social-work decisions are always wrong. Social workers are criticized when they fail to protect a child from harm and, when they do so, they are accused of trampling roughshod over parental rights. They can't win. However, as the British Association of Social Workers (1981) recognized, social workers are in a 'risk-taking' business where blame, although undeserved, is an occupational hazard. Inquiries into child-abuse deaths serve an important social function. It seems to be agreed that, in addition to having a cathartic value, inquiries should serve to: discover the facts surrounding the tragedy; draw conclusions from the facts; make recommendations designed to prevent similar tragedies. Although the form of the inquiries has perturbed many social workers, the repetition of recommendations without corresponding action has been even more disturbing. This was made clear in the Carly Taylor Inquiry Report (Leicestershire Area Health Authority 1980: 24), which included among its recommendations a bitter comment on:

> the plethora of recommendations in the various reports of similar inquiries in recent years; we have studied nine of them, and while we agree with the majority of their general recommendations, many of them are largely repetitive of others, it would be pointless for us to repeat them. We would only say that, if they had been studied and followed by those concerned at all levels in this case, it is reasonable to assume that the troubles with which we have been concerned might well not have occurred.

In order to avoid duplicating information contained in a previous publication (Greenland 1986), the comments in this section will be limited to two main issues. The first relates to the issue of procedural fairness. The second is concerned with what might be called the hazardous fall-out from child-abuse inquiries. By way of background it should be noted that in June 1985 a consultative paper, *Child Abuse Inquiries*, was issued by the Department of Health and Social Security (DHSS 1985). This described three types of inquiry into serious cases of abuse: case review by management; inquiry by a review panel, conducted by people specially appointed by the local agency; and statutory inquiry instigated by the Secretary of State for Social Services. The last type of inquiry is to be reserved for cases which raise major national concern and have national policy implications. Unlike the other two forms of inquiry, witnesses are compelled to appear before a statutory inquiry under section 26 of the Child Care Act (England and Wales) 1980.

Although it is generally agreed that the enormously expensive[6] public statutory inquiries should be reserved for exceptional cases, the current decision-making process is, to say the least, labyrinthine – if not capricious. For example, following the death of Jasmine Beckford in July 1984, the London Borough of Brent held two internal inquiries before 28 March 1985 when the non-statutory review panel, chaired by Louis Blom-Cooper, QC, was appointed. Meanwhile, during the sentencing of Jasmine's mother, Beverley Lorrington, the Common Sergeant, Judge Pigot, in an extra-judicial utterance, observed that the social worker has shown a 'naïvety almost beyond belief'. Encouraged by this insulting and injudicious remark, the press launched a sustained attack on the character and conduct of the Brent social workers. The fact that they had not been charged with any crime and lacked the means to defend themselves was, apparently, of no concern to the news media. The peculiarly British sport of social-worker baiting reached new depths when, during the Beckford inquiry, a journalist was rebuked by the chairman for publishing wildly inaccurate and malicious information about a key witness. When requested by the chairman to do so, the journalist refused to apologize.

Although these problems are not confined to this case, the Beckford inquiry report (Brent 1985), being well documented and recent, illustrates the unfair burden faced by the social workers. Unlike a criminal trial, an inquiry is an inquisitorial rather than an adversarial process. But this fact would not be obvious to inexperienced witnesses. While they cannot legally be compelled to do so, social workers, as employees of the local authority which ordered the inquiry, can hardly refuse to testify. In some cases, however, family physicians have obstinately refused to give evidence. As a result they have been relieved of the ordeal of cross-examination and, of course, the hostile press publicity which usually follows. The social workers in the Beckford case were subjected to the ordeal of being examined and cross-examined by eighteen barristers and solicitors as well as the Panel of Inquiry. They were, however, fortunate in being legally represented by NALGO, their union. In addition to individual legal costs, the overall cost of the Beckford inquiry was £250,000.

The astonishing events which followed from the publication of the Beckford inquiry reports confirmed the worst fears expressed by Olive Stevenson in her reflections on the Maria Colwell inquiry. She said:

> We must at least acknowledge that the launching of an inquiry is like casting a huge stone in a pond. The ripples spread outward often involving many who did not expect it and, more important, in ways they did not anticipate. The emotional cost is very, very high and can only be justified if the inquiries appear to play a constructive part in protecting the lives of other children.
>
> (Stevenson 1979: 1–3)

The ripples in the Colwell case turned into waves which threaten to engulf the hapless social workers who were involved with Jasmine Beckford. Although she had no knowledge of the Beckfords until after the tragedy, Valerie Howarth, Director of Social Work at Brent, who had already accepted a new post in Cambridgeshire, was not allowed to take up the appointment.[7] The two social workers who were involved with the Beckfords were dismissed from their employment. Since then, both of them have experienced considerable humiliation and harassment in their attempts to find other jobs.[8] The ordeal of these two social workers, which is by no means over, will do nothing to encourage others to seek employment in the treacherous field of child abuse.

8 Conclusions

It is generally conceded that the early US estimates of child-abuse deaths, at between 2 and 5 per cent of all abused children, were grossly exaggerated. Although the true incidence is impossible to determine, it is usually assumed (American Medical Association 1985) that, depending on the age of the victims, an estimated death rate of less than 1 per cent is to be expected. The limitations of this gross estimate will be considered in chapter 2. Since the term 'child abuse and neglect' includes victims ranging in age from birth to 16, or 18 years in some jurisdictions, and diverse conditions including emotional and sexual abuse, calculating a death rate for such a heterogeneous population makes little sense. A much more accurate and meaningful measure would be to calculate CAN deaths in age-specific terms, as a proportion of all deaths to children in the same jurisdictions and period. Examined in this fashion, it will be seen that the CAN deaths form a relatively small proportion of all child deaths due to avoidable causes officially defined as 'accidents and adverse effects'. This includes motor-vehicle traffic accidents, poisoning, falls, and drowning.

The controversy in the UK regarding the incidence of child-abuse deaths appears to have been resolved with the publication by Adelstein et al. (1982). These authors claim 'that the estimate of 700 deaths a year being due to non-accidental injury is incompatible with any but the wildest view of the inaccuracy of death certification'. Support for this view is provided by Creighton (1984) who estimates the incidence of CAN deaths in England and Wales at between forty-four and seventy-four annually.

With the passing of the rhetoric about the virtual epidemic of child-abuse deaths, it is reassuring to discover that abuse and neglect severe enough to maim or destroy young children is comparatively rare. However, due to the moral panic associated with child abuse, this conclusion may not be welcomed by the professional community. This can be demonstrated by the angry response to Gil (1970) in the USA and to Peckham and Jobling (1975) in the UK. Gil's conclusion, that physical abuse cannot be considered a major maimer of children, was fiercely contested by Fontana (1970) and Helfer (1970). Peckham and Jobling, who suggested that the incidence of deaths due to battering at 750 cases per year might be an exaggeration, were similarly rebuked by Howells (1975 and by Franklin (1975).

In the heat of the debate, the main point, made by Peckham and Jobling (1975: 686), was overlooked. It is repeated here because similar sentiments serve both to inform and to guide this study.

> Clearly child abuse is a very important problem. However, such acts of violence of this nature in society can be dealt with adequately only if the nature and the extent of the problem is fully understood. The diagnosis of child abuse as a cause of death can be extremely difficult, but exaggerated estimates could hinder the development of a full understanding and distort attempts to help these tragic families.

Since CAN deaths are rare events, major differences in the findings and in the conclusions of studies of this problem should be expected. Yet consistencies between studies are likely to be significant. This is especially true in relation to the major studies describing the characteristics of the victims and the perpetrators. The US DHHS (1981a) study with an estimated 1,000 fatalities, reported that almost three-quarters of the victims, 74 per cent, were aged 5 years or less. The American Humane Association 1981 study (1983), with 585 fatalities, reported that the average age of the victims was 3.3 years. On this basis it seems reasonable to conclude risk of death from CAN declines with the age of the child.

The smaller studies, providing clinical information, are equally consistent in reporting that a high proportion of fatal CAN victims were premature or underweight infants. The incidence of congenital malformations and/or illness in the victims is also reported to be much higher than expected. In other words, these infants show characteristics or behaviours that could identify them as being 'at risk'. This is particularly so since a substantial proportion of them were previously reported to a child-protection agency as victims of abuse or neglect.

The characteristics of the perpetrators are also well described in the literature. A high incidence, ranging from 20 to 40 per cent, of young single mothers is frequently reported. But even in two-parent families, the male and female perpetrators are likely to be well under 30 years of age. In the large majority of cases, in almost all studies, these parents are described as unskilled or unemployed and poorly educated. A high proportion of the men have criminal records, many of them for violence.

Although adults who seriously injure or kill children share many common characteristics, they are not a homogeneous group. While some of them are clearly dangerous to children under all circumstances, the majority are not entirely unfit to care for children in conditions that are not unduly stressful. Some young parents who provide excellent care for their new-born infants may be exceedingly aggressive in response to a demanding and non-compliant toddler. The reverse may also be true. A previously competent mother, in an advanced stage of pregnancy, or in a state of post-partum depression may, in an explosion of rage, attack an older child. These examples will serve to indicate that serious assaults on children are, almost invariably, situationally specific events. Ill health or excessively demanding behaviour in the child, maternal distress or depression, an unstable or unhelpful male partner, when combined with social isolation, poverty, and poor housing, may precipitate a perilous or lethal family situation. The infant's powerlessness and inability to escape defines him as the victim.

Crime, poverty, emotional instability, poor health, substandard housing, social isolation, and dependency on a range of welfare services are commonly described features of severe child abuse and neglect culminating in death. This ill-omened concatenation of descriptors is, of course, traditionally associated with social or multi-problem families. Whether this entity exists in fact, or whether the evidence associating severe CAN with multi-problem families is inadequate, need not be debated here. But at least two points are beyond dispute. First is the intimate association between poverty and the increased risk of post-neonatal deaths in all jurisdictions. Second is the growing conviction that the traditional forms of casework intervention provided by child-protection agencies are inadequate to protect the lives of already identified high-risk children. Almost by definition, high-risk children, their siblings, and their parents are likely to have a multitude of problems, but the risk of severe injury or death decreases with the child's age. This means that the socio-medical intervention, designed to protect the children and assist the parents, must concentrate on identifying and remedying the specific hazards which contribute to the child's vulnerability.

2

CAN deaths in the USA – epidemiological studies

Every year, more than a million children in the United States are seriously abused by their parents, guardians, or others, and between 2,000 and 5,000 children die as a result of their injuries.
(*Journal of the American Medical Association* 9 August 1985: 254.6.796)

Although as TV addicts we have become inured to murder, it is still shocking to learn from the American Medical Assocation that, as a result of abuse and neglect, the lives of between 2,000 and 5,000 American children are destroyed each year. But this information will not surprise the US federal health authority, because it was warned about this in 1981 by Christoffel and her colleagues.

Using 1976 data, Christoffel, Kiang, and Stamler (1981: 57) reported that 'homicide was the fifth leading cause of death in children age 1–4 in the U.S.' 'Rates are even higher for children under one.' The 1982 statistics provided by the World Health Organisation (1985) referring to child deaths from birth to 14, shows that the situation has not improved. Of the almost 60,000 recorded deaths of children under the age of 14 years in 1982, 8,612 (14.3 per cent) died as a result of 'accidents and adverse effects'; 3,288 (5.5 per cent) died as a result of 'motor-vehicle traffic accidents', and 1,023 (1.7 per cent) died as a result of 'homicide and injury purposely inflicted by other persons'.

While homicide, which includes only a fraction of deaths due to child abuse and neglect, represents a relatively small proportion of all the violent deaths in the USA, wasting more than a thousand young lives a year is, by any standard, intolerable. Even worse is the fact that very little is known about these deaths and what can be done to prevent them. In an attempt to grapple with a part of this problem, the National Center of Child Abuse and Neglect (NCCAN) in 1984 funded three demonstration projects designed to inquire into child fatalities due to abuse and neglect. These pilot projects, based in New York City, St Louis, Missouri, and Illinois, in conjunction with the Louisiana Department of Health and Human Services, which may take several years to complete, will be of considerable practical and theoretical interest.

Meanwhile, in order to gain an understanding of the epidemiology of CAN deaths in the USA, this chapter considers the data obtained from more than twenty American studies (tables 2.1 and 2.2) published in the past twenty years.

A remarkable finding is the wide range in the estimates of the incidence of CAN deaths. For example, Schloesser (1964) from Kansas, in a survey of eighty-five cases, found fourteen deaths, representing 164.0 deaths per 1,000 cases. In contrast, the NCCAN (1981) study, based on 652,000 CAN cases, estimated 1.5 deaths per 1,000. Since these data are based on quite different populations, the rates are unlikely to be comparable. This is because these studies fall into two main types. First is the hospital-based and second the community-based research. Hospital-based studies involve either prospective or retrospective research designs. Since in prospective studies the data collection is designed to answer specific questions, they have a much higher degree of reliability than do retrospective studies. In regard to community-based studies, it should be noted that except for the surveys by Schloesser (1964), Gil (1978), US DHHS (1981a), New York City Mayor's Task Force (1983) and Los Angeles ICAN study (1986), most of the base-line data were obtained from child-abuse registers which have a low level of reliability. Since there are fewer of them, the results of hospital-based studies will be examined first.

Hospital-based studies

Table 2.1 showing data from seven hospital-based studies published between 1967 and 1976, illustrates the wide variation in the estimated incidence of deaths due to CAN. The variations cannot be explained by the type of study, i.e. prospective or retrospective. They may, however, be due to factors such as the age of the children, the nature of the initial injury, and whether or not, following discharge from hospital, children were adequately supervised by a child-protection agency. The way in which a case is defined for research purposes is also relevant. This can be illustrated by reference to two prospective studies, one by Ebbin *et al.* (1969), from Los Angeles, and the other by Smith and Hanson (1975), from Birmingham, England. The criteria for inclusion in Ebbin's study were: '(i) admission of the battery by a parent or parent surrogate, or (ii) a statement by the child or a responsible witness confirming the battery, or (iii) evidence of previous severe injuries that were probably inflicted.' As a result of these stringent criteria, only 50 of a possible 106 children were included. They ranged in age from 1

Table 2.1 *US hospital-based studies*

Hospital-based data USA Author(s)	Type of study	Location	Date of study	No. of cases	No. of deaths	Rate per 1,000
Elmer and Gregg 1967	FU*	Pittsburgh	1949–62	50	8	160.0
Ebbin et al. 1969	Prosp.**	Los Angeles	1966–7	50	3	60.0
Gregg and Elmer 1969	Retro.***	Pittsburgh	1949–62	113	1	8.8
Rowe and Leonard 1970	Prosp.	New Haven	1967–9	118	1	8.4
O'Neill et al. 1973	Prosp.	Nashville, Tenn.	1968–72	110	8	72.0
Lauer, Broeck, and Grossman 1974	Retro.	San Francisco	1965–71	130	6	46.0
Goldson et al. 1976	Prosp.	Denver	1971–2	140	6	42.0

*   Follow-up study.
**   Prospective study.
*** Retrospective study.

month to 14 years, with a median age of 19 months. Data on the excluded cases were not, unfortunately, provided.

In contrast to Ebbin's study, with three deaths (60 per 1,000 cases), the comparable UK study by Smith and Hanson (1975), based on 134 cases, revealed twenty-one deaths (156 per 1,000 cases). In Smith's study 82 per cent of the children were under 2 years of age. The mean age, 18.5 months, was similar to the children in Ebbin's cohort. Unlike Ebbin *et al.*, Smith and Hanson included cases where the parents 'could give no adequate explanation of their child's injuries.' These unexplained injury cases were included with those where the parents had confessed to battering. In the absence of additional data, it seems reasonable to conclude that the higher rate of deaths in Smith's cohort is, most likely, due to the broader or different definition of a 'case'.

Valuable information about the variation within hospitals about the decision to identify and report cases of child abuse and neglect is contained in a sophisticated study by Hampton and Newberger (1985). Using the data from the US *National Study of the Incidence and Severity of Child Abuse and Neglect* (US DHHS 1981a), Hampton and Newberger (1985: 66) report that, of the 652,000 children in the study, 212,400 (32.5 per cent) were known to the local child-protection agency. At the same time, 77,000 (11.8 per cent) of these children were identified by hospitals. Their study, based on a sample of 805 cases, concluded that compared to other agencies, hospitals identified abused children who were

> younger, Black, lived in urban areas and had more serious injuries. Hospitals failed to report to child-protection agencies almost half the cases that met the study's definition of abuse . . . Disproportionate numbers of unreported cases were victims of emotional abuse and came from families of higher income.

Exceedingly disturbing was the finding that, even when the injuries were ranked as 'serious', over half the cases were unreported by the hospitals. However, in respect to CAN deaths, representing 0.3 per cent of the population sampled, there were no unreported cases.

Community-based studies

Table 2.2, showing the results of fourteen community-based studies published between 1964 and 1986, also reveals wide variations in the rate of deaths. However, unlike the hospital-based studies, a marked reduction in death rates over time can be observed. This trend is also associated with substantial increases

Table 2.2 US community-based studies

Community-based data Author(s) USA	Type of study	Location	Date of study	No. of cases	No. of deaths	Rate per 1,000
Schloesser 1964	Survey	Kansas	1962–3	85	14	164.0
Simons et al. 1966	Case reg. [1]	New York City	1964–5	313	16	51.0
Allen et al. 1969	Case reg.	Minnesota	1963–8	123	7	56.9
Gil 1970	Survey	USA	1967	5,993*	134*	34.0*
Shaheen, Husain, and Hays 1975	Case reg.	Missouri	1974	1,462*	11	7.5
Friedrich 1976	Case reg.	Texas	1974–5	2,509**	104	41.4
Gonzalez-Pardo and Thomas 1977	Case reg.	Kansas	1972–5	1,505	7	4.6
Berger 1978	Case reg.	New Orleans	1977	1,600	25	15.0
Penn. Med. 1978	Case reg.	Pennsylvania	1977	4,498	26	5.7
McCarthy et al. 1981	Case reg.	Georgia	1975–8	2,446**	38	15.5
Texas Dept. 1981	Case reg.	Texas	1975–7	73,752**	267	3.6
US DHHS 1981a	Survey	National study	1979–80	652,000	1,000***	1.5
Jason et al. 1982	Case reg.	Georgia	1975–9	4,221**	51	12.0
AAPC Inc. 1986	Case reg.	National	1984	727,292†	500	0.68

[1] Case reg. – case register.
*   It is impossible to reconcile these numbers with the data in Gil 1970.
**   Confirmed or validated cases.
*** Estimated.
†   or 616,310 = 0.81 per 1,000.

in the size of the populations studied. In this context the very high rate of deaths, 164 per 1,000, observed by Schloesser (1964), needs to be explained.

Schloesser's data were based on the responses of thirty-seven physicians reporting fifty cases of child abuse during 1962–3. Questionnaires were sent to 1,000 physicians and returns were received from only 337. Additional cases were provided by the county health departments. At the other extreme, the data from Gil's 1967–8 (1970) study came from a nationwide epidemiological study of child abuse. Data for the US *National Study of the Incidence and Severity of Child Abuse and Neglect* (1981a) were based on a sample of child-protective service agencies located in ten states in a twelve-month period from May 1979 to April 1980.

The incidence of CAN deaths is also influenced by the definition of abuse and neglect employed by the researchers. Schloesser's (1964) interest was limited to physical abuse, including severe neglect and starvation. Over 80 per cent of her cases reported by physicians involved life-threatening injuries. Gil (1970) defined child abuse as 'when an adult physically injures a child, not by accident, but in anger or deliberately'. Since then, the legal definition of child abuse has been expanded to include emotional and sexual abuse. While always deplorable, these forms of abuse are rarely fatal. This fact was well illustrated by the US NCCAN (1981) study. Of the estimated total of 652,000 maltreated children (10.5 per 1,000 US children), less than half (48.4 per cent) had been physically abused or neglected. Of the remainder, 6 per cent had been 'sexually exploited'; 21 per cent had been 'emotionally abused'; 27 per cent had been 'educationally neglected', and 9.1 per cent had been 'emotionally neglected'. This broad definition of child abuse accounts for the relatively low incidence of deaths (1.6 per 1,000) reported in this study.

Finally, it may be useful to explain the relatively tentative nature of these estimates. This can be done with reference to the 500 fatalities reported in *Highlights of Official Child Neglect and Abuse Reporting, 1984* (American Association for Protecting Children, Inc. (AAPC) 1986). Strange though it may seem, calculating the incidence of fatalities per 1,000 cases is by no means simple. This is because it is difficult to determine if the denominator, the total population of children at risk, should include unsubstantiated cases or not. Similar problems occur in choosing between the total number of families reported or the total number of children within the families. In fact, the denominator can be determined in three ways. First is the total number of cases, i.e. 616,310. Second is the 722,704 children whose age is given. Third is the 727,292 children whose sex is given. The best solution was to present the highest and lowest possible rates. In this way it can be stated with some confidence that according to the AAPC 1986 data, the rate of CAN deaths in 1984 ranged between 0.68 and 0.81 per 1,000 reported cases.

Before sampling the results of several major community-based studies, it is necessary to explain the problem of dealing with 'confirmed' and 'unconfirmed' cases. Since reporting child abuse is mandatory across the USA, considerable effort is involved in determining whether a reported case is valid or not. Except when the child is obviously unmarked and in rude health, determining whether an injury was caused by an accident, rather than abuse, may well defy the most expert examination. Defining neglect may be equally difficult. As will be seen from the following examples, only about half the reported cases are 'confirmed'. In addition, there is growing evidence of bias in the reporting procedures. As a result, White, educated, middle-class parents are much less likely to be reported as abusers. This problem is further complicated by the fact that reports of abuse submitted by professionals, physicians, nurses, teachers, and social workers are more likely to be 'confirmed' by a child-protection agency than, say, by reports from family members or neighbours. For this reason it is misleading to use the confirmed or unsubstantiated case rate as a true measure of the incidence of reported abuse. For example, the 1984 AAPC report (American Association for Protecting Children 1986: 12) states, '90 percent of substantiated cases in the 1984 National Study were opened for protective services, whereas 16 percent of unsubstantiated cases were opened.' The same report estimates that of the 1.7 million children who were reported to have been abused in 1984, an estimated 727,000 (42 per cent) were considered to be 'substantiated' cases. Comparable data from some earlier studies show similar trends. The US DHHS (1981a) study showed a 'substantiation' rate of 42.7 per cent. Based on an analysis of 7,502 cases reported in Georgia, Jason and her colleagues (1982) showed a 'confirmation' rate of 56.3 per cent. This means that 43.7 per cent of reported cases were either 'non-confirmable' or 'ruled out'. Jason (1982) also claims that there is substantial bias in reporting procedures. The main point to be made here is that, in determining the incidence of fatalities in a population of child abuse and neglect cases, it is vital to know if the denominator includes or excludes the unsubstantiated cases.

The relevance of this information is simply demonstrated by reference to Friedrich's (1976) epidemiological survey of physical child abuse in Texas. Of approximately 4,000 cases reported in

1973, 2,509 (62 per cent) were confirmed cases. This included 135 cases of sexual abuse and 104 deaths. On this basis, it is possible to calculate the incidence of fatalities in three different ways. If the total number of reported cases, 4,000, is used as the denominator, the incidence of deaths will be 26 per 1,000. Using only the confirmed cases, the incidence is 43 per 1,000. Excluding the 135 sexual abuse cases from the confirmed cases reduces the incidence to 41 per 1,000 cases.

US NATIONAL STUDY OF THE INCIDENCE AND SEVERITY OF CHILD ABUSE AND NEGLECT (1981a)

This carefully crafted national study has produced some startling results. Most outstanding is the finding that deaths from maltreatment represent only 0.16 per cent of all cases. Almost half the estimated 1,000 CAN deaths involved children under 2 years of age. One-quarter were between 3 and 5 years of age. The remainder ranged in age from 6 to 17 years. Seventy-two per cent of the deaths were due to physical assault, including a few cases which also involved sexual abuse. The remainder of these deaths were attributed to physical neglect. In order of frequency, the physical neglect cases were subdivided into three main categories: disregard of avoidable hazards in the home; inadequate physical supervision; failure to seek medical care. This report does not provide data on the proportion of the fatalities involving children who were being supervised by child-protection agencies. However, after the child's death, 87 per cent of the cases were reported to the child-protection agency. The large majority, well over 80 per cent of the reported cases, involved families living in virtual poverty.

CHILD DEATHS IN TEXAS (1981)

This community-based study of 267 deaths attributed to child abuse and neglect in Texas examined data from two main sources. The primary source was the state CAN Reporting and Inquiry System (CANRIS). The supplementary source was child-protection agency records which proved to be of limited research value. CANRIS yielded information on 61 deaths in 1975; 82 deaths in 1976, and 124 deaths in 1977. Based on a total population of 66,719 reported cases (1975–7) the 267 deaths represent a rate of 0.4 cases per 1,000. It is difficult to determine if unsubstantiated cases were included or not. Information was not provided on the total number of age-specific deaths nor on the total population of children at risk in Texas in the years under study.

The Texas study reports that 46 per cent of male and 54 per cent of female victims died as a result of physical abuse. This pattern was reversed for neglect; 64 per cent of the males and 35.2 per cent of the females died as a result of neglect. The median age of the 267 victims was 1.8 years, compared with 10.1 years for children who were abused or neglected but not killed. Among the dead children, 20 (7.5 per cent) were between 5 and 7 years; 12 (4.5 per cent) were 7 to 9; and 22 (8.2 per cent) were 9 or older.

The ethnic variables in the Texas study are of interest. These data show that 45.1 per cent of the victims were 'Anglo'; 29.5 per cent were Black and 23.9 per cent were Mexican-American. This latter group was, however, responsible for 46.5 per cent of all the medical-neglect cases. The comparable percentages for the other ethnic groups were Anglo 18.5 per cent; Black 21.1 per cent. In other words, compared to the Anglos and Blacks, Mexican-American children in Texas were twice as likely to die from medical neglect. By definition, 'medical neglect' implies a wilful failure or refusal on the part of a perpetrator to provide the child at risk with needed medical attention. This assumes that medical services are equally and readily available to the children who need it. But the recommendations from the Texas (1981) study indicate that Mexican-Americans do not have equal access to medical services. It seems that due to problems with the US immigration authorities, Mexican-Americans are reluctant to use the services provided by public hospitals in Texas.

The authors of the Texas study (Texas Department of Human Resources 1981: 1) conclude: 'we are dealing with severely troubled and multi-problem families, who through desperation, inadequate parenting skills, or social isolation have engaged in abusive and neglectful behaviour implicated in the deaths of their children.' Apart from observing that one-quarter of the victims were involved with a child-protection agency at the time of their death, the researchers draw no conclusions from this finding.

CHILDHOOD FATALITIES IN NEW YORK CITY, 1983

Although this report provides one of the most recent and comprehensive studies of child abuse and neglect deaths, its statistical content is extremely limited. However, in order to glean as much information as possible, a brief description of the structure of the research is provided. The purpose of this exploratory and descriptive study was to identify key events in the lives of abused and neglected children and their families, before and after their death. The sample studied, identified from death certificates, was of

children under 6 years who died during the first six months of
1980, whose deaths were recorded as due to homicide, accident,
malnutrition, exposure, and sudden infant death syndrome (SIDS)
among children over 1 year of age. Deaths listed as 'pending further study' were included among the ninety-six deaths.

The preliminary causes of death were classified as: accidental:
48 (50 per cent); homicide: 23 (24 per cent); pending further
study: 24 (25 per cent). A SIDS case was reported in a child over
the age of 1 year. One-quarter of the accidental deaths were due to
motor vehicles, and 44 per cent were deaths due to fires which
were not classified as arson.

An expert panel was assembled to review the records obtained
from participating agencies. The cases were classified as follows: 45 *cases*, abuse or neglect involved; 24 *possible cases*,
circumstances unclear; 27 *non-cases*, circumstances without
abuse or neglect. The *possible* and the *non-cases* provided a
useful basis for comparison with the CAN *cases*. Although the
numbers are small, the consistent trends in the distribution
of data between the three groups provide a useful basis for
identifying high-risk situations. The relevant information is
assembled in Table 2.3.

In regard to sex and age of the victim, table 2.3 shows 64 per
cent of males among the *cases* compared to 50 per cent *possible
cases* and 56 per cent *non-cases*. The excess of male victims
among the *cases* is unexpected. Although the differences are not
great, the higher proportion of younger infants, under 6 months,
among the *cases* should also be noted. This is confirmed by the fact
that the *case* victims were, on average, six months younger than
the *non-case* victims. The difference reflects the higher incidence
of *non-case* deaths occurring out of doors.

The classification of deaths in the three groups reveals that
among the 27 *non-case* victims, 8 (29 per cent) died as a result of
motor-vehicle accidents. Among the 24 *possible cases*, 4 (16 per
cent) 'unsupervised' children were killed by a car. There were no
motor vehicle-accident deaths among the *cases*.

Deaths by fire were frequent in the New York City (1983) study.
But the 25 (26 per cent) deaths were by no means equally distributed. Eleven (44 per cent) were found among the *cases* compared
to 7 (28 per cent) each among the *possible cases* and *non-cases*.
Eight of the 11 deaths due to fire, among the *case* victims, involved
children who were left unattended.

The lack of adequate supervision and a generally hazardous
environment is, of course, characteristically associated with
CAN. This is well confirmed by the literature, which shows

Table 2.3 *The characteristics of the* cases, possible cases, *and* non-cases, *from the 1983 study,* . . . Child Fatalities in New York City.

Characteristics	Cases		Possible cases		Non-cases	
*Deceased child	No.	%	No.	%	No.	%
Sex: Male	29	64.0	12	50.0	15	56.0
Female	16	36.0	12	50.0	12	44.0
Total	45	100.0	24	100.0	27	100.0
Ages: % under 6/12		24.0		16.0		18.0
Median age	21 months		22.5 months		27 months	
*Siblings (prior to death)	%		%		%	
Lasting harm/injury	44.0		4.4		—	
Dead siblings	14.0		12.0		—	
*Parents	%		%		%	
Single-parent family	20.0		8.0		7.0	
Mother's ethnicity						
Black	65.0		64.0		17.0	
Hispanic	23.0		32.0		71.0	
White	7.0		—		8.0	
Median age at first pregnancy	18 years		17 years		20 years	
Adult occupations	%		%		%	
Professional/ managerial	4.0		4.0		15.0	
Unskilled/ unemployed	80.0		54.0		44.0	
Contact with health-care system before child's death	72.0		54.0		22.0	
History of family violence	44.0		4.0		—	
Arrest records of household members	36.0		17.0		15.0	

*Only three of the ten elements in table 2.3 reach an appropriate level of statistical significance. They are:
Mother's ethnicity: $\chi^2 = 19.69\,(4)\,p < 0.01$.
Contact with health-care system: $\chi^2 = 4.94\,(2)\,p < 0.05$.
Family violence: $\chi^2 = 11.99\,(1)\,p < 0.01$.

that a high proportion of siblings are victims of child abuse and neglect (Elmer 1967; Baldwin and Oliver 1975; Smith, 1975). A similarly high incidence of deaths or 'lasting harm' to siblings was revealed by the New York City (1983) study. Table 2.3 shows that a sibling had died in 14 per cent of the *cases* and 12 per cent of the *possible cases*. No sibling deaths were reported among the *non-cases*. The comparable data for 'lasting harm or injury' to siblings were: *cases* 44 per cent; *possible cases* 4.4 per cent; and none for *non-cases*. An extremely heavy burden of ill-health and handicaps was found among the 96 dead children (and their siblings) in the New York City (1983) study. Handicaps, defined in a somewhat arbitrary fashion,[1] were reported in 29 per cent of the *cases*; 33 per cent of the *possible cases*; and 26 per cent of *non-cases*.

The New York City (1983) study provides a wealth of information on the relationship between poverty and death due to CAN. It was found that 80 per cent of the adults involved as *cases*, when classified by occupation, were unskilled or unemployed, compared to 54 per cent of the *possible cases*, and 44 per cent of the *non-cases*. In respect to Medicaid or Public Assistance status, 90 per cent of the *case* families had such contact, compared to 67 per cent of the *possible cases*, and 36 per cent of the *non-cases*. Similarly in regard to the mother's education, it was found that *case* mothers had a lower grade level, 9.7, compared to 11.4 for *possible cases*, and 11.5 for *non-cases*.

Over 30 per cent of all families had been reported for suspected child abuse or neglect before the child died. These reports were heavily weighted towards *case* families. Almost half of them (49 per cent) had been reported to the child-protective services, compared to 17 per cent of *possible cases* and 4 per cent of *non-cases*. One-fourth (24 per cent) of the *case* children who died were under active supervision of a child-protection agency.

Taking all of these factors into account the authors of the New York City (1983: 19) study concluded:

> The data on child and family characteristics indicates that the children came from multi-problem families; some suffered from severe pathology or severe dysfunctions. These data provide a crucial context for understanding and interpreting the findings in this report. The difficulty of treating these families partially explains what happened, or did not happen, when these families came into contact with various human service and health programs before and after the death of the child.

A PROFILE OF SUSPICIOUS CHILD DEATHS IN LOS ANGELES COUNTY,
1986

In order to gain a better understanding of the nature and causes of
suspicious childhood deaths in Los Angeles County, ICAN, a
multi-disciplinary group representing the major public agencies,
was formed in 1978. Inspired, no doubt, by the medical 'death
rounds' model used in some teaching hospitals, the ICAN committee reviews all the deaths of children up to the age of 10 years,
where child abuse or neglect is suspected. The presence of one or
more of the following thirteen factors was used as a criterion for
inclusion: drug ingestion; cause of death undetermined after
investigation by coroner; head trauma (subdural, subarachnoid,
and subgaleal); malnutrition/neglect/failure to thrive; bathtub or
other type of drowning; suffocation/asphyxia; fractures; sudden
infant death syndrome (SIDS), where history and condition of
body raises suspicion, or child was over 7 months of age at death;
blunt force trauma; homicide, child abuse, or neglect; burns
(except where cause is clearly not abuse and neglect, such as auto
accident, accidental house fires, etc.); sexual abuse; gunshot
wounds. The ICAN group reviews about one-fifth of all child
deaths reported to the coroner each year. In this way 107 deaths
were examined in 1981; 154 in 1982; 107 in 1983 and 130 in
1984. Over this period between 25 per cent and 28 per cent of the
deaths were defined as due to homicide. Most of the remaining
deaths, while not directly due to child abuse or neglect, appeared
to 'involve conditions reflecting abuse or neglect'.

The Los Angeles County (1986) report provides valuable information, most of it very disturbing, about the 130 deaths in 1984.
At the outset 7 cases were rejected because they did not fit the criteria. Of the remaining 123 cases, well over half were children
under 1 year of age. Almost one-fifth were under the age of 2
years. Ninety-three per cent of all the children ranged in age from
birth to 5 years. The remainder (7 per cent) ranged in age from 5
to 10 years. In respect to ages of victims, the Los Angeles, Califor-
nia, deaths correspond quite closely to the CAN deaths in Ontario,
Canada. The proportion of male (54 per cent) over female victims
was also similar. However, unlike Ontario, there were considerable differences in the distribution of racial groups in the Los
Angeles cohort. The proportion of Black children whose deaths
were identified as suspicious was twice as high as the proportion of
Black children in the general population. In contrast, the proportion of the White children who were victims, was almost half that
of the general population. The proportion of Spanish-surnamed

children was equal to the population of Hispanic children. Race was also a factor in the types of deaths. Most of the White children died as a result of homicide. The deaths of Black children were most frequently attributed to 'accidents'. On the other hand, almost half the deaths of the Hispanic children were recorded as being due to 'natural' causes. The overall distribution of deaths by causes was: neglect, 59 per cent; abuse only, 20 per cent; abuse and neglect, 20 per cent; and sexual abuse, 2 per cent.

An unusual feature of the Los Angeles cohort was that 15 deaths (12 per cent) in the abuse/neglect group were drug related. At the autopsy 5 of the children were found to have drugs, usually cocaine, in their systems. In the remaining cases either the child was reported to have had drug-withdrawal symptoms at birth or the mothers were reported to have been abusing drugs.

In about one-fifth of the ICAN cases, the victim and/or the family was previously known to the child-protection agency. This was usually associated with some previous abusive episode. Hardly surprising was the finding that 63.4 per cent of the familes had a record of prior contact with public assistance programmes, including cash, food stamps, Medi-Cal, or social services. The ICAN report (1986: 35) concludes:

> There was a significant number of children whom it appears had been victims of maltreatment prior to their deaths. It also appeared that many of these children had not been visible enough or perhaps seriously enough injured to have received the types of services which might have prevented their deaths.

Summary and conclusions

This review of the epidemiology of CAN deaths in the USA serves three main purposes. It demonstrates that the early estimates of mortality were grossly inaccurate. It suggests the need for a more effective means of determining the incidence of deaths due to non-accidental injuries. Finally, in emphasizing the close connection between poverty and child mortality, it is hoped that child-health specialists and policy makers will recognize the urgent need to remedy these gross injustices. Effective professional intervention in these difficult cases demands urgent political action at every level of government. Failing this, it may well be impossible to prevent this needless waste of young lives.

The wide variation in the early estimates of mortality due to child abuse, ranging from 5–11 to 27 per cent (Kempe and Helfer 1972: 103), should have warned us to treat these figures as treacherous for research purposes. Although the reasons for the exaggeration need not concern us now, it is important to remember that the death rates specific to hospitalized cases cannot properly be generalized to other populations without strict control for the age of the victims, nature of the injury, and history of previous abuse. The ages and socio-economic status of the parents/perpetrators should also be regarded as important discriminating variables. The results of community studies based on child-abuse registers also need to be treated with caution.

As far as influencing social policy and improving professional intervention are concerned, the cohort studies (New York City, 1983, and Los Angeles, 1986) are extremely valuable. However, their effectiveness could be improved, at little extra cost, by relating these deaths, in an age-specific fashion, to all the other 'accidental' deaths of children in the same jurisdiction. Although data are scarce, there is good reason to believe that many 'accidental' deaths to children are associated with the lethal combination of poverty, adverse environmental conditions, parental stress, and the absence of effective child- and family-support services. The very high incidence of 'accidental' deaths involving Black children in the Los Angeles study is an example of the need for broadening instead of narrowing the scope of the community's action to protect its children.

Evidence of the close relationship between poverty, family stress, and child abuse and neglect in the USA is provided in the *Highlights of Official Child Neglect and Abuse Reporting*, published annually since 1976 by the American Humane Association (now the American Association for Protecting Children). The report for 1984, which provides data on more than 772,000 documented cases, reveals that the most common form of maltreatment, affecting 54.6 per cent of the children, was 'deprivation of necessities'. This is not surprising because almost half the abusive families were receiving some form of public assistance; 36.6 per cent of the caretakers were unemployed and 37.4 per cent of the families were headed by a single female. Data on 500 fatalities, from the same report, show that the average age of the dead children was 2.6 years. Deprivation of necessities accounted for 44 per cent of these deaths. In 28 per cent of these cases the responsible parent or caretaker was a single female.

With these depressing figures in mind, it should by now be obvious that little progress can be made in reducing the incidence of deaths due to child abuse and neglect until the problem of poverty afflicting some 35 million Americans, mostly women and children, is effectively dealt with. This issue was eloquently explored by Dr Carol Nadelson (1986: 952). In her presidential address to the American Psychiatric Association, titled, 'Health care directions: who cares for patients?', Nadelson reminds us of the appalling consequences of the 'feminization' of poverty in the United States. Concerned also about the moral and social contract which physicians have or should have, to provide health care for all those who need it, regardless of means, Dr Nadelson calls for political action. She says:

> In supporting this contract [to provide health care], we must also be aware that our society has not even made a commitment to provide food or shelter to needy children. The great numbers of hungry and homeless are testimony to failed or denied social responsibility.

3

CAN deaths in Ontario – a cohort study

To speak for the dead, to protect the living
(Ontario Coroner's Office motto)

The high level of anger and anxiety provoked by the death of children makes this a difficult field for a cohort study. This is especially true for research involving access to records of children who died or were assumed to have died as a result of abuse or neglect. Surmounting the ethical problems involved in gaining access to case records was the first hurdle. An even more difficult task was to ensure that all the relevant records were available for study. This problem was solved through the generous co-operation of the Chief Coroner of Ontario, Dr Ross Bennett. In addition to providing access to all the child-abuse and neglect deaths as determined by the individual coroners and coroners' inquests, and notified to the Provincial Child Abuse Register over a period of ten years from 1973 to 1982, I had virtually unrestricted access to all the records involving the deaths of children. Deaths due to injuries or conditions occurring at home were subject to close scrutiny. The causes of death in these cases were usually listed as, 'sudden infant death syndrome', 'suffocation', 'other accidental causes and adverse effects', and 'injury undetermined'. Cases with any suspicion of abuse or neglect were then discussed with one of the coroners, all medical specialists with considerable experience. In this way it was possible to add a few previously unidentified cases to the child-abuse list. It was a pleasant surprise to discover that the Ontario cohort consisted of exactly one hundred cases. While every effort was made to include all the CAN deaths, it would be naïve to imagine that we were completely successful. In fact three missed cases have already been identified. In two separate cases, after lengthy police investigations, the parents confessed to deliberately suffocating their children who were thought to have been sudden-infant-death-syndrome victims.

The cases involving coroner's inquests and criminal trials were particularly valuable for research purposes. They made it possible to secure access to a wide range of documents, including medical and child-protection records as well as the testimony of experts. In the absence of the trials and inquests, it was still possible to secure additional information on an informal basis. The results are reported in the following order: epidemiology; the victims; the perpetrators; situational factors; typology of cases; inquests, criminal charges, and dispositions; discussion and conclusions.

Epidemiology of CAN deaths in Ontario, 1973–82

SOURCES OF DATA

Although 'Child battering and other maltreatment' is included in the 'International Classification of Diseasees', 9th revision (World Health Organisation 1977–8), this category is notoriously under-reported in Ontario's *Vital Statistics* (Ontario, Office of the Registrar General). For example, *Vital Statistics* for 1983 report only two CAN deaths, while nine are listed in the Provincial Child Abuse Register. However, as previously indicated, the cohort of one hundred CAN cases, which provides all the data for this chapter, was made available by the Chief Coroner of Ontario. The supplementary data, used for purposes of comparison, come from the Provincial Child Abuse Register and from the reports on vital statistics published annually by the Registrar General of Ontario.

The expanded definition of CAN in the Child Welfare Act, Ontario, 1978, to include mental ill-health and sexual molestation, and the addition of a penalty for failing to report the abuse, resulted in a substantial increase in the number of reported cases. However, as table 3.1, column 2, shows, the increase in 1977 anticipated the legislative changes. This was probably due to the publicity associated with the deaths of Kim Anne Popen in 1976 (Allen 1982) and Vicki Star Ellis in 1977 (Greenland 1980a). For reasons which are difficult to explain, the number of reported cases declined in 1980, 1981, and 1982.

Since the rate of child-abuse reporting is influenced by a number of extraneous factors, it is necessary to establish some relationship between CAN and the population of children at risk. Equally important is the link between the number of CAN deaths reported annually by the Coroner of Ontario and the number of 'accidental and violent' deaths reported annually by Ontario's Registrar General. This relationship is examined in table 3.1. Column 1 confirms that over a period of ten years, from 1973 to 1982, there was a steady decline in the number of children in Ontario between the ages of 0–14 years.[1] Column 2 shows the number of children reported to the CAN register in the same period.

Table 3.1 *Reported cases of CAN and CAN deaths, related to the population of children, 0–14 years, at risk in Ontario, 1973–82*

Year	1	2	3	4
1973	2,169.5	598	0.275	10
1974	2,151.4	562	0.261	11
1975	2,130.3	769	0.360	13
1976	2,037.8	746	0.359	14
1977	2,037.8	1,045	0.512	15
1978	1,998.5	1,762	0.881	9
1979	1,941.0	1,170	0.602	9
1980	1,914.6	719	0.375	6
1981	1,886.5	603	0.319	7
1982	1,876.2	713	0.380	6

Column 1   Population of Ontario ages 0–14 years in 1,000s.
Column 2   Number of cases reported to the provincial CAN register in Ontario.
Column 3   Rate per 1,000 children, age 0–14 years, at risk.
Column 4   Number of CAN deaths reported by the Chief Coroner of Ontario.

Note: There is a statistically significant relationship between the CAN deaths and the population of children, 0–14 years, at risk ($r = 0.66\,(8)\,p < 0.05$).

The relationship, or lack of relationship, between the number of reported cases and the at-risk population of children, age 0–14 years, is confirmed in column 3. This shows that the rate of reported abuse, per 100,000 children, ranged from 0.261 in 1974 to 0.881 in 1978 and to 0.380 in 1982. These varying rates confirm the arbitrary nature of child abuse reporting in Ontario. Column 4 shows the actual number of child-abuse deaths.

Since many of the CAN deaths are included in *Vital Statistics* under the category of 'accidental and violent' deaths, table 3.2 examines this relationship in the context of the population of at-risk children from birth to 4 years in the period from 1973 to 1982. Column 1 records the slowly declining number of children in the birth-to-4 years age range. Column 2 shows the decreasing number of 'accidental and violent' deaths per year. Column 3, showing the number of 'accidental and violent' deaths, per 100,000 children, confirms that, in relation to the population at risk, the incidence of deaths attributed to accidents and violence in Ontario has decreased. Columns 4 and 5, showing the number and rate of child-abuse deaths, per 100,000 children, age 0–4, at risk, indicates that compared to accidental and violent deaths, CAN deaths show a more modest decline in incidence. The proportion of CAN deaths to accidental and violent deaths, shown

Table 3.2 *Accidental and violent deaths and CAN deaths, compared to the population of children, 0–4 years, at risk in Ontario, 1973–82*

Year	1	2	3	4	5	6
1973	634.1	230	36.2	10	0.157	4.3
1974	637.0	226	35.4	11	0.172	4.8
1975	632.9	193	30.6	13	0.205	6.7
1976	607.2	184	30.3	14	0.230	7.6
1977	603.8	171	28.3	15	0.248	8.7
1978	604.2	143	23.6	9	0.148	6.2
1979	603.6	137	22.6	9	0.149	6.5
1980	603.6	135	22.3	6	0.099	4.4
1981	593.0	145	24.4	7	0.118	4.8
1982	597.4	100	16.7	6	0.100	6.0

Column 1 Population of Ontario ages 0–4 years in 1,000s.
Column 2 No. of accidental and violent deaths per year, involving children age 0–4 years.
Column 3 Accidental and violent deaths, rates per 100,000 children, age 0–4 years, at risk.
Column 4 No. of deaths due to CAN per year.
Column 5 No. of CAN deaths per year; rates per 100,000 children, age 0–4 years, at risk.
Column 6 CAN deaths as a percentage of accidental and violent deaths per year.

Note: Due to the small numbers involved, the relationship between the CAN deaths and the population at risk is not statistically significant.

in column 6 as percentages, is relatively stable. This suggests that the number of children whose deaths are attributed to CAN bears a fairly constant relationship to the number of children at risk. This contrasts with the incidence of reported child abuse which does not show such a dependence.

SEASONAL INFLUENCES

The paper by Macfarlane (1982) on seasonal variations in post-neonatal mortality (PNM) in England and Wales, shows that in 1968–79 PNM was much higher in winter than in the summer. This trend was particularly noticeable in respect of deaths due to acute respiratory infections, bronchitis, influenza, and pneumonia. Deaths due to accidents increase in the summer months.

Table 3.3 shows that slightly less than one-third, 32 per cent, of the CAN deaths occurred in the four summer months, June, July, August, and September. Thirty-five per cent of male and 28 per

Table 3.3 *Distribution of CAN deaths and 'other' infant deaths[†] by sex and by winter, summer, and other months, Ontario, 1973–82*

Winter months (November, December, January, February – 120 days)	Male	Female	Both
CAN deaths	25	24	49
Percentage of CAN deaths	46.0	52.0	49.0
All infant deaths*	286	199	485
Percentage of all infant deaths	35.9	34.0	35.1

Summer months (June, July, August, September – 122 days)	Male	Female	Both
CAN deaths	19	13	32
Percentage of CAN deaths	35.0	28.0	32.0
All infant deaths*	251	187	438
Percentage of all infant deaths	31.5	31.9	31.6

Other months (March, April, May, October – 123 days)	Male	Female	Both
CAN deaths	10	9	19
Percentage of CAN deaths	19.0	20.0	19.0
All infant deaths*	260	200	460
Percentage of all infant deaths	32.6	34.1	33.3

* Infant deaths, age 0–12 months, Ontario, 1978.

Note: 'The percentages refer to the distribution of these deaths over three seasons. 'All infant deaths' are randomly distributed over the three seasons, winter, summer, other. The distribution of the CAN deaths over the three seasons is statistically significant: ($x^2 = 11.53\,(2)\,p < 0.01$).

cent of female deaths occurred in this period. The remaining months, March, April, May, and October, accounted for 19 per cent of the deaths. The differences between the sexes, 19 and 20 per cent, respectively, were minimal. Since, on a common-sense basis, it is easy to assume that the risk of a CAN death would be greater in the winter months, when parents and children are more likely to be confined at home, some alternative explanations were explored. First, however, it should be noted that there are 120 days in the 'winter' months, compared to 122 in the 'summer' and 123 in the 'other' months. This means that the statistical significance of the difference, noted in table 3.3, is substantially increased.

Table 3.4 *Victims by age and sex, one hundred CAN deaths, Ontario, 1973–82*

Age	0–12 months	–2 years	–3	–4	–5	*–11	Totals
Males	29	16	4	4	—	1	54
%	53	29.6	7.4	7.4	—	1.8	100
Females	28	9	2	2	1	4	46
%	60.9	19.6	4.3	4.3	2.1	8.8	100
Totals	57	25	6	6	1	5	100
** %	15.2	11.7	12.5	7.8	8.6	44.1	100
*** %	75.6	5.2	3.4	2.5	2.5	10.8	100

*   Includes two age 6 years; two age 7 years; and one age 11 years.
** Percentage of all deaths in Ontario, age 0 to 9 years, 1978.
*** Percentage of all deaths in Ontario, age 0 to 9 years, 1978, due to accidents, poisoning, and violence (ICD AE. 138–150, 8th revision. Ontario (1978), *Vital Statistics*).

Note: The differences between the age distribution of the CAN compared to the other deaths are statistically significant. (χ^2 = 69.73 (4) p < 0.01). The differences between the sexes are not significant.

Assuming, for the purpose of this analysis, that the seasonal distribution of the CAN deaths is the same as the distribution of all infant deaths in Ontario, the data provided by *Vital Statistics*, concerning all infant deaths, for children age 0–12 months, have been incorporated in table 3.3. These data show that the distribution of the deaths over the three seasons are more or less as expected. The small differences are not statistically significant. This is also true for the sex distribution of the victims.

It should be noted that the 1,373 deaths, reported in the Ontario *Vital Statistics* for 1978, refers only to infants age 0–12 months. The hundred CAN deaths, reported in this chapter, involve children age 0–12 years.[3] Unfortunately, it proved impossible to obtain access to age-specific data by causes of death. However, an analysis of deaths by month of death, for all ages, showed that it was very similar in distribution to the deaths of 0–12-months infants.

Victims

AGE AND SEX

Table 3.4, showing victims by age and sex, confirms that 95 per cent were age 5 years or less. The majority, 53 per cent males and

Table 3.5 *Birth order of victims and family size, CAN deaths, Ontario, 1973–82*

Family size		No. of children	
1 Only child		29	(28.47)*
2 Older of two children	2		
younger of two children	30	32	(35.52)
3 Oldest of three children	—	—	
second of three children	4		
youngest of three children	13	17	(15.57)
4 Oldest of four children	1		
Youngest of four children	1	2	(4.82)
5 Oldest of five children	2		
Youngest of five children	2		
Fourth of five children	1	5	(1.12)
6 Youngest of six children	1	1	(0.52)**
Family size not known		14	
Total		100	

* Comparative family size frequencies, 1981 census, Ontario. ** Six or more children.

Summary

Total of only children	29
Total of youngest children	47
Total of oldest children	5
Total of other children	5
Family size not known	14
Total	100

Note: The different frequencies of family size shown in table 3.8 and in the Ontario 1981 census data are statistically significant (χ^2 = 16.07 (5) $p <$ 0.01).

60 per cent females, died in the first year of life. Of the remainder, 54 of the victims were boys and 46 girls.

BIRTH ORDER AND FAMILY SIZE

Table 3.5, showing birth order of victims and family size, confirms that 29 were only children and 47 were the youngest children. Over 60 per cent of the victims were members of small families with one or two children. More than three-quarters of these

Table 3.6 Injuries at death or causing death by victims' age and sex, Ontario, 1973–82

Injuries or cause of death *	Age						Totals		
	0–12 months		–5 years		5 + years				
	Male	Female	Male	Female	Male	Female	Male	Female	Total
All head and brain	20	15	11	10	—	1	31	26	57
Neglect/malnutrition	7	7	3	1	—	2	10	10	20
Internal injuries	2	1	4	3	—	—	6	4	10
Asphyxia/choking	2	1	—	1	1	2	3	4	7
Other fractures	—	2	1	—	—	—	1	2	3
Multiple bruising	1	—	1	1	—	—	2	1	3
Other injuries**	2	—	3	1	—	—	5	1	6

* More than one injury was recorded in some cases.
** Includes one each of shaking, burns, drowning, stabbing, pneumonia, and exposure.

Note: The differences between the types of injuries and the victims' age and sex are not statistically significant.

victims came from families with three or fewer children. In this respect, the size of the hundred CAN-death families corresponded almost exactly with the expected distribution shown in the 1981 census data.

INJURIES CAUSING DEATH

The injuries recorded at the time of death, or given as the cause of death, are displayed in table 3.6. This shows that head and brain injuries were the cause of death in more than half the cases. Neglect and malnutrition, including dehydration, was the cause of death in 20 cases. Next, in order of frequency, were the internal injuries accounting for 10 deaths. These included torn bowel and ruptured liver caused by massive blows.

PREVIOUS INJURIES

Sixty-three victims (32 males, 31 females) had sustained previous injuries. The details, abstracted from the coroner's or the pathologist's reports are summarized in table 3.7. The presence of healing fractures was noted in 18 (28 per cent) of these cases. Other bruises and lacerations were noted in 16 (25 per cent) cases. In 2 cases, signs of a previous subdural haematoma were reported. The unexpectedly high incidence of previous injuries in this cohort should be noted.

Table 3.7 *Previous injuries by sex of the victims in sixty-three* CAN deaths, Ontario, 1973–82*

Type of injury	Male	Female	Total
All skull and brain	1	1	2
Facial bruises and lacerations	—	1	1
Neglect, malnutrition, failure to thrive	3	5	8
Healing fractures	6	12	18
Other bruises and lacerations	11	5	16
Other**	12	12	24
Total injuries***	33	36	69

*   32 male and 31 female victims.
**   Includes hospital admissions for unexplained injuries and not-stated injuries.
*** Some of the victims had several previous injuries.

PHYSICAL DEVELOPMENT AND NUTRITIONAL STATUS

With the exception of four cases, information on heights and/or weights of the victims at the time of death was obtained from the Ontario Coroner's Office records. Using the standard Growth and Development Record (Tanner, Whitehouse and Takaishi 1966), the appropriate centile height and/or weight was calculated from the available age- and sex-specific data. In this way, it was determined that 47 per cent of the victims were at or below the 3rd centile for height, weight, or both. These 3rd-centile cases were not equally distributed among the sexes. Twenty-five (54 per cent) of female victims were at or below the 3rd centile, compared to 22 (40.7 per cent) males.

Since 'failure to thrive' is defined (Whitten 1981) as being below the 3rd centile for height and weight, 16 of the victims (10 males and 6 females) fell into this category. An additional 19 (12 females and 7 males) were at or below the 3rd centile for weight, and 12 (7 females and 5 males) were at or below the 3rd centile for height. In summary, it can be stated that, including the 16 definite failure-to-thrive cases, 47 per cent of the victims were stunted in growth in respect to height, weight, or both. Information about the number of victims who were premature or underweight at birth was not available.

Although they are widely used to assess the growth of children, a disadvantage of the standard height/weight/age grids is the assumption that there is an ideal weight in relation to age, regardless of the child's length. This is a particular problem in assessing the nutritional state of very long infants who may be of average weight according to the standard growth charts. Similar difficulties arise in assessing genetically very small infants who, although below the third centile for height and weight, are well nourished.

In an attempt to overcome these difficulties, McLaren and Read (1975) developed an alternative classification of nutritional status based on a numerical relationship between height, weight, and age. Using the observed weight as a percentage of ideal weight/length and age, McLaren and Read provide the following categories of nutritional status:

Overweight/obese	110
Normal range	90–110
Mild malnutrition	85–90
Moderate malnutrition	75–85
Severe malnutrition	75

Since this classification is standardized for children up to the age of 5, it was only possible to classify 84 of the 100 victims. The results, in a compressed form, can be seen in table 3.8.

The distribution of cases, according to the McLaren–Read (1975)

Table 3.8 *Nutritional status*

Classification*	Males	Females	Total
Overweight/obese	2	4	6
Normal	14	15	29
Mild/moderate malnutrition	16	13	29
Severe malnutrition	9	11	20
Insufficient data**	13	3	16
	54	46	100

* Based on McLaren and Read 1975.
** Includes victims over the age of 5 years.

classification, reveals that 49 per cent of the victims suffered from severe, mild, or moderate malnutrition. Six were classified as being overweight or obese. This distribution is very close to the comparable categories derived from the Tanner–Whitehouse (1966) growth charts showing that 47 per cent of cases were at or below the 3rd centile for height, weight, or both. Yet only 16 cases fell into the failure-to-thrive category compared to the 20 per cent of severe-malnutrition cases defined by McLaren and Read.

An unexpected finding was that only 12 of the 47 victims who were stunted in growth died as a result of neglect or malnutrition. Twenty-six were battered-child-syndrome (BCS) victims. Four died at the hands of baby-sitters. Three died as a result of being severely shaken, and two were assaulted by mentally ill parents. In the 49 cases, classified according to McLaren and Read (1975) and showing 'mild, moderate or severe malnutrition', only 10 deaths were due to neglect or malnutrition. Most of the remainder were BCS deaths.

At the other end of the growth scale, 18 victims (10 males and 8 females) were at or above the 90th centile for height, weight, or both. Eleven were at or above the 90th centile for height, 2 were at or above the 90th centile for weight, and 5 were at or above the 90th centile for height and weight. The majority of these infants, 16 (88 per cent) were less than a year old; half of them were age 3 months or less.

Perpetrators

The suspected perpetrator was identified in 98 cases. Forty-three were female and 36 male. In 19 cases, both parents or partners

Table 3.9 Suspected perpetrators by age, sex, and relationship to victim, Ontario, 1973–82

Perpetrators	Age														Not known		Totals	
	-14		-19		-24		-29		-44		45+							
	M	F	M	F	M	F	M	F	M	F	M	F	M	F	M	F
Mother	—	—	—	9	—	12	—	10	—	3	—	—	—	4	—	38*
Father	—	—	1	—	5	—	4	—	2	—	1	—	—	—	13	—
Mother and father	—	—	1	2	5	6	2	—	1	1	1	1	2	2	12	12
Common-law partner/boy-friend	—	—	2	—	4	—	6	—	1	—	—	—	5	—	18	—
Mother and common-law partner	—	—	1	1	3	3	2	2	1	—	—	—	—	1	7	7
Baby-sitter	—	2	—	1	—	—	—	—	—	1	—	—	2	3	2	7**
Foster-/step-father	—	—	—	—	—	—	2	—	—	—	1	—	—	—	3	—
Father + girl-friend	—	—	—	—	1	—	—	—	—	—	—	—	—	1	1	1
Totals	—	2	5	13	18	21	16	12	5	5	3	1	9	11	56	65
Per cent	—	3.0	9.0	20.0	32.1	32.3	28.5	18.4	8.9	7.7	5.3	1.5	16.0	17.0	100	100

* Includes 17 married mothers.

** Includes two whose sex is not known.

Note: The differences between the perpetrators in the various age groups are not statistically significant.

were jointly responsible for the victim's death. The relationship between perpetrators and victims, by sex, is shown in table 3.9.

Natural parents were the perpetrators in 63 per cent of cases. Mothers were involved in 38, fathers in 13 and both in 12 cases. A father and his girl-friend were responsible for one death. Mothers and their common-law partners or boy-friends were responsible for 7 deaths. Acting alone, common-law partners or boy-friends were responsible for 18 deaths. Nine deaths occurred while the victims were being cared for by baby-sitters. Five of the baby-sitters were females, 2 were male and in 2 cases the baby-sitters' sex was not known. Two step-fathers and one foster-father were the perpetrators in 3 cases. No step-mothers were involved.

As a group the female perpetrators were much younger than the males. Well over half, 55 per cent, of the women were under the age of 24 years, compared to 42 per cent of the men. Somewhat unexpected is the relatively small proportion of teenage parents among the perpetrators. Table 3.9 shows that 12 (21 per cent) of the 57 mothers were under the age of 19 years. The corresponding figure for the fathers was 2 (7.7 per cent). Three teenagers, common-law partners, or boy-friends were involved as male perpetrators. At the other end of the age range, the presence of 4 perpetrators, age 45 or older, should be noted. Three of them were male and one was female.

In an earlier study, Greenland (1980a) showed that CAN injuries, divided into acts of commission and omission, are related in a statistically significant way to the sex of the perpetrators. Compared to females, male perpetrators were more likely to injure children by acts of commission such as hitting, kicking, slapping, throwing, etc. In an attempt to determine if this pattern applied to CAN deaths, the relationship between the perpetrators and the victims was explored in table 3.10. For this purpose, the injuries were grouped under four main headings; neglect, brain/head, abdominal, and other injuries. Although the numbers are small, the patterns of injuries causing death are quite clear. Both natural parents and single/separated mothers were responsible for 70 per cent of the neglect deaths. At the same time, married mothers were much more likely to be responsible for violent deaths. This was also true for male common-law partners. Except for the neglect deaths, involving 60 per cent of female perpetrators, the differences between the sexes, in relation to acts of commission, were negligible.

SOCIO-ECONOMIC STATUS

Precise information about the socio-economic status of the victims' parents was rarely available. Some case records provided

Table 3.10 *Suspected perpetrators and type of injury causing death, Ontario, 1973–82*

Perpetrators	Neglect	%	Brain/head injuries	%	Abdominal injuries	%	Other injuries	%	Total
Father	1	5.0	9	16.3	—	—	4	21.1	14
Married mother	2	10.0	11	20.0	3	30.0	3	15.8	19
Mother and father	6	30.0	3	5.5	1	10.0	2	10.5	12
Single/separated mother	8	40.0	9	16.4	1	10.0	3	15.8	21
Male common-law partner*	—	—	14	25.4	4	40.0	3	15.8	21
Mother and common-law partner	1	5.0	4	7.3	—	—	2	10.5	7
Baby-sitter	2	10.0	5	9.1	1	10.0	2	10.5	10
Totals	20	100.0	55	100.0	10	100.0	19	100.0	104**

* Includes 1 foster-father and 2 step-fathers.
** More than one injury was recorded in some cases.

Note: The differences between the perpetrators, male, female, and both, and the type of injury causing death are statistically significant ($x^2 = 11.25$ (2) $p < 0.01$).

fairly detailed descriptions of either abject poverty or modest affluence. The police were often surprised to find serious child abuse where the father was employed and the house was clean, well furnished, and comfortable. Based on what could be gleaned from information about the parents' ages, educational levels, means of support, and type of housing, the majority of cases could be classified in the UK Registrar-General's social classes IV or V.[4] In 37 cases there was evidence to suggest that the parents were unemployed and in receipt of general welfare assistance. This includes about 20 single or separated mothers who were supported by family benefits allowances. In sharp contrast to the frequent descriptions of poverty, there were 6 cases in which one of the parents had the equivalent of a white-collar or social class II occupation. These included a chiropractor, a nurse, a teacher, and a university student.

Situational factors

NATIVE CHILDREN ON RESERVES

Of the nine native Indian children who died as a result of CAN, five deaths occurred on reserves. One death occurred in a bush camp off the reserve. The mother, in this case, was leading a vagrant life. Since the high rate of mortality and morbidity of children on reserves is a matter of great public and professional concern (Ministry of Indian Affairs and Northern Development 1980), the following case vignettes may help to illuminate a part of the problem.

Case 1. Female, age 6.548 years. Cause of death, malnutrition. This child and her 5-year-old sister were deliberately starved and neglected by both parents. The mother was age 23 and the father 26. The older child died and the life of the younger was saved by prompt medical attention. Two younger children, ages 2 and 4, were found to be well nourished and cared for. Some months earlier the victim and her sister were treated for failure to thrive and placed in the care of a local children's aid society. The children were returned to their parents and the case closed without any investigation or follow-up.

Case 2. Male, age 0.808 years. Cause of death, pneumonia and malnutrition. At death, age 9 months, the victim was 62 cm in length and weighed 4.8 kg. This is the height and weight of a healthy infant at 2 to 3 months. There were four other children in this family. Both parents, mother 38 and father 55, were on probation for alcohol-related offences. They were charged with 'failure to provide the necessaries of life' and given a two-year suspended sentence.

Case 3. Female, age 1.488 years. Cause of death, cerebral oedema, bruises, and bite marks. The victim and her 2½-year-old brother were left for twenty-six hours in the care of a 12-year-old baby-sitter. The 24-year-old mother was found guilty of 'failing to provide' and put on probation for a year.

Case 4. Male, age 1.263 years. Cause of death, subdural haemorrhage, and multiple bruising. Two to three months before his death, the victim was admitted to hospital on two occasions suffering from 'pneumonia, gastroenteritis, and anaemia'. He was described as 'poorly cared for'. At death at the age of 16 months, he weight 8.1 kg. This is the normal weight for a healthy 6- to 7-month-old boy. The mother, found guilty of assault causing bodily harm, was sentenced to eighteen months' imprisonment.

Case 5. Male, age 2.17 years. Cause of death, exposure-frozen. While his mother was in hospital, the victim was left in charge of a 12-year-old baby-sitter who inadvertently let the fire go out. During the night the victim fell out of bed. Next morning he was found on the ground frozen to death. No charges were laid. The coroner's jury, all Indians, made the following recommendation:

> Shouldn't have two adults leave at the same time; should have lots of wood and food and have a reliable adult stay there or check them once in awhile. Before leaving kids they should check that everything is checked out to avoid accidents, like gas or matches with the baby-sitter.

MENTAL ILLNESS: NINE CASES

A high incidence of mental illness, especially severe personality disorders, among abusive parents, has been noted in several studies, Gil (1970), Smith and Hanson (1975), Lynch and Roberts (1982). One of the few researchers to include a comprehensive psychiatric assessment of his cases and control parents, Smith (1975) reported that 76 per cent of the 125 mothers and 64 per cent of the 89 fathers had an 'abnormal personality'. The incidence of psychotic illness was low. Although hints of mental illness, character disorders, or mental retardation were available in many more cases in this study, a formal psychiatric diagnosis was recorded in only nine cases: two were male and seven were female. One of the men had a diagnosis of personality disorder and reactive depression. The other man, who made previous attempts on the life of his 7-week-old son, was found to be psychotic and 'unfit to stand trial'.

The seven female perpetrators included three who were single or separated and four who were married. They had an average age of 28.6 years, range 20 to 38 years, and were older than the female perpetrators in the other groups. Four of these mothers had been diagnosed and treated for depression. Two had symptoms of paranoid schizophrenia. One had a long history of manic-depressive illness with frequent admissions to hospital. Six of the seven women, where this information was available, were taking tranquillizers. One of these women was also reported to be a heavy user of drugs and alcohol. The victims of four of the six women taking drugs, including the heavy drug user, showed characteristic signs of 'overkill'. An 8-month-old infant had forty-eight stab-wounds. The others died of multiple injuries, including fractures, to the head and body. In six of the nine cases, the victim's plight had already been identified by a children's aid society. Three cases were on the equivalent of a high-risk register. Warnings or help-seeking behaviour (Greenland 1971a) by the mother was evident in seven of the nine cases.

PREGNANCY

The critical role of pregnancy and the post-partum state in the aetiology of child abuse was mentioned in chapter 1. In the Ontario cohort nine (15 per cent) of the sixty battered-child-syndrome deaths occurred in the mother's post-partum period – up to two months following the birth. Three of the four mothers, known to be pregnant at the time of the victim's death, appeared in the BCS group. However, only one of them was a perpetrator. In two cases, common-law partners were the perpetrators. In the post-partum group, four mothers and five fathers were the perpetrators. This finding suggests that pregnancy and the post-partum period may be as stressful for men as it is for women. The literature on spousal abuse, Fagan, Stewart, and Hansen (1982) confirms that a current pregnancy is highly correlated with physical assaults on women by their male partners.

BABY-SITTERS: NINE CASES

Gil's (1970) typology of child abuse, to be considered in the next section, includes baby-sitter cases. In order to simplify this presentation, these cases will be examined here as 'situational' events. It will be seen that, although the range of injuries causing death include battered child syndrome, neglect and homicide, the infants who were killed while in the care of baby-sitters form a distinct group. They should be considered separately because child-abuse literature pays very little attention to the abuse and neglect of children by baby-sitters and other temporary caretakers.

In an earlier study of child abuse in Ontario, Greenland (1973) noted that baby-sitters were abusers in twenty-seven (2.4 per cent) cases. It was surprising to discover that baby-sitters were responsible for 9 per cent of the CAN deaths. Only two of the victims were females. The ages of both sexes ranged from 0.230 to 2.5 years. Five of the baby-sitters were female, two were male. The sex was not stated in two cases. In three cases, the baby-sitters were children. One was a 12-year-old girl who was suspected of killing a boy, age 1.4 years. He died from a subdural haemorrhage caused by a blow to the head. The second case involved a group of boys on an Indian reserve. They were left to look after a girl, age 1.4 years, who died as a result of cerebral oedema. Her body was covered with bruises and bite marks. In the third case a native child, age 2.17 years, froze to death while being cared for by a 12-year-old baby-sitter. In case 6, the male infant, age 0.230 years, died from intracranial haemorrhages due to whiplash injuries. At the time of his death the victim was suffering from severe colic. His aunt was charged with manslaughter.

In three cases, involving a girl, age 2.5 years, and two boys, ages 0.852 and 1.301 years, the prodromal symptoms included the observation, 'S/he falls a lot.' In case 7 the infant was admitted to hospital with suspected encephalitis three days before his death. In case 8 the infant had several minor falls three to four days before her death. The baby-sitter reported this to the victim's father. In case 9 the family physician, who questioned suspicious bruising on the child's body, was also told 'he falls a lot.' The autopsy revealed that the three infants died as a result of massive blows to the head inflicted, it was suspected, by baby-sitters. During the trial, in case 9, it was revealed that the 21-year-old baby-sitter had a history of disturbed and impulsive behaviour which made her unfit to care for an infant. In case 10, a male, age 1.375 years, was killed by a 23-year-old male baby-sitter. Death was due to a massive abdominal haemorrhage due to a lacerated liver. The man was charged with homicide.

A typology of CAN deaths

The various attempts to develop typologies of child-abuse cases have been reviewed by Smith (1975). Most of them, it seems, were designed to illuminate the psychodynamic elements of abusive situations. They tended to be primarily concerned with labelling various psychopathic behaviours. However, as Smith (1975) pointed out, 'There has been no evidence to show that such categories or similar clusters are valid or whether they are useful, as an aid in the determination of high risk patients.'

Gil (1970) argues that the conceptualizations involved in developing a typology of child 'abuses' may help to 'avoid fruitless arguments between those who believe that child abuse is caused by the psychopathology of the perpetrators and those who see the phenomenon related primarily to cultural, social and economic factors.' Although there is considerable heuristic value in the seven-factor typology developed by Gil (1970) the limited sources of data prevented its use in the present study.

Table 3.11 shows the suspected perpetrators distributed into five categories:

Battered child syndrome (BCS) Defined by Kempe *et al.* (1962)
Neglect These cases include all the acts of omission causing death, such as starvation, dehydration, left unattended, drowning in the bath, etc.
Homicide These represent impulsive criminal acts causing the infant's death.
Discipline and inappropriate handling The cases in this category involve excessive shaking by the adult caretaker of an otherwise well-cared-for infant.
Other Unclassified.

BATTERED CHILD SYNDROME (SIXTY CASES)

Sixty cases seem to fit, almost perfectly, the classic battered child syndrome (BCS) described by Kempe and his colleagues. Like Kempe *et al.* (1962), we found that the victims were very young. Thirty-two (53.3 per cent) were age 12 months or less, and only one was older than 5 years. Nine of the fourteen infants who died in the post-partum period (under 2 months of age) were victims of the BCS. The balance between the sexes, thirty males and thirty females, was equal at all ages.

The most frequent cause of death was head injuries including haematoma, intracranial haemorrhage, subarachnoid haemorrhage, and subdural haematoma with or without a fractured skull.

Table 3.11 *Suspected perpetrators and typology of one hundred CAN deaths, Ontario, 1973–82*

Perpetrators	Typology of cases					
	BCS*	Neglect	Homicide	Discipline	Other	Totals
Single/ separated mother	7	8	6	—	—	21
Common-law partner**	16	—	3	2	—	21
Married mother	15	2	—	1	—	17
Father	7	1	3	1	1	13
Mother and father	4	6	—	—	2	12
Baby-sitter	5	2	—	1	1	9
Mother and common-law partner	6	1	—	—	—	7
Totals	60	20	12	4	4	100

* Battered child syndrome.
** Includes one foster- and two stepfathers.

Note: The difference between single/separated and married mothers and the typology of cases is statistically significant ($\chi^2 = 11.61$ (1) $p < 0.01$).

These features were present in forty-eight (80 per cent) of deaths. The next most frequent cause of deaths was abdominal injuries, including ruptured duodenum and lacerated bowels. These injuries occurred in twelve (20 per cent) cases. The most outstanding feature of the battered-child-syndrome cases was the multiplicity of injuries and the high proportion of previous injuries including evidence of healing fractures and old bruises. Among the sixty BCS cases, a total of 109 injuries, average 2.0 per case, were recorded by the pathologists. Combinations, such as fractured ribs, multiple bruising and dehydration or fractured skull, contusions and bruising, or subdural haemorrhage and healing fractures, were frequently reported. Bite marks and cigarette burns were noted in only two cases.

An analysis of these data shows that the male common-law partners averaged 2.4 injuries per victim; both parents averaged 2.2 injuries and the remainder 1.8 injuries. This suggests that the attacks by male common-law partners on unrelated infants tended to be more indiscriminate and violent.

In twenty-five (45 per cent) cases, there was a record of previous injuries to the victims. In nine (16 per cent) cases, it was reported that a sibling had either sustained a serious injury or had died as a result of such an injury. In twenty-two (40 per cent) cases, the victim's family was either known to be involved or was currently involved with a children's aid society before the death.

A closer examination of these data reveals that, where the mother was the suspected perpetrator, thirteen (86 per cent) were or had been actively involved with a children's aid society. The corresponding proportions for the other groups of perpetrators involved with a children's aid society were: both parents, two (50 per cent); fathers, two (33 per cent); male common-law partners, six (37 per cent); and mothers and common-law partners, three (50 per cent). The numbers are too small to permit useful tests of significance.

Among all the adults who were included in this study as suspected perpetrators or partners of perpetrators, at least ten had been children's aid society wards. Eight of them appeared in the fifty-five battered-child-syndrome cases, three as perpetrators. Two were fathers, and one, a mother, was involved with a common-law partner. Three of the men were fathers where mothers were the perpetrators. Two of the mothers, former children's aid society wards, were living with common-law partners who were perpetrators.

The perpetrators consisted of twenty-three males and twenty-seven females. In ten cases, both parents or the mother and her

Table 3.12 The relationship between perpetrators and victims in the sixty battered-child-syndrome cases compared to the total number of perpetrators in each category, Ontario, 1973–82

Relationship	Total no. of perpetrators	Battered-child-syndrome cases (BCS)		BCS cases as percentage of total no. of perpetrators
			%	%
Married mother	17	15	25.0	88.2
Mother and common-law partner	7	6	10.0	85.0
Common-law partner	19	16	26.7	84.2
Baby-sitter	9	5	8.3	55.0
Father	13	7	11.6	53.8
Mother and father	12	4	6.6	33.0
Single/separated mother	21	7	11.6	33.0
Other	2	—	—	—
Total	100	60	100.0	60.0

Note: The difference between the relationship to victims in the battered-child-syndrome and other cases is statistically significant (x^2 = 20.19 (1) $p < 0.01$).

male common-law partner were equally responsible for the victim's death. Table 3.12 shows the relationship between perpetrators and victims in the battered-child-syndrome cases compared to the total number of perpetrators in each category. These data are arranged in descending frequency in order to show the relationships most and least frequently involved in the BCS deaths. It will be seen that the mother's common-law partner, who is not the victim's biological parent, accounted for twenty-two (36.6 per cent) of the BCS deaths. In sixteen (26 per cent) cases, he acted alone. In six (10.0 per cent) cases, the common-law partner and the victim's mother were jointly responsible for the death. In Scott's (1973b) study, involving twenty-nine fatal battered-baby cases, the average age of the male perpetrators was 24.3 years with a range of from 18 to 35 years. Less than half (48.3 per cent) were biological fathers. In the present study, only eleven (18 per cent) of the perpetrators were biological fathers. The average age of the thirty-three male perpetrators was 23.3 years, with a range of from 17 to 36 years.

That fifteen (88.2 per cent) of the seventeen married mothers in this series were perpetrators in the BCS cases is unexpected. Together with the common-law partners (84.0 per cent), they formed the largest group of perpetrators. The high proportion of mothers among the BCS cases is not due to differences in age. The female perpetrators in the four categories, married mother, mother and common-law partner, father and mother, and single/separated mother, had an average age of 20.5 years, range 15–30 years. Since they included one 15-year-old and three 17-year-old mothers, the thirteen perpetrators who were single/separated or living with common-law partners formed a slightly younger group.

NEGLECT (TWENTY CASES)

A combination of neglect, dehydration, malnutrition, strangulation, starvation, exposure, and pneumonia was given as the cause of death in twenty cases. With the exception of three baby-sitters, the perpetrators were all parents of the victims. Eight of them, including three unmarried mothers, age 16, 17 and 18, were single or separated women.

The victims, ten males and ten females, ranged in age from 26 days to 6.5 years. In only five cases were the heights and weights of these infants in the normal range, 10th to 97th centiles. These data were not available in one case. The remainder were at or well below the 3rd centile for height and weight. Some mixture of poverty, isolation, parental incompetence, and the lack of adequate social supports were clearly responsible for fourteen (70 per cent) deaths. Children's aid societies were involved in six of these cases. Physicians and public health nurses were active in at least two cases.

In addition to some of the social factors mentioned above, there was evidence of personality disorders or other psychopathology in four cases. In case 1 the parents deliberately starved and neglected two children, including the 6.548-year-old female victim, but provided adequate care for two younger children. In case 11 the victim, who died as a result of dehydration, was found on autopsy to have healing fractures of her arms and ribs. Her sister had died earlier from a fractured skull. In case 12 the male victim, age 1.019 years, who died from dehydration and malnutrition, was found to have severe genital bruising. The suspected perpetrator, the male common-law partner, was charged with manslaughter. The victim in case 13 was a 0.482-year-old female. In addition to suffering from 'emaciation and neglect', she had multiple contusions and abrasions. Her 26-year-old, divorced mother, living with a boy-friend, had refused the help offered by a public health nurse. There was no inquest or trial.

HOMICIDE (TWELVE CASES)

Although they had much in common, it is inappropriate to lump the twelve homicide cases in with the BCS cases. This is because, except for case 14, which involved a sustained sadistic abuse of a male infant by his foster-father, the other deaths were caused by a single physical assault. The victims, ten boys and two girls, ranged in age from 0.343 to 6.4 years.

One of the perpetrators, a 33-year-old single mother, had a long history of alcoholism. While intoxicated, she threw her 4-month-old infant over a balcony. He fell 60 feet and died from multiple injuries. Because of the mother's history of irresponsible behaviour, this case was well known to the children's aid society. The victim in case 15, age 1.26 years, was described as well developed and cared for. He was choked to death by his 22-year-old father who could not stand the baby's crying. In case 16, the victim, age 1.424 years, was killed by his mother's 18-year-old boy-friend. The 17-year-old mother, who was six months pregnant, her boy-friend, and the victim were in a cinema when the assault occurred. The boy-friend hit the victim on the head to stop him from being a nuisance. He waited until the show was over before reporting the death to the police.

INAPPROPRIATE HANDLING AND DISCIPLINE (FOUR CASES)

Two of the four victims, a male, age 0.477 years, and a female, age 0.808 year, died from whiplash injuries caused by a severe shaking. One of them suffered from a subdural haematoma. The perpetrators were fathers, age 24 and 39. They seemed to have lost patience with the infants and vented their frustration by shaking them to death. Similar whiplash injuries, with a subdural haemorrhage, caused the death of a male age 0.230 years. The perpetrator was a 33-year-old aunt who was baby-sitting. In the fourth case, the victim, an 11-year-old girl, was reported to have been obstreperous and unwilling to do her share of the housework. She was beaten about the head and killed by her step-father, who had previously abused her.

OTHER, UNCLASSIFIED (FOUR CASES)

The following cases could not be fitted into the typology. In case 17, the male victim, age 0.208 years, died from a fractured skull. His father, a university student who was caring for him while his wife was at work, said that, while carrying him out to the car, he slipped on ice and fell on the baby. The coroner and police thought that the head injury was inconsistent with the father's explanation. Their supsicions were increased by radiological evidence of healing fractures. Since there were no witnesses an open verdict was returned.

Case 18, a *cause célèbre* in Toronto, involved the death by 'hypernatremia', of a 4-week-old infant who was being closely supervised by social workers. Two of the four previous children died as the result of abuse or neglect, and two were removed by the court and put up for adoption because of the mother's inability to care for them (Greenland 1980a).

Case 19 This male, age 1.164 years, drowned in a bath while in the care of a baby-sitter. He was allowed to stay overnight with a young single mother who had abused and neglected her own children. Next day the victim was found dead in a bath of water. His body was covered with fresh bruises and abrasions. The babysitter claimed that her children must have put him in the bath while she was asleep. There was no explanation for the injuries and, in the absence of witnesses, no charges were laid.

Case 20. This female, age 4.471 years, died from a head injury when a door fell on her. She had previously been abused by her father who suffered from a personality disorder and depression.

Inquests, criminal charges, and dispositions

In her 1977 study of fifty-four CAN deaths in Canada, Robertshaw (1981: 112) reported that in ten (18.5 per cent) cases no inquests were held and no charges were laid by the police. In Ontario, however, under the Coroner's Act, Ontario, 1982, the coroner has the authority as well as the responsibility to investigate all deaths which are the result of violence, misadventure, negligence, misconduct, or which are sudden and unexpected. When charges are laid by the police, the coroner is required to terminate his investigation. Sometimes the police charges may follow from an inquest. In two cases in this series, charges were laid in this way. Once the charge is disposed of, the coroner may, in exceptional circumstances, decide to hold an inquest. In rare cases the decision to lay charges may be delayed for many months. This protracted delay may lead the coroner to conclude that the public interest would not be well served by an inquest.

Since the Chief Coroner's Office of Ontario has a long-standing interest in the problem of child abuse and neglect, and an excellent reputation for the most painstaking inquiries into suspected CAN deaths, it was surprising to discover that no inquests were held or charges laid in thirteen cases. The main features of these cases are illustrated by the following case vignettes.

Case 21, 1977. Male, age 0.117 years. Both parents, described as mentally retarded, lived in 'total squalor'. Death was due to 'bowel infection, severe dehydration, renal failure, cerebral hypoxia and cardiac arrest'. The infant was below the 3rd centile for height and weight. On the day before his death, the infant was taken to a medical clinic suffering from 'a bowel disorder and diarrhoea'. He was sent home. Following the death, his two siblings, age 3½ and 2 years, were removed by the children's aid society.

Case 22, 1975. Female, age 0.668 years. Mother, age 18 years, intellectually dull. Both parents regarded as immature. Victim had been hospitalized for 'failure to thrive'. Height and weight at death was below the 3rd centile. Death was attributed to SIDS and neglect. Victim had not been fed or changed for fifteen hours. Up to the time of her death, this child had been seen weekly by a physician. The mother also had counselling on nutrition from a public health nurse. An older sibling was found to be suffering from anaemia and malnutrition. Perhaps with tongue in cheek, the coroner recorded 'Medical care has been excellent throughout.'

Case 20, 1980. Female, age 4.471 years. Mother was 23, and father 26. Since they were suspected of abuse when victim was a year old, the children's aid society had supervision. The victim, who was treated by the family physician for 'feeding problems', was admitted to hospital 9.7.76 with dehydration and gastro-enteritis. The parents failed to visit during the twelve days of her hospitalization. Mother had a miscarriage in August 1979. Father admitted to mental hospital, 10.10.79, with diagnosis: 'Personality disorder and reactive depression.' On 22.11.80 a door fell on victim and killed her. Cause of death was 'Cardio-pulmonary arrest and subdural haemorrhage'.

A search of the Coroner's Office records concerning this cohort of 100 CAN deaths revealed that charges were laid by the police in sixty-two cases, involving thirty-two (61.5 per cent) male and thirty-seven (58.7 per cent) female perpetrators. Although charges were apparently not laid in the rest of the cases, this does not preclude the possibility of charges being laid at some later date if new evidence becomes available. For example (case 22), in 1984 a young mother was found guilty of infanticide and given a suspended sentence. The victim, age 0.104 years, died in 1979 as a result of a subarachnoid haemorrhage. This mother was charged with infanticide in 1982, after she had been found guilty of assaulting her 5-week-old son. It should be noted that in seven cases both perpetrators or partners were charged jointly for the same offence. This explains why the number of perpetrators exceeds the number of victims.

The following data, shown in tables 3.13 a, b, c, d, e, and f, are grouped according to charges. This otherwise convenient arrangement conceals the fact that in some cases, as a result of plea bargaining, the original charge of, say, manslaughter, was reduced to the lesser charge of assault causing bodily harm. In other words, the categories used here may not be as precise and as immutable as the legal charges seem to imply. An additional complication is that the disposition was not known in eight cases, involving two (6.4 per cent) male and six (16.6 per cent) female perpetrators.

Tables 3.13 a, b and c show that charges of homicide or manslaughter were laid against twenty-six (81.2 per cent) men and seventeen (45.9 per cent) women. However, if the eleven infanticide

Table 3.13 *Types of criminal charges and dispositions by the perpetrator's sex, Ontario, 1973–82*

(a) *Manslaughter,* * *26 cases:*

Dispositions	Male perpetrators	Female perpetrators
Life imprisonment	1	—
10 years	2	—
7	—	1
5	3	1
4	2	—
3	1	2
90 days to 2 years	6	4
Not guilty or acquitted	2	—
NGRI**	—	1
Suspended sentence	—	1
Not known	2	1
Total persons charged	19	11

* Sec. 217, CCC (Canadian Criminal Code). Maximum penalty is life imprisonment.
** Not guilty by reason of insanity.

Note 1 : Of the 19 males charged with manslaughter, 10 were common-law partners of the mother; and one each was a foster-father, step-father and a baby-sitter. The remainder were fathers of the victims.

Note 2 : The differences in the length of sentences imposed on male and female perpetrators are not statistically significant.

(b) *Homicide,* * *13 cases*

Dispositions	Male perpetrators	Female perpetrators
Life imprisonment	1	1
10 years	1	—
2–4½	2	1
Not guilty/dismissed	2	—
NGRI**	1	3
Not known	—	1
Total persons charged	7	6

* Sec. 212, CCC. Maximum penalty is life imprisonment.
** Not guilty by reason of insanity. The man was found unfit to stand trial.

Note: Of the 7 males 5 were common-law partners of the mother, and one was a step-father.

(c) *Infanticide,* * *11 cases*

Dispositions	Mothers
Imprisonment, 3 months–2 years	2
Suspended sentence of 3 years	2
Probation, 2–3 years	2
Released on appeal	1
Sent for psychiatric treatment	1
Not known	3
Total charged	11

* Sec. 216, CCC. Maximum penalty is 5 years' imprisonment.

(d) *Criminal negligence,* * *3 cases*

Dispositions	Male perpetrators	Female perpetrators
18 months' imprisonment	1	—
21	—	1
3 years'	—	1
Total persons charged	1	2

* 'Causing death by criminal negligence', Sec. 203, CCC. Maximum penalty is life imprisonment.

(e) *Failure to provide the necessaries of life,* * *3 cases*

Dispositions	Male perpetrators	Female perpetrators
Suspended sentence	1	1
Psychiatric treatment	—	1
Not known	—	1
Total persons charged	1	3

* Sec. 197, CCC. Maximum penalty is 2 years' imprisonment.

(f) *Assault, causing bodily harm,* * 6 cases

Dispositions	Male perpetrators	Female perpetrators
5 years' imprisonment	1**	—
2–4	1	1
2	—	1
9–18 months'	2***	2
Total persons charged	4	4

* Sec. 245, CCC. Maximum penalty is 5 years' imprisonment.
** Common-law partner.
*** Plus 3 years' probation.

cases are included, the number of women charged with these offences is increased to twenty-eight (75.6 per cent). With respect to the lesser offences of failing to provide the necessaries of life, maximum penalty two years' imprisonment, and assault causing bodily harm, maximum penalty five years' imprisonment, tables 3.1 e and f show that seven (19.4 per cent) women and five (16.1 per cent) men were charged in this way. This suggests that the courts treat the male perpetrators more severely than the female.[5] The differences in the severity of punishments accorded to the male perpetrators compared to the female perpetrators is confirmed by the sentences. Sentences of imprisonment ranging from five years to life were imposed on nine (29.0 per cent) men and three (8.3 per cent) women. Women had similar advantages in respect to the non-penal dispositions. Grouping the categories of 'not guilty', 'not guilty by reason of insanity', 'referred for psychiatric treatment', 'suspended sentence and probation', it will be seen that thirteen (35.1 per cent) women and seven (22.5 per cent) men were disposed of in these ways.

Of the thirty-two male perpetrators charged, only eleven (34.3 per cent) were biological parents. Of the remainder, seventeen (53.1 per cent) were common-law partners or boy-friends of the natural mother. There were two step-fathers, one foster-father, and one male baby-sitter. Among all the male perpetrators, these non-biological parents received the most severe punishments. Two received life sentences; two, ten years; two, five years; and five between two and four-and-a-half years. One was found unfit to stand trial, two were not guilty as charged. In two cases, the sentence was not known. The remainder received prison sentences with a minimum of nine months. Although this information was rarely available, in a few cases it was reported that some of the common-law partners had substantial criminal records, often involving violence. This may account for the relatively severe sentences imposed on them.

Discussion and conclusions

A common criticism of child-abuse research is that its source of data tends only to reflect the reported cases which come, often very dramatically, to public attention. The other cases, which may well form the majority, are rarely accessible to researchers. While this observation may apply to CAN deaths research, the possibility of concealment is substantially reduced by virtue of the Coroner's Office and the legislation requiring the medical certification of all deaths by cause.

Analysis of the 100 CAN deaths, in the context of the *Vital Statistics* provided by the Registrar General of Ontario, leaves no doubt that the CAN deaths form a distinctive sub-population of the 'accidents, poisoning, and violence' deaths (AE. 138–50, 'International Classification of Diseases and Accidents', 8th revision; AE. 250–76, 'International Classification of Diseases', 9th revision) (see WHO 1977–8). Using the year 1978[6] for purposes of comparison, it was observed that, up to the first year of life, an approximately equal number of girls and boys died as a result of accidents and violence. Table 3.4, showing CAN victims by age and sex, indicates that there were slightly more deaths among boys than girls. However, after the first year of life, there is a rapid increase in the proportion of male deaths in both populations. But, unlike the CAN deaths, which decline in incidence after age 4, deaths due to accidents and violence increase rapidly with age reaching a peak for both sexes at 20–24 years.

Any doubts that might exist about the circumstances causing a death can usually be resolved by a report on the victim's socio-medical background and the post-mortem examination. A history of repeated accidents, previous hospital admission for unexplained injuries, or reports of abuse and neglect to the victim or his siblings, must obviously increase the index of suspicion. Equally significant at the autopsy is evidence of previous abuse, neglect, malnutrition, and failure to thrive. In view of the finding (Table 3.7) that 63 per cent of the victims had previous injuries, including healing fractures, bruises, and lacerations, and the finding (table 3.8) that 20 per cent were suffering from severe malnutrition, this combination of conditions should be, in the absence of alternative explanations, regarded as pathognomic of CAN deaths.

In studying the issues raised by the high incidence of 'failure to thrive' in this population, the victim's role in precipitating the attack must be considered. Unfortunately, except for such odd comments as 'he was a very poor eater', 'never slept', 'suffered from colic', 'cried a lot', and 'refused to be comforted', the records provided very little information about the temperament of the victim and the quality of the parent–child relationship. But these and related observations suggest that some children may indeed be temperamentally more difficult to raise than others. This possibility is accepted in the ecological model of development suggested by Samaroff and Chandler (1975). They see 'multiple transactions between environmental forces, caregiver characteristics, and infant attributes as continuing, reciprocal contributions to the events and outcomes of child development.' Thus, it is necessary to consider the possibility that the infant's failure to thrive, despite the best efforts of the parents, may provoke the aggression which eventually culminates in his death.

An equally important question is whether the hundred CAN deaths, examined in this chapter, are part of the spectrum of child abuse or whether, phenomenologically, they should be located in the context of intrafamily homicide. The former position assumes that the deaths are best explained as an unintended consequence of the violence toward children which, according to Gil (1970), is endemic to our culture. The intrafamily homicide explanation assumes that, while socio-economic and cultural factors are relevant, the criminal act is mainly the result of severe psychopathology.

In addressing these issues, Kempe et al. (1962) placed child murder by a psychotic parent at the extreme end of the child-abuse spectrum. A similar position was taken by Steele and Pollock (1968). They also claimed that murderous attacks on children are, phenomenologically, quite different from abuse where the perpetrator's objective is to hurt rather than destroy the victim. The former group, they say, includes more pathologically disturbed individuals. Scott (1973b) suggests that in some cases, since the child may frustrate his wishes, the perpetrator's intention is not so much to hurt or kill but merely to eliminate a source of frustration and annoyance.

Except in a few cases where this information was part of the record, the design of the present research precluded the possibility of studying or attributing motives to individual perpetrators. However, the typology of deaths, shown in table 3.12, is designed as a modest contribution to the debate on the aetiology and dynamics of child abuse in its most extreme form. Although there is an inevitable overlap between homicide, battered child syndrome, and neglect deaths, each of the categories has some unique features. The twelve homicide cases will be considered first.

HOMICIDE

The term 'homicide', in this context has been generally reserved for cases in which the death was caused by a single massive blow to the head or body, delivered, it must be assumed, with murderous intent. The victims ranged in age from 2 months to 6 years. Except for one who showed signs of failure to thrive, the victims were all unusually healthy. In six of the twelve cases, the perpetrators were single or separated mothers, ranging in age from 17 to 33 years. All of them were living in extremely stressful situations, and only one of them was considered to be mentally ill. Among the men who killed in a 'homicidal' fashion, three were fathers and three were unrelated. One of them, a common-law partner, was found unfit to stand trial due to mental illness. In another case, a foster-father subjected the victim to sadistic treatment over several months before killing him. In two cases, very young men, ages 17 and 18, killed infants in the circumstances described by Scott (1973b), 'because they were being a nuisance'. This suggests that these offences are probably due to gross immaturity, impulsiveness, lack of compassion, and poor judgement.

MENTAL ILLNESS

Since mental illness is commonly employed either to explain or to excuse criminal offences, references to it were frequently found in the hundred CAN deaths records. However, only in nine cases involving two male and seven female perpetrators was there clear evidence of pre-existent and severe psychiatric illness. In at least four cases, involving mentally ill female perpetrators, a disinhibiting or paradoxical reaction to the prescribed medication may have precipitated the homicidal assault. In view of this and the other observations, it seems reasonable to conclude that psychotic or mentally ill perpetrators were not responsible for much more than about 10 per cent of the CAN deaths.

DISCIPLINE

The inappropriate use of force by adults to secure compliance, obedience, or submission in children is illustrated by the four 'discipline' cases involving one female and three male perpetrators.

One of the cases involved an 11-year-old girl whose head was beaten by an irate step-father. The other three cases involved fretful infants, ages 2, 5 and 9 months, who were shaken to death by exasperated parents or parent substitutes.

NEGLECT

The professional preoccupation with the battered child has, to a considerable extent, obscured the plight of children who suffer and die as the result of neglect including starvation. Eight of the twenty perpetrators were young, single, or separated mothers. The victims, also very young, ranged in age from 2 to 13 months. They all died from malnutrition or dehydration, but two of them showed signs of previous injuries as well as neglect. The neglect deaths could be attributed to a combination of factors, including maternal incompetence, adverse environmental conditions, and an inefficient child-protection service. Gross incompetence of the child-protection services, including physicians and public-health nurses, was a contributing factor in at least five additional cases. In three or possibly four cases, it seems that the starvation and neglect were deliberately used as a means of destroying unwanted children. For this reason, it seems best to assume that 'neglect' covers a range of quite different behaviours and motivations.

BATTERED CHILD SYNDROME

Most of the data provided in this chapter conform to the classical description of the battered child syndrome (BCS) by Kempe and his colleagues. However, in describing this syndrome, without providing data, Kempe *et al.* (1962) mention that the perpetrators are usually the parents or foster-parents. In a later study of child abuse in the USA, Gil (1970) records that in one-third of the cases the male perpetrator was not the victim's biological parent. Similar data were provided in the UK by Creighton (1980b). She reported that 'Natural Mother and Substitute Father' were the perpetrators in 22.1 per cent of cases.

Since Gil (1970) and Creighton (1980b) were reporting on child abuse and not specifically on child-abuse deaths, some differences between their findings and the data presented here should be expected. Analysis of the data concerning the sixty BCS cases confirms that twenty-two (36.6 per cent) of the male perpetrators were common-law partners or boy-friends of the victim's other. Acting alone or in partnership with the mother, these non-biological parents appear to have inflicted more and often more violent injuries on the infant victim. Although it was not possible to trace the criminal careers of these men, the available information confirms Scott's (1973b) impression,[7] that young infants left in the care of male common-law partners have a great risk of being severely abused or killed.

The data presented here also indicate that the risk of a BCS death appears to be greater in the presence of a current pregnancy or post-partum state. Aristotle's notion, that mothers are fonder of their children because they have a more painful share in their production and are more certain that they are their own, is not supported by Table 3.12 which shows that mothers were the perpetrators in half the sixty BCS deaths. The thirty BCS cases involving mothers are of particular interest because of the high incidence of revealed psychopathology. Five of these mothers, including two who were clearly psychotic, suffered from severe psychiatric disorders at the time of the tragedies.

This discussion would not be complete without some reference to the role of socio-economic factors. Since the sources of data on this topic were by no means complete or reliable, the conclusions presented here should be regarded as tentative. With this caution in mind, it is reasonable to conclude that the majority of the parents of the hundred infants whose deaths were due to CAN were young, poorly educated, unskilled, unemployed, and, most likely, dependent on welfare allowances. Although it may be impossible to confirm this statistically, it seems that the link between child-abuse deaths and poverty is as strong in Ontario as it is in the USA and the UK.

4

CAN deaths in the UK – children at risk

Last week we all watched and read as officialdom trundled to its conclusions on the death of one, small, abandoned and broken child [Jasmine Beckford]. Newspapers and politicians thundered for action, as they always do. As they did for Maria Colwell. As they did for Tyra Henry. As they did for Heidi Koseda. But while they thunder you can act.

(Mail on Sunday, 8 December 1985: 26)

Unlike the previous chapter which described a total population of CAN deaths in Ontario, Canada, the aim of this one is to examine an unrepresentative sample of CAN deaths in England and Scotland. As far as can be determined there were none in Wales in the period under review. The majority of the cases examined here involved at-risk children who were already under the protection of social workers. Because they form, as it were, a biased sample, an epidemiological analysis of these data would not be useful. But in order to provide a foundation for what follows, some statistical information will be presented on the characteristics of the victims, the perpetrators, and the situation in which the tragedy occurred. This information will be prefaced by a brief review of the vital statistics and the relevant research data. A comparison between the UK and the Ontario cases will be presented in the summary and conclusions section.

At the outset it should be noted that since the reporting of child abuse and neglect is not mandatory in the UK, no official statistics are available. In the absence of official statistics, the best source of information is the annual reports, *Trends in Child Abuse* (1977–82), published by the National Society for the Prevention of Cruelty to Children (NSPCC) (Creighton 1984). This will be considered as an example of community-based research. The hospital-based research will be examined first.

Hospital-based research

Table 4.1 provides data on eight hospital-based research projects published in the decade ending in 1982. The variations in the

Table 4.1 UK hospital-based data

Hospital-based data Author(s) UK	Type of study	Location	Date of study	No. of cases	No. of deaths	Rate per 1,000
Jackson 1972	Retro.	London	pre-1970	100	2	20.0
Cooper 1975	FU*	Newcastle	1965–71	136	14	102.9
Hall 1975	Retro. ***	Preston	1963–72	68	7	102.9
Hall 1975	Retro.	Preston	1970–2	29	5	172.4
Smith 1975	Prosp. **	Birmingham	1970–4	134	21	156.7
Speight et al. 1979	FU	Newcastle	1974–5	60	1	16.6
Roberts et al. 1980	FU	Oxford	1958–70	332	9	27.1
Lynch and Roberts 1982	FU	Oxford	1966–75	42	1	23.8

* Follow-up study.
** Prospective study.
*** Retrospective study.

estimated incidence of deaths range from Jackson (1972), 20.0 per 1,000 cases to Hall (1975), 172.4 per 1,000. As indicated in chapter 2, with reference to the study by Smith (1975), these differences are most likely due to variations in the definitions of a 'case'. Incidence rates may also vary due to chance factors. This is likely since the populations studied, for example by Hall (1975) and Lynch and Roberts (1982), are relatively small.

Community-based studies

Vital statistics for 1984, concerning child deaths in England and Wales in 1984 (World Health Organisation 1985) provides the background information for this section. In 1984 there were 10,870 deaths to children from birth to age 14 years. Of these, 'accidents and adverse effects' were responsible for 1,001 (9.2 per cent) deaths in this age group. 'Motor vehicle traffic' and 'other transport accidents' caused 479 (4.4 per cent) deaths. 'Homicide' and 'other violence' were responsible for 90 (0.82 per cent) deaths. It seems reasonable to assume that most of the CAN deaths which were not classified as homicides would be included in the larger category of 'accidents and adverse effects'. Information on the incidence of sudden infant deaths, to be mentioned later, was not available in the vital statistics. However, as Creighton (1984) demonstrates, there is a connection between some SIDS cases and CAN deaths.

The community studies shown in table 4.2 also indicate wide variations in the rate of CAN deaths. These range from Baher *et al.* (1976), 160 per 1,000 cases, to Creighton (1984), 7.6 per 1,000 cases. These variations are not surprising because, in addition to the relatively small number of cases, the follow-up periods also vary in duration from one year to over twenty years. Despite these differences, homicide and other forms of violence are not major causes of deaths to children in the UK. This is confirmed by Creighton (1984: 6). Based on an extrapolation of the 1977–82 data, she estimates that the national figure for CAN deaths ranges from '44 to 74' per year. This figure is much less alarming than the estimate provided by Hall (1975) whose study was based on a population of injured children seen in a hospital emergency department. In a period of three years, from 1970 to 1972, Hall (1975) found twenty-nine definite abuse cases, including five deaths. In this way a mortality rate of 17.2 per cent was derived. Applied to an estimated 4,400 abuse cases seen in emergency departments all over England and Wales, 17.2 per cent yields 757

Table 4.2 UK community-based data

Community-based data Author(s) UK	Type of study	Location	Date of study	No. of cases	No. of deaths	Rate per 1,000
Skinner and Castle 1969*	NSPCC Retro.***	London	1969	78	4	51.2
Castle and Kerr 1972**	NSPCC Prosp.	England	1970	292	3	10.2
Baldwin and Oliver 1975	Retro Prosp.†	NE Wiltshire	1967–71 1972–74	60	6	100.0
Baher et al 1976	NSPCC Prosp.	London	1971–3	25	4	160.0
Rose 1976	NSPCC Case reg.	Leeds, Manchester	1973–4	124	1	8.6
Creighton and Owtram 1977	Case reg.	Manchester, Leeds, Newcastle, etc.	1975	562	9	16.0
Creighton 1980b	Case reg.	Manchester, Leeds, Newcastle, Northampton, Notts., etc.	1976	644	7	10.8
Oliver 1983	Case reg.	NE Wiltshire	1960–81	560	41	73.0
Creighton 1984	NSPCC Case reg	Manchester, Rochdale, Calderdale, Leeds, etc.	1977–82	4,679	36	7.6

*   Excludes accidents.
**   All reported cases, plus F.U. of 78, 1969 cases.
*** Retrospective.
†   Prospective.

as the annual number of deaths to be expected in the whole population. This primitive arithmetic provided the foundation for the *Sunday Times* headline (11 November 1973): 'Two babies battered to death each day'.[1] A decade later this estimate was described by Adelstein *et al.* (1982) as being 'incompatible with any but the wildest view of the inaccuracy of death certification.' But this caution has not diminished the enthusiasm of the press for alarming headlines. A recent example of this comes from a *Daily Telegraph* article (10 December 1986), based on a NSPCC press release which reports a '68 per cent increase in reports of children seriously or fatally injured (59 to 99). The headline reads, "CHILD ABUSE DEATHS SOARING; Parents 'killing 3 or 4 weekly' ".' On the other hand, in an earlier report, Creighton (1984) claimed that 'the continuing decline in the proportion of fatal and serious injuries, and of re-injuries, demonstrates the efficacy of the management of child abuse in the NSPCC Special Units Register Areas.'

Some of the difficulties involved in collecting data on CAN deaths is described by Creighton (1984: 21). For example, the thirty-six children who died in suspicious circumstances, and were notified to the NSPCC Special Units Registers, included three children from one family who were killed by their father in a murder–suicide incident. This was one of the two murder–suicides in which four of the the thirty-six children died. Only two children in this cohort had been previously injured. In addition to the thirty-six children who were registered as 'suspicious' deaths, three more deaths were reported. Two were cot deaths and one child died of bronchial pneumonia. They were reported to the register when the post-mortem examination revealed evidence of old injuries. As a result of police investigations, two parents admitted injuring their children. Creighton (1984: 21) states that twelve registered children died during the study period, 1977–82. Ten of them died from 'natural causes'. Included here were two children who, on autopsy, were found to have suffered recent fractures.

Although its focus was post-neonatal mortality (PNM), involving children age 1 week to 2 years, the multi-centre study of 988 deaths in the years 1976–9 (Knowelden, Keeling, and Nicholl 1984) provides valuable information on the incidence of violent deaths as well as on the sudden infant deaths. The first point to be made is that death certificates provided an unreliable basis for classifying PNM. The next important finding was that trauma was responsible for only forty-seven deaths (47.5 per 1,000). The coroners gave verdicts of 'infanticide' in nine cases, but the authors conclude that there might well have been a further fifteen 'violent deaths'. The remainder of cases were regarded as 'genuine accidents'. On this basis it can be assumed that twenty-four deaths were probably due to CAN. In this way the rate of deaths due to CAN for children, age 2 or less, can be estimated at 25 per 1,000. While appreciating that violence plays only a small part in infant deaths, Knowelden's conclusions leave no room for complacency. In reviewing this study *The Lancet* (9 February 1985: 322) made the following points which provide a useful point of departure for this review of CAN deaths in the UK:

> In the new inquiry [Knowelden, Keeling and Nicholl 1984], out of 297 infants who had a clinically apparent illness or non-specific symptoms before they died, avoidable factors attributed to inappropriate behaviour on the part of the parents occurred in 24%. More surprisingly, 131 infants had been seen by the general practitioner and in 64%, the avoidable factor was an inappropriate action by the GP. This was seen as an indictment of the quality of primary care and one recommendation relates to the training of family doctors. Of the sixty-nine admitted to hospital, just over a quarter were deemed to have been handled inappropriately by the hospital staff.

SOURCES OF DATA

The data for this section come from three main sources: official published and unpublished reports on thirty CAN deaths; [2] thirty-three NSPCC Special Units cases; five Area Review Committee cases.

Official reports have been published on thirty CAN deaths. Since this information is in the public realm, the names of the victims and the local authorities concerned are mentioned when necessary. Information on some of these caes has been supplemented by data provided on a confidential basis by coroners, pathologists, police, and others involved in the initial investigations.

Two cases, Clark in 1975 and Menheniott in 1978, have been excluded from this study. Since he was 19½ years old when he was killed, the case of Stephen Menheniott was excluded. The decision to exclude Richard Clark, age 3.6 years, was much more difficult. Although he suffered from a massive cerebral haemorrhage caused by a blow to the head, and his foster-parents were convicted of assault, Richard Clark survives in a vegetative state. While this case cannot be classified as a CAN death, it will be referred to again because it provides valuable information on 'help-seeking' behaviour which was ignored.

Data sheets on thirty-three deaths collected by the NSPCC

Special Units Research Office, from 1976 to 1980, provide the second source of UK cases. To protect the confidentiality of these records, all identifying information was obliterated at source. To avoid using the same material twice, cases that were the subject of Area Review Committee Inquiries were abandoned. Five deaths which are not strictly attributable to child abuse or neglect have been retained. These cases are mentioned in Creighton and Owtram (1977) and Creighton (1980b) annual reports on the NSPCC's Special Units Registers.

LIMITATIONS OF DATA

Unlike the hundred Ontario cases, the UK material is not a representative sample. At least thirty of the sixty-eight cases involved children and families who were known to or under the supervision of a child-protection agency. Many of these victims or their siblings had previously been defined, formally or informally, as high-risk cases. For this reason the family backgrounds in these cases may include a high degree of pathology. To some extent, however, the revealed pathology may also reflect the searching inquiry conducted into the circumstances leading to the victim's death. It seems reasonable to regard these cases as being at the extreme end of the child-abuse spectrum.

The thirty-three NSPCC cases provide a more representative sample of CAN deaths occurring in the industrial heartland of England. Although the quality of the NPSCC research data has obviously improved in recent years, there were many gaps in the data provided for the years 1976–80. For this reason, NPSCC data is omitted from some of the tables.

The five cases provided by Area Review Committees, which prefer not to be identified, are in almost all respects very similar to the NSPCC cases. But unlike the NSPCC material, the Area Review Committee cases include an analysis of the lessons to be learned from each of these tragedies.

EPIDEMIOLOGY

Table 4.3 shows the sixty-eight deaths arranged by year, source, and sex of the victims. The UK and NSPCC cases are treated separately. For both cohorts, the greatest number of deaths occurred in the years 1978 and 1979.

Table 4.4, which examines the distribution of cases by months and sex of the victims, shows no statistically significant differences. The same is true for the analysis of the thirty-five UK deaths by days

Table 4.3 Sixty-eight CAN deaths in the UK, year, sources, and sex of the victims

Years	UK cases*			NSPCC cases			All UK cases		
	Male	Female	Total	Male	Female	Total	Male	Female	Totals
1972	1	—	1	—	—	—	1	—	1
1973	2	2	4	—	—	—	2	2	4
1974	—	1	1	—	—	—	—	1	1
1975	3	1	4	—	—	—	3	1	4
1976	5	—	5	3	2	5	8	2	10
1977	1	1	2	5	1	6	6	2	8
1978	2	4	6	2	6	8	4	10	14
1979	2	4	6	7	3	10	9	7	16
1980	3	1	4	1	3	4	4	4	8
1981	—	—	—	—	—	—	—	—	—
1982	1	1	2	—	—	—	1	1	2
Totals	20	15	35	18	15	33	38	30	68
%			100			100			100

* Subject to official enquiries.

Table 4.4 *Distribution of sixty-eight UK deaths by months and sex of victims*

Month	Male	Female	Total	%
January	5	1	6	8.8
February	5	1	6	8.8
March	1	2	3	4.4
April	4	3	7	10.3
May	2	1	3	4.4
June	4	5	9	13.3
July	1	3	4	5.9
August	3	2	5	7.4
September	5	1	6	8.8
October	3	2	5	7.4
November	2	4	6	8.8
December	3	5	8	11.7
Totals	38	30	68	100

Note: The sixty-eight CAN deaths are randomly distributed over the months of the year ($\chi^2 = 6.50\,(11)\,p < 0.05$).

of the week. Except for a slight tendency to peak on Sundays (seven cases), the deaths were randomly distributed over the week. The thirty-three NSPCC deaths showed quite a different distribution. Eleven (33 per cent) of the deaths occurred on Thursdays. There were none on Fridays. Re-examination of these data provided a prosaic explanation for what might otherwise be termed the 'Bloody-Thursday' syndrome. Five of the eleven deaths occurring on Thursdays involved two families. In one case, three children were strangled by their father in a murderous rampage. In the other case, two children were asphyxiated when their father, in a fit of pique, set fire to their home.

VICTIMS

Table 4.5 shows the victims by age, sex, and source of data. In both cohorts, males exceed the females at the rate of 56 to 44 per cent. Except in the first year of life, the distribution of ages in the two cohorts is similar. Three of the six children over five years of age were strangled by their father.

Table 4.5 *Victims by age, sex, and source of data, sixty-eight UK deaths*

	0–12 months		2 years		3 years		4 years		5 years		5–14 years		Totals	
	NSPCC	UK	NSPCC	UK	NSPCC	UK	NSPCC	UK	NSPCC	UK	NSPCC	UK	NSPCC	UK
Males	8	5	6	6	1	3	1	1	—	3	2	2	18	20
Totals	13		12		4		2		3		4		38	
Females	9	5	4	4	—	3	1	2	—	—	1	1	15	15
Totals	14		8		3		3		—		2		30	
Totals	17	10	10	10	1	6	2	3	—	3	3	3	33	35
Totals	27		20		7		5		3		6		68	
Per cent.	39.70		29.40		10.30		7.40		4.40		8.80		100	
UK Mortality Statistics*	78.20		5.10		8.30						8.40			

* Office of Population Censuses and Surveys (1974).

Note: Compared to 'All' child deaths in the UK, 1973, the age distribution of the sixty-eight CAN deaths is statistically different ($\chi^2 = 100.86$ (4) $p < 0.01$). The difference between the sexes is not statistically significant.

Table 4.6 *Injuries at the time of death or cause of death by age and sex, sixty-eight UK deaths*

| Injuries or cause of death* | Age | | | | | | | | |
| | 0–12 months | | –5 years | | 5 + years | | Totals | | Total |
	Male	Female	Male	Female	Male	Female	Male	Female	
All head and brain	9	8	8	6	—	2	17	16	33
Internal injuries	4	3	6	4	—	1	10	8	18
Neglect/malnutrition	—	—	7	2	1	—	8	2	10
Asphyxia/strangulation	2	2	1	1	2	1	5	4	9
Burns and scalds	—	—	2	4	2	1	4	5	9
Other fractures	4	1	—	2	—	1	4	4	8
Multiple bruising	—	3	1	—	—	—	1	3	4
Other injuries**	1	3	1	5	—	—	2	8	10

* More than one injury was recorded in some cases.
** Includes bite marks, stab wounds, cigarette burns, and anal injuries.

Note: There is a statistically significant difference between the victims under 1 year of age and the others in relation to the injuries ($\bar{x}^2 = 18.36\,(6)\,p < 0.01$). The differences between the sexes are not significant.

Table 4.7 *Previous injuries sustained, by sex of the victims in 31* of the 35** UK deaths*

Type of injury	Male	Female	Total	%
All skull and brain	1	3	4	5.8
Facial bruises and lacerations	13	11	24	35.3
Neglect/malnutrition and failure to thrive	6	3	9	13.2
Healing fractures	7	4	11	16.1
Other bruises and lacerations	2	7	9	13.2
Abdominal	—	2	2	2.9
Other***	5	4	9	13.2
Total injuries	34	34	68	100.0

* Some of the victims had several injuries.
** 18 male and 13 female victims.
*** Includes scalds, bite marks, and cigarette burns.

Note: The differences between the sexes in the type and frequency of previous injuries are not statistically significant ($\chi^2 = 7.75\,(5)\,p > 0.05$)

INJURIES AND CAUSE OF DEATH

Table 4.6, showing injuries at the time of death or the cause of death, confirms that thirty-three (48 per cent) of the victims died as the result of head or brain injuries. The most frequent cause of death ws given as intracranial haemorrhage with or without skull fractures. Next in frequency were the internal or soft-tissue injuries which included torn bowel or ruptured liver due to severe blows. The large majority of victims age 12 months or less died as a result of head or soft-tissue injuries. Multiple injuries were very common at all ages. With the exception of the ten deaths due to neglect and/or malnutrition, there was little difference in the distribution of injuries by sex of the victim. Table 4.6 shows that eight boys and two girls died as the result of neglect.

PREVIOUS INJURIES

The high-risk status of this cohort is confirmed by the fact that thirty-one (88.5 per cent) of the thirty-five victims had sustained previous injuries. Table 4.7 shows that facial bruises and lacerations were reported in 35 per cent, and healing fractures in 16 per cent of cases. Neglect/malnutrition and failure to thrive, other bruises and lacerations, and other injuries, including scalds, bite-marks, and cigarette burns, each accounted for 13 per cent of cases.

GROWTH AND DEVELOPMENT

Data on the heights and weights of the thirty-three dead children in the NSPCC cohort were not available. However, with the generous co-operation of coroners and pathologists, it was possible to obtain some of this information in thirty of the thirty-five UK fatalities. In three (8.5 per cent) cases, the victims were well below the 3rd centile for height and weight. In four (11.4 per cent) cases, the victims were below the 3rd centile for height, and nine (25.7 per cent) were below the 3rd centile for weight. On this basis we can conclude that sixteen (45.7 per cent) of the victims were severely stunted in respect to height, weight, or both. Only two of them were premature babies. Another was listed as having a 'low birth weight'. The six victims whose deaths were due to neglect or malnutrition were at or below the 3rd centile for height, weight, or both. Of the ten remaining victims in this category, nine deaths were due to the battered child syndrome and one was due to homicide. Eleven of the BCS victims were in the normal range, 10th to the 90th centile, for height and weight. Three were at or above the 90th centile for height and weight. One of them, a month-old girl, was killed by her 21-year-old father who had a previous conviction for violence. The second case involved a 1-year-old boy who was killed by his 22-year-old father. His death was due to a severe shaking, causing head trauma and retinal haemorrhages. In the third case, involving physically well-developed children, a recently adopted 3-year-old girl was killed by her step-mother.

PERPETRATORS

Table 4.8 shows the suspected perpetrators by age, sex, and relationship to the victims. The sixty-eight deaths involved forty-three male and forty female perpetrators. In fifteen (22 per cent) cases, the perpetrators were male and female partners. Both parents were the perpetrators in ten (14.7 per cent) cases. Mothers and their common-law partners were the perpetrators in three (4.4 per cent) cases. In the two remaining cases, a father and step-mother, and step-grandparents were the perpetrators. In regard to the ages of the perpetrators, there appeared to be very little difference between the sexes: 60 per cent of the male and 65 per cent of the female

Table 4.8 Suspected perpetrators by age, sex, and relationship to victim, sixty-eight UK deaths

	Ages in years											
	-19		-24		-29		-44		Not known		Totals	
Perpetrators	M	F	M	F	M	F	M	F	M	F	M	F
Married mother	—	3	—	3	—	5	—	3	—	3	—	17
Father	4	—	10	—	1	—	6	—	—	—	21	—
Mother and father	—	—	1	5	6	2	1	1	2	3	10	10
Male common-law partner**	1	—	3	—	2	—	—	—	1	—	7	—
Single/separated mother	—	—	—	2	—	1	—	1	—	1	—	4
Adoptive/foster-mother	—	—	—	1	—	2	—	—	—	1	—	4
Mother and common-law partner	—	—	—	2	2	1	1	—	—	—	3	3
Father and step-mother	—	—	—	—	1	—	—	1	—	1	1	1
Step grandparents	—	—	—	—	—	—	—	—	1	1	1	1
Totals	5	3	14	13	12	11	8	5	4	9	43	40
%	11.6	7.0	32.5	32.0	28.0	27.0	18.6	12.0	9.3	22.0	100	100

* No. of perpetrators exceeds no. of victims.
** Includes one step-father and one 15-year-old brother.

Note: The distribution of the sexes among the age-groups is not statistically significant.

Table 4.9 *Suspected perpetrators and type of injury causing death, sixty-eight UK cases*

Perpetrators	Neglect		Brain/head injuries		Abdominal injuries		Other injuries		Total
Father	2		10		3		6		21
Married mother	1		9		1		6		17
Both parents	3		3		1		3		10
Common-law partner	—		1		4		2		7
Single/separated mother	2		1		1		—		4
Adoptive/foster-mother	1		3		—		—		4
Mother and common-law partner	1		1		1		—		3
Other*	—		1		1		—		2
Totals	10	14.7%	29	42.6%	12	17.6%	17	25%	68	100%

* Step-father and a 15-year-old brother.

Note: In respect to the type of injury, relationship, and sex of the perpetrators, the differences are not statistically significant.

perpetrators were between the ages of 25 and 29 years. The value of this information is reduced by the fact that for four (9.3 per cent) males and nine (22.5 per cent) females, the age was not given.

Table 4.9 examines the data on suspected perpetrators and the type of injury causing the victim's death. Between them, fathers, mothers, and both parents were responsible for twenty-two (75.8 per cent) of the deaths due to brain and head injuries. This distribution is quite different from the comparable data for Ontario. This is partly explained by the relatively small number of common-law partners and the absence of baby-sitters in the UK cohort.

PREGNANCY AND POST-PARTUM STATES

In three of the thirty-five UK cases, mothers were pregnant at the time of the victim's death. In another three cases, the mother had given birth within two months of the infant's death. In two of these cases, new-born infants, one male and one female, died as a result of blows to the head inflicted by their fathers. One of these men, a 21-year-old 'aggressive psychopath' with a criminal record, had previously assaulted his daughter. The other man, age 17, had kicked his wife during the final weeks of her pregnancy and also slapped his son when he was only a few weeks old. In the third post-partum case, a year-old male was killed by his 22-year-old father. The victim had previously suffered fractured ribs and legs.

One of the pregnant mothers, who killed her 3½-year-old daughter, had two other children aged 2 and 5 years. Her request for a termination of pregnancy was refused by her GP. Instead he prescribed 'medication for nerves'. The victim, who died from a fractured skull, had extensive bruising all over her body. In a previous attack by her mother, she sustained a fractured arm and severe bruising to her head, face, and pelvis. In the two remaining cases involving pregnant mothers, both parents were considered responsible for the death. The victims, males age 1 and 2 years, had been seriously injured or neglected on previous occasions. In one case, the victim's 3-year-old half-brother had also been abused. In the third case, the victim, who died of 'malnutrition, hypothermia, and neglect', had previously been treated for gangrenous toes due to neglect. The parents, aged 24 and 28, had three other children, ages 2, 4 and 6.

CRIMINAL CHARGES AND DISPOSITIONS

Since most of the thirty-five UK deaths provoked considerable media attention, it was not surprising to discover that the

Table 4.10 *Criminal charges and dispositions by the perpetrator's sex, 35 UK deaths*

Dispositions	Homicide and manslaughter		
	Male	*Female*	*Total*
Life imprisonment	2	—	2
10–15 years	2	—	2
5–9 years	3	1	4
2–4 years	3	3	6
1–2 years	—	2	2
Guilty, sentence not known	5	4	9
Probation/suspended sentence	—	4	4
Not guilty as charged	1	1 *	2
Totals	16	15	31 **

* Charged with infanticide and acquitted.
** In four cases both parents were charged.

Note: The differences between male and female offenders, in respect to
         sentences, are not statistically significant.

seriousness of the offences was reflected in the criminal charges. Table 4.10 shows that the charge of homicide or manslaughter was preferred in thirty-one cases. The parents were jointly charged in four of these cases. In two cases the perpetrators were found not guilty as charged. This included an acquittal in a case of infanticide. The sentence in eight cases was five years to life imprisonment. This involved seven male and one female perpetrators. Of the eight perpetrators receiving sentences from one to four years, three were male and five female. The tendency for women to be treated more leniently than men is confirmed by the fact that four of the women and none of the men were given suspended sentences or put on probation. In respect to the minor charges, men and women were treated more or less equally.

TYPOLOGY OF CASES

The highly selective nature of the sixty-eight UK deaths, compared to the hundred Ontario deaths, is reflected in the typology of cases displayed in table 4.11. This shows that there were forty-five (66.1 per cent) battered-child-syndrome cases; thirteen (19.1 per cent) homicides; and ten (14.7 per cent) neglect/malnutrition cases. Most noticeable is the absence of baby-sitter and discipline

Table 4.11　*Suspected perpetrators and typology of sixty-eight UK deaths*

Perpetrators	Typology of cases			
	BCS*	Homicide	Neglect	Total
Father	15	4	2	21
Married mothers	12	4	1	17
Mother and father	7	—	3	10
Male common-law partner**	4	3	—	7
Single/separated mother	2	—	2	4
Adoptive/foster-mother	2	1	1	4
Mother and common-law partner	2	—	1	3
Other***	1	1	—	2
Totals	45	13	10	68
%	66.1	19.1	14.7	100

*　　Battered child syndrome.
**　 Includes one step-father and one 15-year-old brother.
*** Includes one father and step-mother and one case of step grandparents.

Note:　The different frequencies among classes of perpetrators and types of cases, BCS v. homicide and neglect, are not statistically significant ($\chi^2 = 1.82$ (6) $p > 0.05$).

cases, which accounted for 13 per cent of the Ontario deaths. Another difference is in the greater frequency of homicide cases (19.1 per cent in the UK, 4 per cent in Ontario) and the smaller proportion of neglect cases.

Conclusion

In the course of this chapter, reference has been made to the differences between the sixty-eight UK and the hundred Ontario deaths. By way of a conclusion, various elements of data will be examined, step by step, in order to define and comment on the sources and significance of the differences and similarities. The result will, it is hoped, serve to limit the not uncommon tendency in the literature to assume that deaths due to child abuse and neglect are, more or less, homogeneous events, having a common aetiology and specific remedies.

SOURCES OF DATA

Unlike the Ontario data, which as far as can be determined represents almost all the CAN deaths in Ontario, the sixty-eight UK deaths include a substantial proportion of previously diagnosed high-risk cases. This is particularly true of the thirty-five UK cases which, because they are well documented, provide the major source of statistical data. The thirty-three NSPCC cases, providing much less detailed information, comprise a much wider spectrum of child-abuse and neglect deaths. They include, for example, two families in which all the children were destroyed as a result of single homicidal acts.

VICTIMS' AGE AND SEX

The different sources of data and definitions of CAN is reflected in the ages but not in the sex distribution of the victims. Although over 90 per cent of the victims in both cohorts were age 5 years or less, the Ontario cohort contained a higher proportion (40 to 27 per cent) of victims age 12 months or less.

INJURIES CAUSING DEATH

The causes of death in children are to a considerable extent age specific. This is especially true in relation to CAN deaths. Head and brain injuries were the most frequent cause of death in both cohorts. But the deaths were not equally distributed over the whole range of ages. For the Ontario victims, age 12 months or less, head and brain injuries accounted for 61 per cent of the deaths. For victims over the age of 1 but under 5, brain and head injuries accounted for 55 per cent of deaths. Of the five victims over the age of 5, only one died from a head injury. The comparable UK data is 12 months, 63 per cent; 5 years, 70 per cent. Only two of the six children over the age of 5 died from head or brain injuries. The small number of cases in the upper age-ranges limit the possibility of determining the extent to which this distribution is statistically significant. For this reason we can only surmise that the risk of death due to head injuries is closely related to the extreme vulnerability of very young infants.

PREVIOUS INJURIES

Although it was impossible to determine how they were caused, the present study confirms a high rate of previous injuries in both cohorts. Unfortunately these data were unavailable in the thirty-three NSPCC cases. The UK data, based on the thirty-five high-risk cases, revealed that thirty-one (88 per cent) of the victims had been previously injured. The comparable figure for the Ontario cohort was 63 per cent.

Analysis of the types of previous injuries revealed considerable differences between the two cohorts. In the UK cohort, facial bruising and lacerations accounted for twenty-four (77 per cent) of previous injuries. 'Other bruises and lacerations' were noted in nine (29 per cent) cases. Healing fractures were present in eleven (35 per cent) cases, and 'neglect, malnutrition or failure to thrive' in nine (29 per cent) cases. In the Ontario cohort facial bruising was noted only in one case, but 'other bruises and lacerations' were noted in sixteen (25 per cent) cases. Healing fractures and neglect/malnutrition were reported in 28 and 12 per cent respectively. The presence of such a high incidence of healing fractures (28 and 35 per cent) in both cohorts confirms the need for radiological investigation in all suspected CAN cases.

PHYSICAL GROWTH AND DEVELOPMENT

Failure to thrive, commonly defined as height and weight below the 3rd centile for age and sex, is not the only measure of mal-development but it is the simplest and the most objective. Sixteen per cent of the Ontario and 8.5 per cent of the UK victims, being at or below the 3rd centile for height and weight, were suffering from 'failure to thrive'. An additional 31 per cent of the Ontario and 36 per cent of the UK victims were at or below the 3rd centile for height or weight. On the basis of these data, it seems reasonable to conclude that about half of the victims, in two of the CAN death cohorts, were either severely stunted in growth or showed signs of malnutrition, or both. If this is so, it is important to ask if a higher level of professional awareness of the significance of physical mal-development, in addition to previous injuries, would have enabled the professionals concerned to be more effective in saving the lives of these vulnerable children.

TYPOLOGY

The very narrow spectrum of the sixty-eight UK deaths compared to the hundred Ontario deaths demonstrates the value of studying a total population rather than the most extreme cases. Although the largest proportion of deaths in both cohorts were attributed to the battered child syndrome, followed by neglect and homicide, the few baby-sitter and discipline cases are not unimportant. This is particularly so in respect to understanding the phenomenology of child abuse in order to reduce its incidence. However, while useful for purposes of analysis, typologies can also be deceptive. An example of this is provided by a closer look at the battered-child-syndrome cases. The proportion of BCS cases in both cohorts (66 per cent UK, 60 per cent Ontario) is similar, but the distribution of perpetrators is quite different. In order of frequency, the perpetrators in the UK cohort were: fathers, 33 per cent; married mothers, 26 per cent; both parents, 15 per cent; common-law partners, 9 per cent; and single/separated mothers, 4 per cent. The corresponding distribution for the Ontario BCS cohort were: fathers, 13 per cent; married mothers, 17 per cent; both parents, 12 per cent; common-law partners, 21 per cent; single/separated mothers, 21 per cent. Except to assume that these differences are uniquely associated with the sources of data and the definition of 'cases' in each jurisdiction, the considerable variation in the type and frequency of the perpetrators is difficult to explain.

HOMICIDES

Although 'homicide' is essentially a legal expression, its use in this study has been extended to include sudden or impulsive assaults on children, causing death. This includes several infanticides. Unlike the battered-child-syndrome cases, which usually involve a wide spectrum of assaults including neglect over an extended period, the victims of homicides were frequently well cared for and adequately nourished childen who were killed by single catastrophic acts. In most of these cases the assailants were parents or parent surrogates.

Finally, by way of a summary, it can be stated that, while the professional terminology and rhetoric concerning CAN may be similar in the USA, the UK, and Canada, the data presented here reveal substantial jurisdictional differences in both the definition and the social response to CAN deaths. The nature of these differences, in respect to the victims and perpetrators, has practical as well as theoretical implications. Considering the practical issues first, it may be useful to call attention to an important conclusion from the Knowelden, Keeling, and Nicholl (1984: 2) study of post neonatal mortality. They report:

Death in the period 1 week–2 years was significantly related to young maternal age, to the mother's smoking, short interval from the previous birth, and short gestation period; to lower birth weight, more frequent admission to a special care baby unit, and to less breast feeding. There was evidence of an increased risk of infant death in this period in lower social class families with more other children, having more family problems and living in less satisfactory housing. Death was associated with delayed contact with ante-natal services, but with more out-patient attendances and admissions to hospital prior to the terminal event.[3]

If this constellation of morbid factors seems familiar, it is because very similar patterns are revealed in the trajectory of events which anticipated many of the CAN deaths examined in this and the previous chapter. On the other hand this conclusion is best tempered by Creighton's (1984: 33) finding that the incidence of fatal and serious injuries among physically injured registered children has declined since 1977. A similar finding has been reported in the USA by Gelles and Strauss (1985). While Creighton's (1984) report shows a decline in the number of fatalities and serious injuries, her view that this is due to improved intervention is not supported by data. Without denying the efficacy of the NSPCC Special Units, it must be pointed out that a more likely explanation for the decline in fatalities and severe injuries can be found in the changing population of clients and problems. Two factors are particularly relevant. One relates to the overall decline in the proportion of children under 5 years of age and the corresponding increase in the number of older children who were registered. It will be remembered that the children under the age of 5 have a substantially increased risk of serious injury and death. The second factor relates to the substantial increase since 1977–81 in the proportion of sexual abuse, neglect, and emotional abuse being dealt with by the NSPCC. The combination of these two factors could indeed account for the much hoped-for improvements observed by Creighton (1984).

5

High-risk families – two case studies

In the eyes of the law, to be a child is to be at risk, dependent, and without capacity or authority to decide free of parental control what is 'best' for oneself. To be an adult is in law to be perceived as free to take risks, with the independent capacity and authority to decide what is 'best' for oneself without regard to parental wishes. To be an *adult who is a parent* is therefore to be presumed by law to have the capacity, authority, and responsibility to determine and to do what is 'good' for one's children, what is 'best' for the entire family.

(Goldstein, Freud, and Solnit 1979: 7)

Although the concept of a high-risk family has no status in law, legal philosophy as well as child welfare legislation play major roles in defining the precise circumstances in which this condition can be said to exist. But even when there is a consensus about the presence of risk to a child or children, there may still be considerable differences in legal opinion about whether the risk is sufficient to justify the limitation or termination of parental rights. Since these issues are inherent in the two cases presented in this chapter, it may be useful to review the reasoning of Goldstein, Freud, and Solnit (1979) outlined in their influential book, *Before the Best Interests of the Child*.

Following the first quotation, Goldstein and his colleagues argue that, for optimal growth, children, especially young children, need parental autonomy, autonomous parents, and privacy. These three conditions, enshrined in (American) law, 'provide parents with an uninterrupted opportunity to meet the developing physical and emotional needs of their child so as to establish familial bonds critical to every child's healthy growth and development.'

In the absence of clear breaches of parental responsibility, defined by law, Goldstein, Freud, and Solnit (1979) state that it is in the child's best interests for their families to be protected from arbitrary interference and state intervention. This view, which apepars as a caricature of 'individualism', conflicts with the 'humanitarian' view that, instead of guaranteeing parental autonomy, the state has a prior interest in protecting children. This separation of parental rights and children's interests provides the *raison dêtre* for attempting to identify families or family situations which clearly threaten the life or the safety of children.

In contrast to this position, Goldstein, Freud, and Solnit (1979) argue that, when state interference is necessary, the rule of the 'least detrimental alternative' should prevail. This means that 'if the state cannot or will not provide something better, the least detrimental alternative would be to let the status quo persist however unsatisfactory this might be.' This is not to say that Goldstein, Freud, and Solnit would allow a child to be repeatedly injured by his parents. On the contrary, they argue that once a parent has inflicted serious bodily injury, 'The child would be removed immediately, parental rights would be terminated, and adoptive parents who wanted a child and could care for him on a permanent basis would be substituted for the original parents.' In support of this somewhat extreme position, they claim that, when abusive parents have demonstrated a capacity to seriously injure their child, 'No amount of supervision from outside can counteract what happens within the privacy of a family.' The trouble with this statement is that, although it can be supported by evidence of numerous tragedies, where infants have been repeatedly abused and finally killed, systematic evidence of successful rehabilitation of abusive families is difficult to obtain.

In addition to serious bodily injury inflicted by the parents, the other grounds for state intervention proposed by Goldstein, Freud, and Solnit are: 1 requests by separating parents for the court to determine custody; 2 requests by a child's long-time caretakers to become his parents or the refusal by long-term caretakers to relinquish him to his parents or a state agency; 3 gross failure of parental care; 4 conviction or acquittal by reason of insanity or a sex offence against one's child; 5 refusal by parents to authorize lifesaving medical care.

Using these rules for intervention, they examined the Maria Colwell case and concluded that, had they been used, her life might have been saved. However, an examination of the Colwell case leaves no doubt that the absence of these draconian powers was not responsible for Maria's death. This view is well supported by the *Report of the Committee of Inquiry into the Care and Supervision Provided in Relation to Maria Colwell* (DHSS 1974).

The primary aim in presenting the following case studies is to illustrate and analyse the trajectory of events, as well as the situational context in which these tragedies occurred. In addition to examining the roles played by the perpetrators and the victims, attention is also focused on the patterns of intervention by the helping and control agencies. The object of this exercise is to learn as much as possible from past mistakes in order to develop more effective ways of protecting children in high-risk situations. Since this process exposes evidence of unsatisfactory and inefficient practices, it may well cause gloom among social workers and glee among our critics. This is unintended and deeply regretted. But to keep this matter in perspective, it is important to remember that the work that was done, often under difficult circumstances and sometimes by inadequately trained and unsupervised staff, cannot be divorced from the socio-economic, political, and legal context in which child abuse was defined, identified, and treated in the UK and Canada in the 1970s and the 1980s. Also, with the other helping professions, social work is obliged critically to examine its practices in order to improve the quality of service provided to clients and especially to children in public care.

Most of the information presented in the case studies comes from official reports. Some of the added elements need explaining. They include the standard growth and development record and the high-risk check list. The growth and development record, which plots heights and weights against predetermined standards, needs little explanation; but one point should be made clear. It is that, while a child's height and weight depend on various factors, including nutrition and the size of his parents, a steady rate of growth, including growth spurts, is an attribute of health. Failure to grow or weight loss in children is almost always a cause for concern. It is also wise to assume that children falling below the 3rd centile for height and weight are likely to need the attention of a child-health specalist.

High-risk check list

The high risk check list (see the appendix, pp. 185–7), developed in an earlier study (Greenland 1980a), also needs explaining. The significant variables relating to the perpetrator and to the child at risk appear frequently in high-risk cases reported over the past ten years in the USA, the UK, and in Canada as well as in the relevant professional literature. A score of over half of the completed items in either section appears to be associated with high risk. But children who have been severely injured by their caretaker in the first year of life probably have a higher degree of risk for repeated assault than older and less severely injured children. This is particularly true when the parents are very young and when there is

increased stress such as that associated with pregnancy and post-
natal depression. However, in the absence of rigorous testing, it
should not be assumed that the high-risk check list has any
demonstrated predictive value. On the other hand it may provide
a means of reaching consensus among interdisciplinary teams
concerned with the assessment of risk. It also appears to be useful
in helping to determine priorities for case management. For
example, increased supports for socially isolated parents and a
reduction in feeding and sleeping difficulties in the child are
likely, on a purely common-sense basis, to increase the parent's
nurturing capacities and reduce the risk of harm to a vulnerable
infant.

Help-seeking and warning behaviour

Attention will also be drawn, in these case studies, to manifesta-
tions of 'help-seeking' and 'warning' behaviour. They are marked
HS and W and become increasingly visible with the benefit of
hindsight. Since the phenomena of help-seeking and warning
behaviour associated with interpersonal violence are described in
chapter 1, additional elaboration is unnecessary.

Case study I   Kim Anne Popen
(11 January 1975–11 August 1976)

> As one listened to the testimony of employees of that Ministry
> [Community and Social Services], one could not help but form the
> impression that, for whatever reason, during the period of the time
> material to the life and death of Kim [Popen], the Ministry muddled
> along. It appeared to have been constantly reviewing, discussing,
> organizing, appointing task forces or the like and engaging consult-
> ants. Then the Ministry did not act effectively upon whatever came
> from such reviews, discussions, task forces, and consultants. Instead
> the Ministry would begin another round of review and discussions
> and re-organization.
> (Allen 1982: 1: 9)

The death of Kim Anne Popen in 1976 unleashed a storm of public protest and hostility toward the child-protection workers. This
tragedy also had a major impact on child-welfare policy and practices in Ontario. This was partly because Kim had previously been
identified as a child at risk, and the efforts made to protect her had
been crude and ineffectual. The most conspicuous feature of the

Popen tragedy was the failure of the various social welfare agencies to communicate and co-operate with each other.

As the quotation heading this case study shows, the lack of co-ordination between the various agencies serving children reflected a period of confusion within the Ministry of Community and Social Services which funds and supervises the children's aid societies throughout Ontario. In his report of the judicial inquiry into the care of Kim Anne Popen, 1982, Judge H. Ward Allen (1982: 1: 9) borrowed a quotation from Petronius to describe the sense of demoralization in the children's aid societies at the time of Kim Anne Popen's first injuries and subsequent death.

> We trained hard, but every time we were beginning to form up into teams we would be re-organized and I was to learn later in life that we tend to meet any new situation by re-organizing and a wonderful method it can be for creating the illusion of progress while producing confusion, inefficiency and demoralization.

Following the case summary, this study is divided into two main sections. The first provides background information on the Popen family up to the time of Kim's birth. This is followed by a sequential record of the events leading to Kim's death. The second, which is based on the report of the *Judicial Inquiry into the care of Kim Anne Popen* (1982), describes the contributions of the various agencies and the quality of interprofessional communications.

CASE SUMMARY

Born on 11 January 1975 Kim Anne Popen first came to medical attention at the age of 2 months when she was admitted to St Joseph's Hospital, Sarnia, Ontario, on 22 March 1975, with a transverse fracture of the upper left humerus with displacement. She also had an upper respiratory tract infection. Since child abuse was suspected, the hospital social worker was instructed to investigate the matter. He failed to do so. On 28 April 1975, less than four weeks later, Kim was readmitted to the same hospital suffering from bronchitis and a diaper rash. She made a good recovery and was discharged on 2 May 1975.

In June the general practitioner who had noted evidence of multiple bruising on Kim's arms, notified the Sarnia police of a 'possible battered child syndrome'. The police, in turn, reported the matter to the local children's aid society. However, by the time Kim was seen again, there was little sign of bruising and so no action was taken. In July a nurse who had cared for Kim in hospital encountered her and her mother in a shopping mall. She noticed that Kim's face was bruised and that her eyes were blackened. Then, on 31 August, when Kim was 8 months old, she was, once again, admitted to hospital with multiple bruises and fractures of the arms and ribs. The diagnosis of 'battered child syndrome' was confirmed and the case was formally reported to the police and to the children's aid society (CAS).

On discharge from hospital, Kim was taken into care by the CAS and placed in a foster home. Meanwhile both parents were charged, under the Child Welfare Act, with failing to protect Kim. The father, Annals Popen, pleaded guilty. The charge against Mrs Popen was withdrawn. The police were concerned that this would allow Kim to be returned to her mother's care. Prophetically, they said that if this happened 'Kim would be in her grave in three months'. Kim died on 11 August 1976, less than three months after her return home from foster care. In December 1977 Jennifer Popen, pleading guilty to a charge of manslaughter, was sentenced to seven years' imprisonment. Annals Popen, sentenced to one year's imprisonment, successfully appealed his conviction.

HIGH-RISK CHECK LIST

Kim Anne Popen suffered her first non-accidental injury at the age of 2 months. Had it been completed at the time, the high-risk check list (see Appendix) would have given considerable cause for alarm. This is mainly because of the mother's age – 16 years – and her history of abuse. She had, it should be noted, already given birth to a child before the age of 13. Also, because she was a newcomer to Canada and not on good terms with her husband's family, stress due to culture shock and social isolation should have been considered in the assessment of risk. There was also some concern about Mr Popen who, it was alleged, was an alcoholic.

The birth of Karie on 6 July, a month before Kim's death, created a desperate situation. In addition to the post-partum state of depression, exacerbated no doubt by a difficult labour, Mrs Popen found it even more difficult to cope with Kim who was already exhibiting signs of disturbed behaviour.

GROWTH AND DEVELOPMENTAL RECORD

At the time of her birth, Kim was regarded as a healthy infant and of normal height and weight. Unfortunately records of her growth and development were not available. At the time of her death, her height, 82 cm, and weight, 10.4 kg, were within the normal range: height, + 50th centile; weight, + 25th centile.

THE POPEN FAMILY

Jennifer Angela Popen, neé Mair, was born in Kingston, Jamaica, on 7 September 1959. Her birth certificate appears to have been altered to read 1957.

In his pre-sentence report on Mrs Popen, after she had been found guilty of manslaughter, the probation officer stated:

> For the preparation of this report we have experienced difficulties in gathering factual information on the offender's background. There have been doubtful statements, changed statements by the offender, and other conflicting stories which could not always be verified.
>
> (Allen 1982: 1: 13–14)

According to Mrs Popen, she lost both her parents. From the age of 6, while living with foster parents, she was physically and sexually abused. Between the ages of 11 and 13 years, Mrs Popen gave birth to a child who is still being cared for by her grandmother. On 13 January 1973 Jennifer was married to Annals Popen. She was 14 years of age and had known Annals Popen for only about six months.

Annals Popen , born 24 September 1939. Mr Popen, who had a Grade 8 education and came to Canada from Jamaica in 1957, was employed as a labourer. He was age 34 at the time of his marriage to Jennifer. Members of his extended family lived nearby in Sarnia, where the Popens had made their home.

Kim Anne Popen, born 11 January 1975. The birth, which took place in hospital, was uncomplicated. Kim was reported to be of normal weight and healthy.

SEQUENTIAL RECORD

(HS – help-seeking; W – warning sign)

1975

23 March   Kim was admitted to hospital with a 'transverse fracture of the upper left humerus with displacement and an upper respiratory tract infection'.

27 March	Following a request for a consultation, the Chief of Pediatrics reported: 'It is extremely unusual to break a solid, long bone such as the left humerus, just by changing the child's hand [sic]. This family should be investigated by, first, a social worker for the environmental and social status the family lives in. I would strongly suspect that the battered child syndrome is present and if we do not protect this child at the present state, she might end up with a fractured skull or some other fractures later on in her life. I think this should, of course, be discussed and kept confidential.' This report was circulated to the other involved physicians, including the family doctor.
3 April	Kim discharged from hospital into the care of her parents. The hospital social worker who was asked to investigate the possibility of child abuse *failed to do so*.
28 April	Kim readmitted to hospital. 'Dehydration, high temperature and a diaper rash'.
2 May	Kim discharged from hospital to the care of her parents.
16 June W HS	The family doctor reported that Kim's aunt brought her to his office with a cut lip and severe bruises over her face, neck, and buttocks. Six weeks earlier, Kim was hospitalized with a broken arm. 'Approximately three weeks prior to the child being brought to his office she was checked by him at the hospital for a respiratory ailment and at that time he observed that she had a black eye.' On the same date the doctor reported to the police and the Public Health Unit that he believed the child was battered.
16 June	The Sarnia police recorded the doctor's call about 'a possible child abuse case'.
17 June	Accompanied by two CAS workers, the police made a home visit and found Kim with her aunt. It was observed that she had a cut lip and tongue, due, it was stated, 'to a feeding battle'. Kim, it was noted, seemed very comfortable with her aunt.

	W	Mrs Popen, who arrived to take Kim home, was 'very defensive and hostile'. The social worker was 'amazed at how upset the child was when Jennifer held her and in particular when she tried to feed her.'
18 June		The CAS supervisor, after hearing a report from the two social workers, agreed that the case merited prompt attention. In fact, no action was taken.
19 June	W	At the doctor's request, Mrs Popen brought Kim in to be examined. Unexplained bruises were noted.
2 July		The police made a follow-up call to the CAS and asked what action was being taken.
July	HS	A nurse, who was in charge of the ward when Kim was in hospital, encountered Kim and her mother in a shopping mall. She noted that Kim's face was bruised and her eyes blackened. This was mentioned informally to a doctor but not reported to the CAS.
31 August	W	Kim was admitted to hospital with bruises, recent fracture of the left humerus, and healing fracture of the left humerus, and healing fractures of her ribs. The rib injuries were, it was estimated, about a month old. Mrs Popen claimed that Kim, age 8 months, having pulled herself over the top of the crib, had fallen on the floor. The hospital social worker was advised and the police and the CAS informed.
	HS	Next day Mrs Popen arrived at the hospital and attempted to take Kim home. This was refused. After discussion with a CAS worker, the parents agreed to 'non-ward' care for Kim. A file on the Popens was opened by the CAS.
5 September		Discharged from hospital, Kim was placed in a foster home under the care of the CAS.
10 September		Kim was transferred to a second foster home.
30 October		Criminal charges were laid by the police under the Child Welfare Act. There were court

adjournments on 29 October, 13 November, 17 November, 9 January, 26 February, and 29 March 1976.

1976

16 February   Despite objections by the Popens' lawyer, a CAS social worker made his first home visit.

20 February   Second home visit by CAS worker who records, 'Mrs Popen is a proverbial liar. Says that her first child died in Jamaica at the age of 7
HS   months. She is isolated, young and inexperienced.'

February   Two police officers visited the CAS to discuss the plea of guilty by Mr Annals Popen and the possibility of withdrawing charges against Mrs Popen. Informed that the CAS was thinking of returning Kim to her parents, one of the police officers said that, if that happened, Kim would be dead within three months.

23 February   Mr Popen pleaded guilty to failing to protect Kim, while the charges against Mrs Popen were withdrawn. Mr Popen claimed that he had no memory of hitting Kim, but according to his wife he did so at weekends while drunk. (This, as will appear later, was untrue.)

25 February   Court ordered a six-month wardship for Kim. As a condition of his probation order, Mr Popen agreed to join Alcoholics Anonymous. He and his wife were also required to attend a Parent Effectiveness Training (PET) course under CAS supervision.

29 February   CAS supervisor transferred the Popen case to an untrained female worker who had been with the agency less than three months. (At this time the previous social worker's case-notes on his relationship with the Popens from 1 September 1975 to 29 February 1976 had not been filed.) Following her first home visit, the social worker recorded that Mrs Popen had revealed some information about her deprived background and the fact that she
HS   *was currently pregnant.*

4 March	Mrs Popen also told the social worker about her 5-year-old son in Jamaica. The probation officer visited at the same time. On the following day there was a brief conversation between the social worker and the probation officer. No plans were made to establish formal lines of communication or to exchange information.
18 March	Home visit to discuss arrangements for the Popens to attend the first session of the PET course on 22 April.
29 March	Mr Popen was placed on probation with a one-year suspended sentence.

Note: Up to this point there was no documented assessment of the Popen family situation or plan of action with defined objectives. But, despite the concern expressed by the police, the CAS workers planned to return Kim to the care of her parents.

15 April	Kim starts making home visits to her parents. The worker, who made home visits, recorded, 'Family situation keeps progressing.'
24 April	Parents report to the social worker that they enjoyed the PET classes. Mrs Popen wants Kim home before the birth of her new baby, due in July. The social worker noted that the home visits have proved to be very disruptive for Kim. 'Her behaviour regressed every time W after her home visit.' Visits were discontinued.
6 May	Social worker told Mr Popen that she was mainly concerned about him. 'I felt that he is moving in the right direction but needs to work harder because he is not there yet. . . . We also talked about Kim's temper and the patience and firmness it requires to cope with her . . . *Kim will have to know who is the boss.*'
27 May	Kim was returned home to the care of her parents. (Since Kim was under a six-month wardship order, ending in August 1976, the decision to terminate it earlier should have been approved by the court.)
27 May	(After Kim's death, Mrs Popen reported that

she had consulted a physician about her temper and the injuries she had inflicted on Kim. He prescribed some medication to help her control her temper. She took the pills as prescribed.)

31 May   During a home visit Mrs Popen reported that
W   Kim had temper tantrums and was hard to manage, but she was much better at weekends
HS   when Mr Popen was at home.

1–16 June   The social worker made several home visits during this period. Early in June she recorded, 'Kim is teething, has flu, and is miserable.' Mrs
W   Popen reported that the doctor had told her that she was putting on too much weight. Unless she watched her diet carefully, she would have a hard time delivering her child.
HS   'This scares Jennifer.'
    'Jennifer now understands what the CAS worker has told her about Kim. . . . When mad she will hurt herself and destroy things. . . .
W   Mrs Popen says she has seen Kim being mean to others and kicking younger babies and animals.'

16 June   Probation officer transferred the Popen case to an untrained volunteer.

17 June–   Difficulties in managing Kim reported to
6 July   social worker. 'Kim hurts herself by bumping
W, HS   into things.'

20 June   Volunteer probation officer made a home visit and recorded: 'Mr and Mrs Popen and Kim all appeared tense at the outset, but gradually, with conversation, that eased.'

6 July   W   Karie Popen, a girl, born, breech birth and difficult labour. Mrs Popen discharged herself from hospital against medical advice.

7 July   Home visits continue. Mrs Popen appeared
W   tired, cold, and distant. She is having problems with Kim who is difficult to manage.
HS   Mrs Popen is afraid that the CAS will remove Kim. *The social worker assured Mrs Popen*

that the CAS will not be asking for a continuation of the supervision order. Mr Popen complained of a bad back and felt unwell. Mrs Popen became upset when the social worker asked her if Mr Popen had a tendency to take out his frustrations on the children. Mrs Popen said she was annoyed because the probation officer had been asking similar questions. 'Jennifer was loving towards Kim. She was smiling and singing most of the time. Her eating habits have almost returned to normal.'

14 July   Home visit by probation officer. She reported, 'Mr Popen pointed out some slight bruises on the edge of Kim's cheeks, caused,
HS   he said, by Kim pinching herself.' He was concerned because even slight injury might lead to Kim's removal by the CAS. She reassured him and said 'he should not worry.'

18 July   The volunteer probation officer, who made a home visit, recorded, 'The atmosphere was so charged with resentment and anxiety that I confronted the Popens immediately on the obvious change in feeling from our previous contact. After an initial attempt to ascribe the change to trivialities, they decided to trust me with their feelings which were totally justified. Mrs Popen's treatment by a representative from another community agency is humiliating to a proud woman who has committed no crime and is not being shown the courtesy she is entitled to. I encouraged her to protest the incident but she is reluctant to risk any trouble. This has upset Mr Popen also, and has damaged the rapport they had established with me as well. However, the release of their feelings regarding the episode and my response to the feelings of injustice acted as a catalyst and we were really opening up areas of opinion and true feelings that were most helpful to me, when unexpected visitors arrived. Hopefully we can pick this up again.
        'The client is fulfilling the terms of his probation with no difficulty.'

26 July	The social worker phoned the probation officer to inform him that the CAS involvement with the Popens would cease.
26 July	Social worker phoned Mrs Popen to arrange a home visit but was put off. After discussing the case with her supervisor, it was decided to apply for an extension of the supervisory order. The court date was set for 4 August.
6.30 p.m.	Home visit by social worker. 'Mr Popen had not come back from work yet. Knowing that I was going to discuss something important, Jennifer had her friend (next-door neighbour) there. She was very nervous and apprehensive.'
27 July	Social worker served notice of hearing on the Popens. Mrs Popen seemed more relaxed. Mr Popen was very co-operative.
4 August	Home visit by social worker. 'Kim was sitting quietly beside her mother watching TV.' Mrs Popen said they were thinking of moving because she did not get on well with the next-door neighbour.
8 August	The volunteer probation officer made a home visit and recorded, 'Kim was once more kind of huddled back on the chesterfield and very withdrawn, not responding when I spoke to her. She would just look at me . . . she was very withdrawn and a little peevish when her mother or dad spoke to her; she was a little irritable.' The volunteer probation officer commented that Kim seemed a little tired. Mrs Popen responded by saying that Kim had a sore lip. This was described by the volunteer probation officer as being 'more like a little swelling and a little discoloured'. Mrs Popen said that it was a 'cold sore' and the doctor had prescribed ointment for it. Mrs Popen also told the volunteer probation officer that Kim had been seen by a new doctor who had discovered something wrong with her blood. 'I don't know whether it's sugar diabetes or what. Maybe this is why she bruises too.'

HS (beside 'Popen responded by saying that Kim had a')

HS (beside 'don't know whether it's sugar diabetes or')

10 August	Health visitor made a routine visit following the birth of Karie on 6 July. She inquired about Kim and was told that she was asleep, having an afternoon nap.
11 August	The social worker was informed that Kim had died as a result of a fall.
12 August	Mr Popen phoned the volunteer probation officer and informed her of Kim's death. He explained that Kim had been riding a toy horse on the porch. Jennifer Popen had gone into the house for something. When she returned to the porch, Kim was lying on the ground. She was taken to hospital and found to be dead.

POST-MORTEM FINDINGS

Kim died as a result of subarachnoid and subdural haemorrhaging due to blows to the head. The external signs of violence to the head, face, and body, which had been inflicted from one to five days earlier, were, it was stated, inconsistent with the story of a fall. There were also unexplained anal and genital injuries.

'The anal injury', it was reported, 'would have been noticeable a week prior to Kim's death, but not necessarily if she merely stood naked in front of the observer. It would have been noticeable to anyone changing her diaper. The anal opening was approximately three times the normal size for a child of Kim's age. From microscopic examination, this injury was inflicted on repeated occasions over a period of several weeks or months.'

Another medical expert stated, 'Such an injury would be caused only by the application of considerable force and the insertion of a large object into the anus on repeated occasions over a period of time. The infliction of the injury would be very painful . . . it was indicative of wilfully inflicted force.'

Judicial inquiry into the care of Kim Anne Popen

Published in 1982, the report of the judicial inquiry provided a scathing indictment of the management of the Popen case by the Sarnia CAS. In his eighty-seven recommendations, designed to improve services for abused and neglected children in Ontario, His Honour Judge Allen (1982: 1: 5–6) concluded:

It is apparent that while many contributed to the neglect of the child, Kim, the effect of the contribution of each of them varied from that of the contribution of each of the others. Some were errors or omissions, but perhaps of a highly technical nature, which had little if any effect upon the result of the sum of the many contributions. Others were errors or omissions which had great bearing upon the ultimate result.

Various departments, agencies and personnel of the Province of Ontario failed the child. Particular responsibility falls upon the Ministry of Community and Social Services.

Judge Allen was particularly distressed by the fact that, although they operated under the same ministry and shared statutory duties in relation to the Popen family, the children's aid society and the probation service staffs failed to co-operate or even communicate effectively with each other. The relationship between the CAS, the police and the Public Health Department appeared to be more or less non-existent. In this respect, it must be concluded that the CAS was operating virtually as a closed system. This, of course, was equally true of the health-care system. The family physician, hospital staff, and public health nurses also failed Kim Anne Popen by providing fragmented and ineffectual care.

CASE-MANAGEMENT

As Judge Allen observed, numerous errors and omissions by professionals responsible for Kim Popen's care were ultimately responsible for her death. Although the circumstances of this case are, by now, depressingly familiar, it may still be useful to explore what might have been done to protect Kim from harm.

Using the information that was available to the CAS well before Kim's death, this review will focus on the response of the various systems involved in the case. Kim's response to the abuse will be considered in the next section. Since the failure to assign a professionally competent person to work with the Popens has already been noted, this matter will be mentioned only in passing. There is also little to be gained by belabouring the obvious lack of interprofessional co-operation and communication. It may, however, be useful to point out that unqualified social workers are likely to experience more difficulty in securing the respect and co-operation of physicians. Some valuable insight into this problem is provided by Hallett and Stevenson (1980).

COMMUNITY RESOURCES

If family members and concerned neighbours, to be considered

later, are excluded, the agencies involved in the Popen case included
a hospital and its medical, nursing, and social work staff, a family
physician, public health nurses, probation officers, police, lawyers, a psychiatrist, and a children's aid society supported by
legislation which makes the reporting of child abuse mandatory.
In this respect, at least, the existing community resources could
not be described as inadequate.

Hospital

In tracing the trajectory of events leading to Kim's death, it will be
seen that, following her admission to hospital on 23 March 1975,
with a fractured humerus and a respiratory-tract infection, the
battered child syndrome was promptly diagosed by a consultant
paediatrician. This information was appropriately conveyed to
the hospital social worker and to the family physician but not,
unfortunately, to the CAS. There was no adequate investigation of
the circumstances in which the abuse occurred. The role of the
upper-respiratory-tract infection, associated pehaps with sleep-
less nights and feeding problems, in precipitating the abuse does
not appear to have been explored.

Kim's second hospital admission, a few weeks later, with dehydration, fever, and diaper rash, was treated as an isolated event. Her
clinical condition was not, it appears, considered in relation to the
earlier diagnosis of battered child syndrome. In this way another
opportunity to intervene effectively was missed. Appropriate
action to bring Kim's plight to the attention of the CAS and the police
was not taken until her readmission to hospital on 31 August 1975
with a new fracture of the humerus and healing rib fractures.

Family physician

Between Kim's first and third hospital admissions, the family physician had ample opportunity to observe evidence of abuse. On
16 June 1975, at the request of Kim's aunt, he examined Kim and
found her to be suffering from a cut lip and severe bruising over
her face, neck, and buttocks. Three weeks earlier he observed
that, in addition to a respiratory infection, Kim had a black eye.
This alarming accumulation of evidence of child abuse eventually
prompted the physician to report the matter to the police and the
Public Health Department. One can only speculate on his reluctance to involve the CAS.

Children's Aid Society

The extraordinary failure of the CAS to maintain collegial relationships and effective communications with the hospital, physicians,

public-health nurses, probation officers, and the police, suggests either that it lacked credibility or that its concept of child protection was very narrowly defined. Operating within a closed system and with a minimum of accountability, the CAS was in an extremely vulnerable position. Without reference to the other involved agencies and unencumbered with information, it was free to make its own diagnosis and impose a form of treatment. Whatever its merits, Parent Effectiveness Training had little relevance to the needs of the Popen family or to the protection of Kim.

The inability of the CAS to establish an appropriate interdisciplinary team for the management of the Popen case was associated with the administrative incompetence and arbitrary decision-making by a senior official. Her failure to assign a social worker to the Popen case until about two months after it was first reported had disastrous consequences. These were compounded by the decision to reassign the case to a new and untrained social worker.

Although there was little doubt among the CAS workers that Mrs Popen was responsible for Kim's injuries, they persisted in the charade of assuming that, while in a drunken stupor, Mr Popen caused the injuries. The net effect was that Mr Popen was charged with a lesser offence and found guilty, while the charge against Mrs Popen was withdrawn. This conspiracy was presumably designed to appease Mrs Popen and to win her confidence. The failure, at the outset, to determine who was responsible for the abuse of Kim clearly contributed to her death. Since an investigative role would, no doubt, conflict with their image as helpers, the CAS workers, rather than avoiding the issue, should have involved the police. The police, as has been noted, were far more aware of the danger to Kim than were the CAS workers.

Psychiatrist

In view of the persistent and unexplained injuries to Kim, the need for a thorough investigation and assessment of the parents should have been given the highest priority by the CAS. In neglecting to make their own assessment, the CAS also failed to make use of a report prepared for the court in March 1975 by an experienced psychiatrist. The following extracts from his report serve two purposes. First, they provide a shrewd, although non-committal, assessment of Mr and Mrs Popen in terms of their psychopathology. Second, in recommending the need for 'objective enquiries' and indicating his interest in knowing 'the facts of the case', which were not available to him, the psychiatrist tacitly invites the co-operation of the CAS. Unfortunately, as far as can be determined, there was no communication between the CAS and the psychiatrist.

Mr Annals Popen

I am really unable to give any opinion as to the likelihood of a repetition at a future date, because I cannot assess in any depth the emotional make-up of Mr Popen. He denies ever having been abused himself as a child and in fact my enquiries from him yield such little abnormality that I wonder about his reliability as an informant. I would think, therefore, that a more accurate assessment of his emotional state will likely result from objective enquiries rather than from any enquiries I might make from himself or his wife.

(Allen 1982: 3.991)

Mrs Jennifer Popen

Mrs Popen impresses me as being a somewhat unreliable informant and she appears rather guarded and evasive in the interview situation. She is not able to give me any explanation that seems adequate or feasible to me with regard to how her baby got hurt physically. I find it very difficult to communicate meaningfully with Mrs Popen and she seems poorly able to think in abstract terms. I wonder about her intellectual level, her degree of formal education or language difficulty, as contributing to the difficulty in communication. . . . In brief then all I can say is that I was not impressed as to her degree of reliability as an informant and I would consider her an emotionally deprived person. She does not impress me as being a very stable person emotionally. None of the facts of the case are available to me and therefore there is little else I can say here.

(Allen 1982: 1: 163)

Parent Effectiveness Training

Lacking the psychiatrist's description of Mr Popen's bland demeanour and Mrs Popen's emotional instability, the CAS arranged for them to take the PET course as a condition of Mr Popen's probation order. This made little sense because the course objectives were to 'help parents communicate with their children.' Later on it became clear that the course was designed for parents who were having difficulty coping with teenage children. This was ironic because Mrs Popen herself was little more than a teenager.

During the judicial inquiry, it was revealed that the PET course leader had not been informed that the Popens were suspected of being abusive parents and that he was not asked to provide a report on their progress. Nevertheless, after attending only two PET sessions, the Popens were informed that, since they were making good progress, Kim would be returned to them. Asked by Judge Allen to explain why the Popens had been directed to take the PET course, the CAS supervisor replied, 'It was the only thing available in this whole community.'

Alcoholics Anonymous

Although details are lacking, it seems that with the assistance of Alcoholics Anonymous (AA) and encouraged by his neighbour, an AA member, Mr Popen had no difficulty in giving up alcohol. In fact, there was no evidence that he ever was an alcoholic. This was an invention by Mrs Popen who claimed that Kim was injured by Mr Popen who was drunk at the time. An adequate assessment would have revealed that this was a most improbable explanation of Kim's injuries.

Probation

The involvement of the probation officer with the Popens started when the family court judge, hearing charges against Mr Popen, requested a pre-sentence report. In preparing this report, the probation officer interviewed a CAS social worker, neighbours, and the Popens. He found Annals Popen to be a very quiet withdrawn person who permitted Jennifer Popen to answer questions addressed to him. Mr Popen told the probation officer that he had no memory of inflicting injuries on Kim but accepted what others had told him. Mrs Popen told the probation officer that she was responsible for Kim's injuries in March 1975 when the baby fell out of the crib.

Although he had access to the police reports documenting the history of Kim's injuries, the probation officer did not communicate directly with the police officers responsible for the investigation. Nor did he request to see the CAS files or discuss the case with the worker who had some knowledge and experience of the Popens. In his criticism of the probation officer's pre-sentence report, Judge Allen made the following points: 1 It failed to alert the family court judge to the suspicion that Jennifer Popen, rather than Annals, may have been responsible for Kim's injuries. 2 It failed to alert the judge to the 'shallow basis' for the CAS social worker's expressed optimism. 3 It made no comment on the psychiatrist's report, especially to his comments on the need for more objective information.

After the probation order was made, the probation officer, who admitted that he had no experience with child abuse, passed on the Popen case to a new volunteer. In preparation for her first case, the volunteer probation officer read the pre-sentence report but did not talk with the police or with the CAS worker. Despite her intuitive doubts about the truth of the matter, the volunteer probation officer, for the purposes of her supervisory duties, accepted as a fact that Annals Popen had injured Kim. Some insight into the doubts in her mind is contained in her monthly report at the end of June 1976: 'According to both Mr and Mrs Popen the situation is so devoid of problems as to seem a little unrealistic. They are expecting their second child in early July and hopefully this will present an opportunity to visit Mrs Popen in an unprofessional capacity and possibly get to know them a little more intimately.'

In her conversations with the volunteer probation officer, Mrs Popen was extremely critical of the behaviour of the CAS worker. Assuming that her complaints were justified, the volunteer probation officer planned a meeting with the CAS worker. Kim's death on 11 August 1976 prevented her from doing so.

Public-health nursing

In relation to Kim Popen and the injuries she received resulting in her death, the public-health nurse is a shadowy figure. Although the family physician reported the abuse to the Public Health Department on 16 June 1975, the Medical Officer of Health took no action. This is also ironic because the Health Department, represented by the same public-health nurse, had regular contact with Mrs Popen from well before Kim's birth until the day before her death. Having made, or attempted to make, contact with the police and the CAS, the public-health nurse performed her 'routine' duties, assuming that the other agencies were doing the same. Thus, on 10 August, in the course of her routine visit to the new baby, Mrs Popen told the nurse that 'Kim was doing very well and was well physically.' The nurse reported that she observed nothing that gave her concern for the welfare or safety of Kim or of the new baby Karie. The value of this observation must be questioned. In the first place, it should be noted that Karie was a breech birth and her mother left the hospital early and against medical advice. Due to the complications of a difficult labour, Mrs Popen was experiencing considerable pain for which she had been prescribed 'sleeping tablets and analgesics'.

After Kim's death Mrs Popen also told the forensic psychiatrist, Dr Selwyn Smith (12 December 1977), that she left hospital early because Kim was crying for her and was not eating properly. There were also problems with Karie. She developed a fever, had diarrhoea, and was a very difficult and fractious baby. 'Mrs Popen was up most of the night for several nights and described how the child would only sleep when she was held or rocked.'

Whether these facts were true or not will never be known because the public-health nurse apparently failed to seek this vital information from Mrs Popen's physician or from the hospital records before making her 'routine' visit on 10 August. In relation to Kim, the nurse said that she had no reason to disbelieve Mrs Popen who denied having any problems. In view of Kim's past history of abuse, this glib statement should surely have been questioned. It is, of course, true that the public-health nurse had no legal authority to insist on examining Kim, but there was nothing to stop her from requesting to do so. With hindsight, at least, such an examination might well have saved Kim's life.

Family

At least two members of the extended Popen family, Annals' relatives, knew that Kim was being abused. Francis Kameka, Annals' nephew, baby-sat Kim and observed Jennifer slap her. He also noticed bruising and discussed this with his parents. Francis failed to report the abuse to the authorities and was unaware of his obligation to do so. On the day of her death, he saw Kim twice. On the last occasion, at about 4.30 pm, Francis observed that 'she was not walking much or playing'. She would not come to him when he called her. Otherwise she appeared to be normal.

Unlike Francis Kameka, Kim's aunt Mrs Fay Popen made strenuous efforts to bring the abuse to the attention of the family doctor and to the CAS. On 6 June 1975 she brought Kim to the doctor's office and showed him the cut lip and bruises. Ten days later, the doctor reported the matter to the police and to the Public Health Department. On 17 June 1975 Mrs Fay Popen showed the marks of Kim's injuries to two CAS social workers and to the police officer who accompanied them. Despite this evidence of interest and concern for Kim's welfare, the CAS worker failed to consult or communicate with Mrs Fay Popen or any other member of the family. This may have been due to Jennifer Popen's claim that Fay Popen was spreading malicious rumours in order to gain custody of Kim.

Neighbours

The Popens were blessed with good neighbours. Unfortunately, except on one occasion, the social worker made no attempt to ask them how Kim was getting on. Had she done so, she might have learned that Mrs V. had witnessed two abusive incidents in the three to four weeks before Kim's death. On the first occasion, Mrs V. was in the Popens' apartment when she heard some sounds of slapping and Kim screaming. She went into the bedroom to find out what was wrong. Jennifer replied that Kim had wet her bed and would be left there. When Mrs V. protested that the bed should be changed, Jennifer refused. 'Kim was left in the corner of her bed, shaking and crying and then falling asleep.'

On another occasion, Mrs V. noticed a bruise around the whole of Kim's neck. Mrs Popen said it was caused by a dress which was too tight.

On the next occasion, while Mrs V. was in the Popens' apartment, Kim, who was sitting in her chair, became ill and vomited. Jennifer Popen responded by slapping Kim from her waist to her shoulder. Mrs V., who described the slaps as 'not being gentle but hard enough', expressed her disapproval.

Finally, after Kim's death, Mrs V. provided the following account of what she observed on 11 August. She saw 'Kim walk into a door, turn around, and fall over her feet.' She commented to Jennifer Popen that Kim did not look well and offered to drive Jennifer and Kim to a doctor. Kim appeared to be in a daze and drowsy and 'wasn't walking right'. Jennifer Popen responded by saying that 'Kim was tired, there was nothing the matter with her and that she would be put to bed.'

Asked by Judge Allen, during the judicial inquiry, why he failed to report the abuse to the CAS, the neighbour, Mr V., said that he did not believe that Mr Popen had ever injured Kim and urged him to plead not guilty to the charge. On the advice of his lawyer, Mr Popen refused to do so because this would prevent Kim from being returned home. Mr V. added that, although actively involved with Mr Popen in the AA programme, no one from the CAS had ever asked him about Kim's care or well-being while she was alive. He was only approached by a CAS worker after Kim's death.

Asked why she failed to report Mrs Popen to the CAS, Mrs V. explained that she told the social worker that she was prepared to help Jennifer. Except for one brief conversation, she was never approached or questioned by the social worker. Judge Allen summarized the situation in this way: 'It would seem that Mrs V. was prepared to tell the social worker, or anyone, of the incident if she were asked, but she was not prepared to volunteer the information. She was not going to "butt in".'

Warning signals and help-seeking behaviour
The sequential analysis and chronology of events leading to Kim's death includes fifteen warning signals and fourteen descriptions of help-seeking. In four cases the warning signals and help-seeking behaviours appear to be combined. This combination was particularly evident in the final weeks of Mrs Popen's pregnancy. From 1 to 16 June Mrs Popen reported to the social worker that 'Kim is teething and is miserable' and 'When mad she [Kim] will hurt herself and destroy things . . . Kim is being mean to others and kicking younger babies and animals.'

Following Karie's birth on 6 July 1976, after Mrs Popen had discharged herself from hospital against medical advice, the social worker and the volunteer probation office both noticed that she was 'tired, cold and distant'. But the significance of these typically depressive, post-partum symptoms does not appear to have been fully appreciated. Between 7 and 13 July Mrs Popen told the social worker that she was having trouble with Kim, who was difficult to manage, and added that she was afraid that the CAS would remove her. At about the same time Mr Popen pointed out to the volunteer probation officer the slight bruises on Kim's cheeks, caused, he said, by Kim pinching herself. Although he expressed concern that the CAS might want to remove Kim, the precise nature of his concern was never elucidated. But some of these concerns must have registered because, between 7 and 23 July, the Popens were told that the CAS would not be applying for a continuation of the supervision order. Then, on 26 July 1976, following a discussion with her supervisor, the social worker informed Mrs Popen that the CAS was going to apply for an extension. On 4 August, when the social worker made a home visit to inform the Popens that a new date had been set for the court hearing, she saw Kim sitting quietly beside her mother watching TV. One week later she was dead.

In view of Mrs Popen's extremely deprived background, her suspicion and distrust of social workers, the range and persistence of her help-seeking behaviours are remarkable. Perhaps, because her stories were often vague and conflicting, the social workers failed to attach significance to the fact that, following rape at the age of 11 or 12, Mrs Popen became pregnant and gave birth to a child. To the first CAS worker, she reported that her child died at the age of 7 months. Without investigating the truth of the matter, he recorded that Mrs Popen was a 'proverbial liar'. About a month later, Mrs Popen told the second CAS worker that she was currently pregnant and that her 5-year-old son in Jamaica was being cared for by her grandmother. Except to regard it as a promising exchange of confidence, the new social worker also failed to grasp the implications of this information. In addition to understanding something of the trauma experienced by Mrs Popen at an early age, it would have been helpful to know if her current pregnancy was planned or not.

Although there is no guarantee that it would have been successful in saving Kim's life, paying attention to the practical problems faced by this very young and isolated mother would, at least, have lent some credibility to the social worker's intervention. Cryptic observations such as 'I felt that he [Mr Popen] is moving in the right direction but needs to work harder because he is not there yet' (6 May 1976) and, to Mrs Popen on the same visit, 'Kim will have to know who is the boss,' were probably counter-productive. But, as the following examples show, despite these confusing, if not negative, messages, Mrs Popen persisted in seeking help by repeating on 31 May 1976: 'Kim has temper tantrums and is hard to manage.' 'She is much better at weekends when Mr Popen is at home', she said on 17 June, and 6 July: 'Kim hurts herself by bumping into things.'

Finally, a few days before her death, when the volunteer probation officer asked about Kim's sore lip, Mrs Popen said that Kim had been seen by a new doctor who had discovered something wrong with her blood. 'This', said Mrs Popen, 'might explain why she [Kim] bruises so easily.' Although there was no evidence to support this statement, a call to the doctor seeking confirmation and some explanation for Kim's tendency to 'bump into things' and 'hurt herself' might have brought the help she so desperately needed.

CONCLUSIONS

If nothing else, this review of the Popen case confirms the poignancy of the observation that 'almost every mistake you could make was made . . . ' From the outset, it was obvious that Kim had not received the protection to which she was entitled by law, and the public demanded to know what went wrong and who was responsible. These questions were answered by the judicial inquiry which, while recognizing the failures of the other professionals, placed the ultimate responsibility for Kim Anne Popen's death on the children's aid society and its senior officials.

In addition to apportioning blame, the judicial inquiry made eighty-seven recommendations which were designed to prevent the repetition of similar tragedies in Ontario. Some of these recommendations have been incorporated into the new Child and Family Services Act, 1984. While this will increase the level of legal protection available to children at risk, it must be recognized that legislation alone will not improve the competence of child-protection workers.

Since the need to assign professionally qualified and experienced staff to work with high-risk child-abuse cases is generally accepted, it follows that the failure to do so should be regarded as a dereliction of managerial responsibility. CAS managers must be similarly responsible and accountable for establishing and maintaining effective interdisciplinary communication between the community agencies concerned with child abuse and neglect. It should be obvious by now that an isolated child-protection agency, making arbitrary decisions without reference to the other involved professionals, is functionally inefficient and courting disaster. However, as Hallett and Stevenson (1980) indicate, successful interprofessional co-operation involves the development of trust, mutual respect, skill, and changes in professional attitudes. This cannot be accomplished overnight, but it is worth working for.

Apart from the problem of professional confidentiality, which is often used to avoid co-operation, there are, it must be recognized, profound differences in professional attitudes towards child protection. For example, even though the battered child syndrome was promptly diagnosed in the Popen case by the consultant paediatrician and communicated to the family physician, for some obscure reason neither of them took the obvious step of reporting the facts to the children's aid society, as they were required to do by law. The CAS, who must have been aware of this breach after Kim's third hospital admission, should have discussed this with the physicians concerned – but failed to do so. In view of this, Judge Allen recommended that regular medical examinations of abused children should be a condition for their return home. This would, at least, provide a base for co-operation between physicians and child-protection workers. Such an arrangement in the Popen case might also have facilitated the discovery of the bizarre injuries to Kim's vagina and rectum which have never been explained.

In addition to being deprived of adequate medical care, Kim Popen was also poorly served by the legal process because she was not legally represented before the court. Her own legal counsel would have, it is to be hoped, insisted on determining who was responsible for Kim's injuries. This vital question was never resolved because in the plea-bargaining process, Mr Popen pleaded guilty to the lesser charge of 'failing to protect' Kim and the charge against Mrs Popen was withdrawn. This shameful but perfectly legal chicanery enabled Mrs Popen not only to resume the care of Kim but also to subject her to further physical abuse.

Having established her innocence by putting the blame for injuring Kim on to her compliant husband, Mrs Popen proceeded to sabotage the CAS worker's inept attempt to help her. She did this not only by lies and deceptions but also by making mischief between the volunteer probation officer and the social worker. This scheme failed because Mrs Popen overestimated the level of communication between her helpers. Intervening in such a formidable situation would tax the resources of many experienced social workers, but it was not without hope. Hope was only lost when the CAS abandoned its primary obligation which was to protect Kim. In this respect, it must be said that Mrs Popen's attitude towards Kim was characteristically ambivalent. She could not face the humiliation of being considered an incompetent mother and losing Kim, but she was emotionally unable to provide an acceptable level of parenting without resorting to violence – or worse. This is not an uncommon situation in high-risk cases. The numerous examples of missed warning signals and help-seeking behaviour provide a vivid testimony to Mrs Popen's inner conflict and the social workers' denial and inability to observe evidence of abuse and to respond effectively to the numerous cries for help.

Case Study II   Jasmine Beckford
(2 December 1979–5 July 1984)

> On any conceivable version of the events under inquiry the death of Jasmine Beckford on 5 July 1984 was both predictable and preventable homicide. Even if it was not predicted, it was certainly preventable at the instance of those public authorities – health, education, social services and magistrates' court – which since August 1981 had had in their disparate ways individual and collective responsibility for her welfare.
>
> (*A Child in Trust*, Brent 1985: 287)

A careful study of the events culminating in the death of Jasmine Beckford leads inexorably to the conclusion that by any common-sense standards her death was both predictable and preventable. The sense of public outrage which followed, aggressively promoted by the press, was probably due to the fact that a comprehensive and expensive network of health and welfare services was ineffectual and insensitive to the needs of these previously abused infants. In contrast to the death of Maria Colwell in 1974, ten years earlier, it cannot be said that 'it was the "system", using the word in its widest sense, which failed her'. Although, except for the perpetrators, no single individuals were actually blamed for Jasmine's death, there is little doubt that her life could have ben saved by a higher standard of professional competence. This case study is organized roughly in the same manner as the Popen case. Following a case summary five main areas are examined:the family background; the external environment; intervention by the control agencies; inter-agency communication and co-operation; sequential analysis of the events culminating in Jasmine's death. This is followed by a summary of conclusions. The primary source of information for this analysis is *A Child in Trust: The Report of the Panel of Inquiry into the Circumstances surrounding the Death of Jasmine Beckford* (Brent 1985).

CASE SUMMARY

Jasmine, born 2 December 1979, was the daughter of 20-year-old Beverly Lorrington who lived with Morris Beckford, also aged 20. Although Morris was not Jasmine's father, her name was changed, shortly after her birth, to Jasmine Beckford. Jasmine's sister, Louise, born 27 May 1981, was admitted to hospital on 1 August 1981 with a broken arm and eye haemorrhages which were due to a non-accidental injury. A few days later, 4 August 1981, Jasmine, then age 1.644 years, was admitted to the same hospital with a fractured femur. This was also assumed to be the result of a non-accidental injury. Both children were placed on the non-accidental injury register, made subject to a place of safety order and taken into care by the London Borough of Brent. Discharged from hospital on 14 September 1981, Jasmine was placed in a foster home with her sister Louise, where both children flourished. Although there was a major difference of opinion within the Borough's Social Services Department about whether Jasmine and Louise should be placed permanently, perhaps with a view to adoption, this matter appears to have been resolved with the magistrates' decision that the children should be reunited with their parents.

Once it was decided that the children would eventually be returned, the parents were granted regular access to the children, including supervised contacts in the parental home. To facilitate the transition, on 13 April 1982 the children were transferred to a residential nursery which provided additional opportunities for the parents to have supervised access. According to the key worker, this arrangement was very successful – 'both parents coped very well beyond anyone's expectation.'

With the assistance of the social workers, Morris Beckford and Beverly Lorrington were rehoused. Jasmine and her sister Louise were returned to their parents' care on 19 April 1982. During this period the children were being 'supervised' by a qualified but inexperienced social worker. This was her first child-abuse case. Except for a two-day multidisciplinary course in 1982, the health visitor assigned to the Beckford family also had little or no experience of child-abuse cases. She visited the Beckfords throughout

1983 but did not see Jasmine after 22 April 1983. Both children were removed from the child-abuse register on 9 November 1983. Chantelle Beckford, a sister to Jasmine and Louise, was born on 11 December 1983.

On 5 July 1984 Jasmine, taken to hospital by her parents, was found dead on arrival. Her death was due to 'cerebral contusions and sub-dural haemorrhage' caused by blows to the head inflicted by Morris Beckford. At the post-mortem, Jasmine was found to be very thin and emaciated as a result of chronic undernourishment. Jasmine had been subjected to repeated battering over several months.

Convicted of manslaughter, Morris Beckford was sentenced to ten years' imprisonment. Beverley Lorrington, found guilty of child neglect, was sentenced to eighteen months' imprisonment. The public inquiry into the death of Jasmine Beckford concluded that the two front-line workers, the key worker and the health visitor, 'while not callous or indifferent to Jasmine's welfare, must take personal responsibility for what happened.'

HIGH-RISK CHECK LIST

Properly evaluated, through full Social Services' assessment and contributions from all the professionals who attended the Case Conferences on 6 and 20 August 1981, the evidence that was available, if only it had been assiduously culled from existing sources, should have led ineluctably to the conclusion that Jasmine and Louise Beckford presented a high risk situation.

(*A Child in Trust* (Brent 1985: 289))

This pragmatic assessment of risk by the Beckford Inquiry Committee is well supported by the high-risk check list (see the appendix). It will be seen that, even at the time of her first non-accidental injury, the risk factors were ominously high. The initial NAI was closely associated with the birth of Louise about two months earlier. Jasmine's subsequent injuries and her death followed from the birth of her sister Chantelle about seven months earlier.

GROWTH AND DEVELOPMENT RECORD

As previously indicated, one of the most shocking features of the Inquiry into the death of Jasmine Beckford was the revelation about the stark, but neglected, evidence of her failure to thrive. When she died at the age of 4.589 years, Jasmine was of normal height – 41 inches. But her weight, 23 pounds, was 15 pounds less than the average for her age.

FAMILY BACKGROUND

Beverley Lorrington, born 2 November 1959, was deserted by her mother when she was 6 months old. She claimed that, as a child, she was the scapegoat of the family and was beaten by her father and stepmother. At the age of 17 she ran away from home and has little contact with her family. She was described by a school psychologist as having a 'significant degree of intellectual handicap'. Before living with Morris, Beverley cohabited with a man who was reputed to have been violent. At Jasmine's birth the midwife recorded that Beverley had had two previous abortions and that Morris Beckford was not Jasmine's father.

A useful description of Beverley Lorrington, at the time of the childrens' first injuries, was provided in 1981 by Ms Joan Court, the independent social worker.

> Miss Lorrington is an appealing, frail looking woman, blind in one eye from a childhood accident. She is reserved and shy, and cannot easily show when she is angry or upset. I think she is devious and quick to 'catch on' and find reasons for what has happened or might have happened. For example, she said if she had broken Louise's arm by rough handling she would have heard it snap. On the other hand she says she may have forced the baby's hand into a sleeve as some of her clothes are too small. And, she said, if she was a battering mother she need not have taken the baby to the hospital at all, as she knows how to set a fracture. She is also very frightened and ashamed. The shame is because she does not know what to say to people who ask where the children are. She is frightened because she thinks she may lose not only her children but Mr Beckford.
>
> (Brent 1985: Appendix C2: viii–ix)

Morris Beckford, born June 1959 in Jamaica, was the third child in a family of eight. When his parents came to England, Morris spent the first nine years of his life in the care of his maternal grandmother. He and two sisters were united with their parents in England in 1968. Four years later Morris and his sister, accused of stealing, were severely beaten by their parents. This led to intervention by the police and the NSPCC. The parents were subsequently prosecuted on a charge of ill-treatment and neglect. Morris and his sister were then taken into care of the Brent Borough Council. Morris attended a special school for educationally subnormal children, where he met Beverley Lorrington. After leaving school he started work for a scaffolding company and was described as 'an excellent employee, very hard working and reliable'. He worked long hours and, at the time of Jasmine's death, earned £12,000 a year, which is more than the salary of an experienced social worker.

Up to 1980 Morris Beckford had no serious offences recorded against him. However, on 19 November 1981 he was convicted of 'assault occasioning actual bodily harm' to Louise (age 0.181 years) and sentenced to six months' imprisonment, suspended for two years and fined £250 plus costs. At work he continued to be conscientious, boisterous, and well liked. At home his relationship with Beverley and the two children was quite different. On one hand he spoiled her with expensive gifts and household appliances. On the other hand he was enraged if the house was in a mess. For example, a new cooker he had purchased had a speck of dirt on the oven door, and he smashed the door in. Morris was also concerned because he thought that Beverley was 'spoiling' the children.

> He was very strict with the children, expecting that they instantly obey him. He wanted to teach them things that were too advanced for them (i.e., alphabet, numbers) and would become extremely angry if they could not learn. From the time Jasmine and Louise came home on trial, they were both subject to physical abuse by their father. There was constant bruising on the children, mainly on their buttocks, legs and lower back. Sometimes there was facial bruising including black eyes.
>
> (Brent 1985: Appendix F.1: lxxii)

Jasmine Beckford, born 2 December 1979. Even before her femur was fractured, on 4 August 1981, Jasmine was not thriving. A few months earlier, the health visitor examined Jasmine and recorded that she was a 'thin, miserable looking child'. Information about Jasmine's temperament and relationships is sparse. However, Joan Court's 1981 observations are most instructive.

> I observed both parents with Jasmine in hospital while they changed her and made her comfortable. Both are very competent in their handling and care, but the mother scarcely speaks to the child at all. She knows this may appear odd and told me she could not behave naturally when other people are around, but I was concerned at the passivity and stillness of the child when the mother washed and changed her, and the way she watched her father and did not look at her mother or smile. Her behaviour at this time was in marked contrast to what I had observed when I first came into the ward, when Jasmine was rolling around the floor with the nurse in charge, giggling and playing happily and full of life and vitality, so I know she can be responsive.
>
> (Brent 1985: Appendix C.2: x)

Following her discharge from hospital on 26 August 1981 Jasmine (and her sister Louise) was placed in a foster home for seven months. Some of the most dramatic evidence presented at the Beckford Inquiry concerned Jasmine's growth spurt during this period. Jasmine, who was weighed by the health visitor every fortnight, 'moved from below the 3rd centile (18 lbs. 4 ozs.) on 17 September 1981 to just below the 25th centile (25 lbs. 5 ozs.) on 1 April 1982.' Unfortunately, although she was reported to be 'pinched and worried' looking, Jasmine's weight was not recorded again until her death two years later. At the post-mortem examination on 6 July 1984 she was described as a 'thin little girl 3ft. 5in. in height and weighing 1 stone 9 lbs [23 lbs].'

Louise Beckford, born 27 May 1981. The fact that Louise was attacked by her father at the age of 2 months suggests that his violence towards both children was indiscriminate. An examination of Louise, after Jasmine's death, revealed evidence of unexplained cuts and bruises. The foster-mother reported that, when she was washing her back or face, Louise would say that her father hit her there. 'She does not talk about her mother or about Jasmine.' An assessment by Dr Hugh Jolly, consultant paediatrician, conducted on 20 November 1984, showed Louise to be undersized, placing her 'well below the 20th percentile and nearer the 10th percentile.' Dr Jolly was also concerned about the child's psychological and emotional development.

> Louise is retarded in her development and her behaviour is of a superficial nature. Her foster-mother tells me that she behaves well towards Chantelle (her baby sister), so long as Chantelle is not crying. If she is crying she will hit her, put her fingers in her eyes, and tell her foster-mother to hit and kick her.
>
> (Brent 1985: Appendix F.3: lxxxi)

Chantelle Beckford, born 8 December, 1983. Dr Hugh Jolly, who also examined Chantelle, concluded that, although she has suffered severe child abuse, 'both physical and emotional', Chantelle is

> a normal child though somewhat below the average in height and in motor development. She is, however, within the limits of normal in both aspects and, given optimal opportunities for living, I believe that she will continue to catch up.
>
> (Brent 1985: Appendix F.3: lxxx)

THE EXTERNAL ENVIRONMENT

Since Morris and Beverley were alienated from their own parents, they were virtually isolated and lacked a normal family-support system. Beverley had few friends; one of them was her step-sister

Carol – herself a single parent. Apart from his workmates, Morris had only one long-standing friend. Another negative factor was that Morris, who was extremely conscientious, worked long hours. As a result, he was frequently tired and irritable with Beverley and the children. This difficult situation was also exacerbated by very poor housing which was a constant source of stress and friction for the Beckfords. Beverley was particularly angry because they were not immediately rehoused following Jasmine's birth.

INTERVENTION BY THE CONTROL AGENCIES

The Brent Social Services Department had the major statutory responsibility for child protection. It is not, however, alone in providing statutory services to children and families. The other key agencies include the health authority, medical practitioners, education department, and the juvenile court. The contribution of each of these agencies will be examined in turn.

Social services

As soon as it was determined in August 1979 that Jasmine and Louise had been the victims of a non-accidental injury, the children were placed on the NAI Register; an interim care order was made by the juvenile court magistrates, and the Brent Social Services assumed full responsibility for the case. The key worker, appointed to deal with the Beckfords, had been employed by the Brent Borough Council since 1974. She was seconded for training from 1977 to 1979 and completed her Certificate of Qualification in Social Work in 1979. Jasmine Beckford was her first child-abuse case. Her case-load at this time varied from twenty to thirty-two cases – with eight to ten child-care cases. Her other duties included a play-scheme and support group for parents of handicapped children, and being on rota duty as a mental welfare officer. Also, for three months, from May–July 1983, while her supervisor was on maternity leave, she acted as senior social worker supervising field workers. Despite this heavy workload, the key worker made seventy-eight home visits to the Beckfords and kept almost one hundred pages of 'meticulous' notes.

The key worker was supervised by a senior social worker and team leader. She, unfortunately, had little or no experience with child abuse. Perhaps for this reason, it was assumed that, once the Beckfords were rehoused, the children could safely be returned to their parents. Little or no thought was given to securing psychiatric consultation to determine if the parents were, in fact, sufficiently mature and stable enough to care for small infants. Also,

perhaps in a misguided endeavour to develop a cordial relationship with the Beckfords, no serious attempt was made to understand exactly how Jasmine and Louise came to sustain such serious
injuries. Instead, it was accepted that Louise's injuries were due to
rough play with her father and that Jasmine had fallen down stairs.

Unfortunately, in accepting this explanation, an important
piece of information, provided by the ward sister, Ms Ritchie, was
overlooked. At the first case conference on 6 August 1981, following the admission of the children to hospital, Ms Ritchie
reported that, although the mother appeared to have a good relationship with Jasmine in the hospital, 'she had not visited very frequently or for very long.' At the next case conference (20 August
1981) Ms Ritchie reported that:

> both parents had spent the normal amount of time visiting the hos-
> pital that could have been expected of them, but obviously felt
> over-powered by the doctors and nurses. However, Ms Lorrington
> seems to have little understanding of very small children, and makes
> no attempt to play with Jasmine or to cuddle Louise.
> (Brent 1985: Appendix G.2: lxxxviii)

This vitally important observation was confirmed later in 1981
by Joan Court who observed the interaction between Ms Lorrington and Jasmine on 24 August 1981.

Police

Following an investigation of the Beckfords' home by an experienced police officer, it became clear that the parents' explanation
of the cause of the injuries received by the children was unsatisfactory. However, since Morris was said to be away from home
when Jasmine 'fell' downstairs and fractured her femur, it was
decided that he would be charged only with 'causing actual
bodily harm' to Louise.

The Court

In making an order committing both children to the care of Brent
Borough Council, the juvenile court magistrates expressed the
'earnest hope' that 'the children will soon be reunited with their
parents.' Their feelings of optimism appear to have encouraged
the social workers to work towards the rehabilitation of the Beckford family.

Family aide

In addition to providing them with a new home, Brent Social Services also arranged for the Beckfords to be helped by a family aide

who would, as it were, serve as a role model. Also of Afro-Caribbean origin, the family aide had the task of teaching Morris and Beverley to relate more effectively to their children. Unfortunately the family aide, who was seconded for social work training, made her final official visit to the Beckfords in August 1983 when Beverley was in the fifth month of her pregnancy.

Health visitor

As with other families with small children, the Beckfords were assisted by a health visitor. Her task was to support and encourage mothers, to monitor the children's progress and advise on what needed to be done to ensure their healthy growth and development. The last health visitor, assigned to the Beckfords from July 1982 to July 1984, who had completed her training in 1974, had a caseload of 385 families. Only two of the families were on the child-abuse register. The Jasmine Beckford Inquiry Report (Brent 1985) was highly critical of the health visitor for four main reasons. First, because she failed to carry out the recommendations of the April 1982 case conference that, 'Beverley Lorrington should be encouraged to take the children to the clinic monthly' and the health visitor should 'visit fortnightly'. Second, because she failed to co-ordinate and share information with the social worker. Third, 'she only too readily followed the case-conference recommendation (9 November 1982) to take the children off the child-abuse register, by removing the children from the replica register, without talking the matter over with anyone, let alone her supervisor.' The fourth criticism, while most severe, is extremely pertinent.

> The visit of 22 April (1982) when Beverley Lorrington had just become pregnant, was the last time the HV saw Jasmine. . . . [Her] irregular and infrequent visits thereafter partook of the same misconceived approach of the social workers. She displayed no concern for the fact that when she did visit the Beckford home Jasmine was either away from home or out somewhere in the vicinity of the home.
>
> [She] . . . in fact made only four visits before the year's end during the later stages of Beverley's pregnancy, and thereafter never got a reply to her ring at the door of the Beckford house. . . . [She] saw no significance in the birth of Chantelle in December of 1984, in relation to the welfare of Jasmine and Louise. All through the first six months of 1984, when the child abuse started up and Jasmine had already received a broken thigh bone, repeatedly fractured, . . . [she] was never called to account by her supervisor in respect of the two children.
>
> (Brent 1985: 295–6)

Educational services

Although the Beckfords were not compelled to send her to school until the age of 5, Jasmine was enrolled in a day-nursery programme from about the age of 3. Her attendance in 1983 was irregular. Since the school authorities had not been told that Jasmine was the subject of a child care order and that her name was on the child-abuse register, the staff were not unduly concerned by her frequent absences. Also, although it was noted that she was very thin and quiet, and that after a long absence she returned to school with bruises and scars, the possibility of abuse was not seriously considered.

Eventually the nursery school arranged for the educational welfare officer to make a home visit. When he did so on 14 July 1983, Ms Lorrington told him that Jasmine had not been very well. At the end of September 1983 the headmistress wrote to the Beckfords asking if they still wanted Jasmine to go to school. In October Morris Beckford visited the school and explained that, due to Beverley's difficult pregnancy, Jasmine was staying with her maternal grandmother – which was untrue. Jasmine did not attend school again.

General practitioners

In addition to the specialists who looked after her in hospital when she was being treated for the fractured femur, Jasmine was seen by three general practitioners. The last one was also consulted by Ms Lorrington during her third pregnancy. A brief summary of the involvement of these physicians is presented in chronological order.

Physician 1. In August 1981 the GP saw both Louise and Jasmine, diagnosed the fractures, and recommended that the children be taken to hospital. Child abuse was not suspected. He was invited to attend the case conference but declined to do so and did not see Jasmine again.

Physician 2. While in the foster home Jasmine and Louise were registered with GP 2. The information concerning the children's medical history, including the NAI, and case conference minutes were kept on file but not passed on to physician 3, even though the Beckford children were not seen again after 19 November 1981.

Physician 3. Following their return home in April 1982, Ms Lorrington took the children to see a new doctor. This physician, who was invited by the key social worker to attend a case conference, declined to do so. Instead she asked for the minutes to be sent to her. She did not, however, take any steps to monitor Jasmine's progress. When questioned about this, the GP said that she 'thought' that Jasmine was being cared for by physician 1. This may explain why, when she was being consulted by Ms Lorrington about her 'difficult' third pregnancy, the GP was apparently unconcerned about Jasmine and Louise.

INTER-AGENCY COMMUNICATION AND CO-OPERATION

The now standard procedures (Hallett and Stevenson 1980) for inter-agency communication and co-operation were well in place in the Borough of Brent in 1981 when Jasmine and Louise Beckford were first identified as abused children. In addition to direct communications initiated by the key worker, four case conferences were held and six statutory case review forms were completed. However, despite these precautions it seems that the educational authorities and the general practitioners were unaware that Jasmine and Louise were subject to care orders and that their names had been placed on the child-abuse register. A review of the case conference reports and review forms helps to explain what went wrong.

6 August 1981. NAI case conference, convened by hospital staff. The professions represented at this meeting included the social services staff, police, medical specialists, health visitors, court officer, and the ward sister. Apologies were received from the GP and the Area Child Health Specialist. Since Jasmine did not start nursery school until the following April, the educational authority was not involved.

20 August 1981. NAI case conference, convened by hospital staff. A similar group of people attended this conference. The GP sent his apologies.

9 December 1981. Statutory case review

Miss Lorrington has made few friends and there appears to be no close friends with whom she can confide in. Mothers at the Under 5's Centre have made efforts to communicate with Miss Lorrington, but she has responded inappropriately.

Mr Beckford has still very high expectations of his children as well as of his co-habitee.

Miss Lorrington finds it difficult to talk to and play with her children and rarely sees to both children at once.

Jasmine and Louise are very well settled with the foster parents.
. . . The children have developed well.

Recommended action
(1)   To continue with parental contact once per week but to change
       venue . . . to parental home; visits to last four hours; social worker
       and family aide to supervise.
(2)   Miss Lorrington to spend Wednesday and Thursday mornings at
       Tree Tops (Under 5's Centre) with aide in order to develop skills
       in parenting as well as relationships with other adults.
(3)   Social worker to meet with Mr Beckford and Miss Lorrington
       once a fortnight to try to enable them to talk about their rela-
       tionship, parenting, and why the children are in care and other
       problems.
                                    (Brent 1985: Appendix G.3: xci)

19 January 1982. Review form
Contact with parents has been once a week for two hours at Tree-
tops, Under 5's Centre. At first Jasmine showed signs of distress
when she saw her father. This is no longer so.
                                    (Brent 1985: Appendix G.3: xcii)

4 May 1982. Case conference. None of the medical and hospital
staff involved in the previous case conferences or the health visitors was present. The GP does not appear to have been invited or
informed of the result of the conference. The following observations were included in the minutes.

Magistrates emphasised their concern that every effort should be
made to rehabilitate the children with their parents . . .
     Parents relaxed, shared in the child care – changing nappies, feed-
ing, playing with the children. Morris's change in attitude is particularly remarkable. He previously was restrained, treated them as
property. Now appears to enjoy them and treating them as individuals, doing things with them, talks to them. Both parents do this
now . . .
     Beverley and Morris have visitors so are not as isolated as they
were previously. Also are communicating with each other . . .
     Rehoused into very adequate 3-bedroomed house with garden
last month . . .
     Both parents are aware of the difficulties the children will have in
re-adjusting . . . (to their return home).
     Place at day nursery 5 mornings a week for Jasmine. She will be
seen by a speech therapist . . .
     'Health Visitor' . . . will continue to liaise with keyworkers . . .
     Beverley to be encouraged to attend Clinic monthly and HV to
visit about fortnightly.
                                    (Brent 1985: Appendix G.4: xciv–xcvi)

25 May 1982. Statutory case review. Several significant matters are revealed in this review. First is the statement that the health visitor and the social worker have 'liaised' and that the HV has started to see Miss Lorrington and the children. Second, 'Morris' attitude to social work help and the children has changed in a very positive direction'. Third, 'M. Beckford and B. Lorrington able to relate to each other and now enjoying each other's company.' Fourth, 'Children happy at home – parents wish to be left to cope, with support, but without the "Authority".'

The use-of-'Authority' issue appears to have been considered at a case conference held on 25 May 1982. In addition to the key worker, her supervisor, and the family aide, this meeting was attended by Morris Beckford. The health visitor, GP, and nursery school staff do not appear to have been invited. A summary of this conference provides valuable insights into the key worker's assessment of the situation.

> The discussion was must [sic] less a process of reaching a decision on specifics than an opportunity for Morris to publicly announce his resentment and humiliation of the social service intervention in his 'private life', and an attempt to set a long-term goal of revocation of the care order. Morris was given time to vent his feelings and spade-work done for future working relationships. Stress was laid on Beverley and Morris being involved in the decision making process of Social Services and allowing Social Services to be privy to their decision making proceesses [sic]. There were may [sic] specifics that need to be taken up with Beverley and Morris during the next 6 months as there was neither time nor appropriate atmosphere to tackle all Morris' feelings and Beverley was unable to attend. I felt Morris left with the idea that there was some positive reasons for what Social Services was doing and it was not just a series of irrational spying exercises. There is no concern over the care of the children nor is it felt that they are at risk in their home on trial.
>
> (Brent 1985: Appendix G.5: cii)

The objectives set by the key worker were, long term, the revocation of the care order. 'Short term is to help Morris and Beverley to make rational decisions rather than emotional reactions.' These objectives were approved by the area manager who was not present at the meeting.

30 September 1982. Statutory case review. Except that Beverley Lorrington attended instead of Morris Beckford, the participants of this review conference were the same as at the previous session. The health visitor was not present and her absence was not explained.

The key worker recorded seventeen visits, including three to
the day nursery where Jasmine was seen. No particular attention
was paid to the fact that Jasmine was not seen on eight occasions.
Despite this, the key worker recorded, 'Children well settled and
cared for at home. Jasmine enjoying the Day Nursery – happy
when she arrives and pleased to leave midday. Jasmine has been
seen by Speech Therapist. Jasmine is behind with her speech but
there is no concern.'

9 November 1982. Case conference. Although invited to do so,
Morris Beckford and Beverley Lorrington did not attend this conference. The GP also sent his apologies. The health visitor, a new
one assigned to the Beckford family, was not present either. In
addition to the two social workers and the court officer, the conference was attended by the day-nursery matron who was not
previously involved. The conference concluded that 'The parents
have: (1) matured. (2) are coping with all aspects of parenting. (3)
are no longer isolated. (4) have maintained their financial situation
without current arrears [sic]. (5) have improved their marital relationship and communication. (6) are now able to identify problems or needs and seek help appropriately. The children have: (1)
responded well to the parenting provided and no longer accept
adults indiscriminately. (2) Jasmine's speech as [sic] improved and
she can articulate sentences. (3) always appears well care for.' The
senior social worker concluded:

> There are no longer any signs of ongoing stress in the family. They
> have made enormous strides in all areas since coming into contact
> with this department. As no worker saw any indicators of potential
> problem areas, any cause for concern about the physical or emo-
> tional care of the children and the parents were continuing full co-
> operation with this department, it was agreed that the children
> could now be removed from the register.
>
> (Brent 1985: Appendix G.7: cxi)

During the period covered by this report fifteen home visits
were made by the key worker. There was no reply on five occasions, and no record of Jasmine being seen between 9 September
and 4 November 1982. Her absences were not explained.

18 April 1983. Statutory case review. In addition to Morris Beck-
ford, the review conference was attended by four staff members.
The absence of the health visitor and the GP was not explained.
The summary included the following highlights:

> Jasmine has moved from the Council Day Nursery to the Nursery
> Class at the local infants school . . .

Morris and Beverley have always made it clear that they want all legal ties to the SS dissolved and need this last vote of confidence and gesture towards their being a totally independent family. There is no cause for concern and no reason to oppose the revocation of the Care Order . . .

(Brent 1985: Appendix G.8: cxv)

Although the reasons for their decision were not provided, on 22 June 1983 the Willesden Magistrates Court declined to revoke the child care order. They suggested that the Social Services Department try again in ten months' time.

6 December 1983. Statutory case review. The key social worker's assessment of the situation included the following information:

Beverley and Morris coping very well and the children happy and settled.

Beverley pregnant and expecting baby middle of December. Morris will take annual leave when Beverley goes into hospital . . .

Morris and Beverley will need some support in the near future to be able to involve Louise and Jasmine with the new baby.

Morris and Beverley have proved that they are willing and able to contact SSD when there is a problem.

Seventeen home visits were made during the period from 19 April 1983 to 23 November 1983. The children were seen only five times. Although the key worker was probably unaware of this, the record shows that Jasmine was absent from nursery school from 7 June to 22 July. She resumed attendance on 5 September but was not seen again after 9 September. Two critical events occurred during this period. The family aide made her last visit on 15 August, and Chantelle Beckford was born on 11 December.

On 13 and 17 February 1984 the health visitor visited the Beckford home. There was no reply on either occasion. This was not reported to the key worker. On 12 March the key worker made a home visit and reported 'All three children appeared well and happy.' On this occasion Beverley Lorrington admitted that Jasmine no longer attended nursery school. When the school was contacted by phone, the key worker learned that Jasmine had not attended school since the previous September. Eight home visits were made between 24 May and 5 July. The children were not seen on any of them.

On 3 July 1984 the key worker hand-delivered a letter informing the Beckfords that she and her supervisor would be visiting on 5 July to start the review procedure leading to recommending that the child care order be rescinded. Two abortive attempts to see the Beckford family were made on 5 July but the door was not answered. Later that day, the parents took Jasmine to hospital where she was found to be dead on arrival. On the next day Beverley Lorrington and Morris Beckford were charged with murder.

SEQUENTIAL ANALYSIS

(W – warning sign; HS – help-seeking)

1981

27 May	W	Louise Beckford born.
8 June	W	Health visitor describes Jasmine as a 'thin, miserable looking child'.
1 August	W	Louise admitted to hospital with broken arm and retinal haemorrhages.
4 August	W	Jasmine admitted to hospital with fractured femur.
6 August	W	Key (social) worker appointed has no previous experience of child abuse. Her supervisor and team leader is equally inexperienced.
20 August	W	Ward sister reports mother 'seems to have little understanding of small children and makes no attempt to play with Jasmine or cuddle Louise.'
20 August		Brent Area 6 social workers to organize future review conferences. 'A smaller meeting will be adequate and only those will be invited that it is felt necessary should attend.'
9 September		Juvenile court magistrates, making the care order, express the hope that the children will be reunited with their parents.
9 November	W	Morris Beckford convicted of assaulting Louise. Insufficient evidence to charge him with causing Jasmine's injury.
12 December	W	Case conference *Decision* : 'Key worker to meet with Mr B. and Ms L. once a fortnight to try to enable them to talk about their relationship, parenting, why the children are in care and other problems.'

1982

March		Beckfords moved into three-bedroom house.
5 April		Arrangements made for the health visitor to 'liaise' with the key worker. *A new health visitor would be taking over in July.* Recommended that Beverley should be encouraged to attend the clinic monthly.
19 April		Children home on trial. Key worker reports, 'There is no concern over the care of the children nor is it felt that they are at risk.' 'Long-term objectives; removal of the care order.' 'Short-term objectives; help Morris and Beverley to make rational decisions rather than emotional ones.'
? April	W	Beverley takes both children to register with GP. They were not examined.
7 May	W	Between 7 May and October 1982 the key worker was alerted on seven occasions regarding Jasmine's non-attendance at nursery school.
4 June	W	Health visitor reports, 'Jasmine looks pathetic and pinched.'
28 June	W	Key worker reports: 'Morris and Beverley have worked extremely hard to improve the housing situation. Morris' attitude towards social work help and the children has changed in a very positive direction. Morris and Beverley able to relate to each other and now enjoy each other's company.' (Brent 1985: Appendix G.5· c)
14 August– 26 September	W	Home visits were made but Jasmine was not seen during this period.
7 October	W	Key worker visits. No reply.
21 October	W	Key worker visits. No reply.
26 October	W	Routine physical examination by school medical officer. Although the percentile chart was on the file, no reference was made to it and no weight or height measurements were

taken. Medical officer was unaware that Jasmine was the subject of a care order and that her name was on the child-abuse register.

28 October   W Key worker makes home visit – Jasmine not seen.

Note: Based on evidence of healing fractures, the post-mortem examination revealed that Jasmine must have been injured some time in the first week of November.

2 November   W Jasmine no longer attends nursery school.

4 November   HS Beverley Lorrington tells key worker that she is extremely unhappy in her relationship with Morris Beckford and talks about leaving him and taking the children with her.

9 November   Key worker to case conference: 'As housing had been considered a major factor in the original stressful situation, and because of the parents' co-operation and improvement . . . the children can be removed from the abuse register as they are no longer at risk.' (Brent 1985: Appendix G.7: cx–cxi)

29 November   Health visitor notified that children have been taken off the child abuse register.

1983

10 January   W Home visit. No reply.

11 January   W Home visit. No reply. (Jasmine starts nursery school.)

20 January   W Home visit. No reply.

18 April   Case review, health visitor absent.

19 April   W Beverley's pregnancy confirmed.

4 April   Health visitor sees Jasmine for the last time.

7 June   W Jasmine absent from nursery school, 7 June– 22 July.

22 July   Magistrates refuse to revoke the child care order.

14 July   W Educational welfare officer makes home visit

re her absence from nursery school. Told that Jasmine has been unwell.

15 August   W   Family aide makes her last official visit.

? September   W   Jasmine returns to nursery school showing signs of bruises and healing scars. Mother says she fell off her bike.

9 September   Jasmine's last day at nursery school. Not seen again.

Note: Post-mortem examination reveals evidence of another major injury in September 1983.

? October   W   Morris Beckford visits school to say that, due to Beverley's difficult pregnancy, the children are staying with their maternal grandparents. (This was not true.)

17 November W   Home visit. No reply.

21 November W   Home visit. Children not seen. Told that they are spending a few weeks with maternal grand-parents (untrue).

22 November W   Home visit. No reply.

23 November W   Home visit. No reply.

5 December   Home visit. Key worker records, 'Beverley and Morris coping well and the children happy and settled. Baby due mid-December.'

6 December   Key worker reports, 'There is no cause for any concern and we feel strongly that this family ought to be relieved of the legal ties to Social Services and will re-apply to the Court in the spring when the children have been home two years.' (Brent 1985: Appendix G.9: cxx)

11 December W   Chantelle Beckford born.

1984

18 January   W   Home visit. Mother says that Jasmine is upstairs in bed with a bad cold. She was not seen.

13 February   W   Home visit. No reply.

17 February   W   Home visit. No reply

12 March	W	Home visit. Key worker reports that the three children were seen. They appeared well and happy. Beverley admits that Jasmine no longer attends nursery school.
11 June	W	Home visit. No reply.
3 July	W	Home visit. No reply. Key worker writes to the Beckfords re visit on 5 July.
5 July	W	Two calls were made by appointment. The door was not answered.
5 July		At about 5.30 p.m. Jasmine, taken to hospital by her parents, was found to be dead on arrival.

CONCLUSIONS

In retrospect, it is obvious that the Jasmine Beckford case was, in almost every aspect, typical of the battered child syndrome described by the late Henry Kempe *et al.* (1962). Both parents brought to their relationship a substantial history of abuse and neglect which incapacitated them as parents and reduced their ability to sustain nurturing relationships with each other and with their children. Although Morris Beckford was identified as the perpetrator of the abuse which finally killed Jasmine, Beverley Lorrington's role caused equal concern. By lying to the social workers, by concealing the children's injuries, and by failing to secure the necessary medical attention, she did nothing to prevent Jasmine's painful and lingering death. She also exposed the two younger children to abuse.

In addition to the burden of their experience as abused children, before they were rehoused in March 1982, the Beckfords lived in squalor. This must have been particularly difficult for Morris who was extremely fastidious and obsessed with cleanliness and order. These personality traits would, almost certainly, have diminished Beverley's self-esteem and her ability to cope with three young infants. Although very little factual information is available, it must also be assumed that Beverley's health would be undermined by two abortions and three births in the space of about six years. Her last pregnancy was described by her physician as 'very tough'. No wonder that she was described by a competent observer as 'a helpless, fragile, victimized young woman'.

Unlike Beverley Lorrington, Morris Beckford was, at least on the surface, healthy, outgoing, and robust. In fact, he had quite a reputation as a body-builder and as an amateur boxer. However, according to Joan Court the independent social worker, in 1981, Mr Beckford suffered from a 'painful and irritating condition which has affected his sexual life for the last two or three years and needs treatment.' Ms Court also reported that Mr Beckford 'can be moody and his anxiety is expressed in perfection. He is quite obsessional about everything being just right on time.'

Given these facts, it is not surprsing to discover that the relationship between Morris and Beverley was by no means harmonious. Ms Lorrington, who had responsibilitiy for caring for the children and housekeeping, was unable to meet Mr Beckford's high standards. They also had major differences in their attitudes towards bringing up the children. Morris, who feared 'spoiling' them, was a harsh disciplinarian. Beverley, on the other hand, was more apathetic and relaxed. An additional complication was that both Jasmine and Louise were afraid of Morris and cried when he came near them. After Jasmine's death, Ms Lorrington revealed that Morris would hit the children to stop them crying. He was particularly hard on Jasmine who was not his child.

On a purely common-sense basis, it is not difficult to define the Beckford family situation as 'high risk'. Unfortunately the inexperienced social workers assigned to this case were apparently unaware of this. They were also unaware of the existence of high-risk check lists. An assessment of this family on the check list, 1978 edition, indicates a high degree of risk for the children. The risk was not only miscalculated – it was inadequately assessed. The key worker and her supervisor leapt to the conclusion that, once the housing problem had been solved and communication between the parents improved, the risk to the children would be diminished. This over-optimistic view was obviously encouraged by the magistrates' *obiter dictum* that the children should soon be reunited with their parents. The magistrates, in turn, were influenced by Joan Court's independent social worker's report in 1981 (in Brent 1985) which concluded:

> I consider the parents have many strengths and would expect that the family could be brought together again providing the environmental conditions are relieved, the older child placed in a day nursery, and the parents receive the skilled case-work help they so urgently need but have not so far experienced. Their medical problems should also be attended to by the health visitor.
>
> (Brent 1985: Appendix C.2: x–xi)

This fairly optimistic assessment, which was promptly accepted by the Social Services Department, was not however based on a comprehensive examination of the facts. Although contrary evidence was available, it was incorrectly assumed that Morris Beckford was Jasmine's father. An interview with the health visitor or the maternal grandparents, and with Beverley's step-sister, who still lived with her parents, would probably have provided a more accurate account of Beverley's tragic situation. In view of the serious nature of the injuries to the children and Jasmine's failure to thrive, a psychiatric evaluation of Beverley and Morris should also have been made available to the magistrates. Also, as far as can be determined, no attempt was made to interview the neighbours who could hardly have been unaware that the children were being abused.

Since accurate evidence about the precise causes of the children's injuries in August 1981 was not obtained, the parents' failure to provide an honest account of what happened was unexplained and then forgotten. In this way the social workers were lulled into a false sense of security. They assumed that the parents were not responsible for what happened to the children. The collusion between Beverley Lorrington and Morris Beckford made it difficult for the social workers to reach any other conclusion. Morris admitted shaking Louise and throwing her up in the air but denied breaking her arm. Jasmine's fractured femur was explained by Ms Lorrington who said that she fell down the stairs. The hospital specialists concluded that the injuries to Louise were 'certainly non-accidental', but there was some doubt about the injury to Jasmine. Although this 'could have been caused by an accidental fall', the detective sergeant who investigated the case was by no means satisfied. He concluded that, although it would have been possible for Jasmine to have fallen downstairs, the stairs themselves were well carpeted with underlay and 'should not therefore have caused the injury.' Another piece of information provided to the police by an independent witness was that Jasmine was injured on 2 August and not on 3 August (when Morris was away from home) as the parents claimed. The most reasonable explanation was provided by the independent social worker (Court, 1981). She said,

> I suspect that father's sudden rage with the baby may be a 'one off' episode, but one cannot be certain about this. I am more concerned about the uncertainties surrounding mother's role, and I suspect she has been under intolerable stress in the last two years.
>
> (Brent 1985: Appendix C.2: x)

After Jasmine's death, Beverley Lorrington confessed that Jasmine's fractured femur was caused by Morris, who kicked her in the leg. Beverley didn't say anything because she was afraid of Morris and didn't want him to leave her.

This additional information, placed in the context of what was actually observed in the hospital in August 1981, suggests the need for social workers, investigating child abuse, to have a much higher index of suspicion. The ward sister, it will be remembered, was concerned because the children were not being visited and because Ms Lorrington had little understanding of small children and made no attempt to play with Jasmine or to cuddle Louise. Similar observations were made by the independent social worker. Unfortunately, perhaps because of their concern about Jasmine's fractured femur, the fact that she was also 'failing to thrive' appears to have been overlooked by the child-health specialists. Also overlooked by the social workers and the health visitor was the fact that, during her seven months' stay in the foster home, Jasmine's weight moved from well below the 3rd centile to close to the 25th centile. But Jasmine's weight was not recorded again until after her death when, at the age of 4½, she weighed only 23 lbs. Since failure to thrive is so closely associated with child abuse and neglect, the simple action of weighing Jasmine and noting her weight loss would surely have saved her life.

The authors of the Jasmine Beckford Inquiry Report (Brent 1985) directed their sternest criticism against the social workers and the health visitor who failed in their primary duty of protecting the children. Without wishing to mute this criticism, it may be useful to trace the direction of the social workers' thinking and actions which caused them, literally, to lose sight of the Beckford children. To start with, it should be remembered that neither the key worker nor her supervisor were experienced with child-abuse cases. Lacking the ability properly to assess the case and determine how the children came to be injured, they were guided in their understanding by the 'rule of optimism'. In practice this means that the workers are required, 'if possible, to think the best of parents' Dingwall, Eekelaar, and Murray 1983). This involves a process of screening out negative information and, as far as possible, limiting decision making to like-minded people. The first step was to take over the interdisciplinary child-abuse conferences and to limit the attendance to selected individuals.

Following the two case conferences, convened by the hospital staff on 6 and 20 August, the remaining conferences convened by the social workers virtually excluded input from the medical specialists. Although initially invited to do so, neither the GP nor the health visitor attended the conferences. Consequently no effort was made to ensure that Jasmine was followed up from an orthopaedic point of view. This error was compounded by the fact that, due to a failure in communication, Jasmine was not registered with or examined by a GP from the time of her return home on 19 April 1982 until her death on 5 July 1984.

Guided, no doubt, by the 'rule of optimism' and lacking competent professional supervision, the key worker was allowed to block evidence which contradicted her beliefs. Although on 4 November 1982 Ms Lorrington told the key worker that she was extremely unhappy in her relationship with Morris Beckford, on 9 November the key worker recorded that, because of the parents' co-operation and improvement, the children, who were no longer at risk, could be removed from the child-abuse register. This treacherous combination of unfounded optimism and inexperience explains the key worker's incorrect assessment of the risk to the children associated with Ms Lorrington's 'difficult' pregnancy and the stress following the birth of Chantelle.

While all the ingredients for a tragedy were present in the Beckford case, perhaps the most egregious fault was the Social Services Department's failure properly to identify the children as their primary clients. This position, which is eloquently argued in the Beckford Inquiry Report (Brent 1985), serves as an appropriate conclusion to this case study:

> Throughout the three years of social work with the Beckfords, Ms W. totally misconceived her role as the field worker enforcing Care Orders in respect of two very young children at risk. Her gaze was focused on Beverley Lorrington and Morris Beckford; she averted her eyes to the children to be aware of them only as and when they were with their parents, hardly ever to observe their development, and never to communicate with Jasmine on her own. The two children were regarded as mere appendages to their parents who were treated as the clients.
>
> (Brent 1985: 293)

6

Strategies for intervention

It is right that we should feel shocked and angry at the social conditions which breed the circumstances in which she [Maria Col-
well] lived and died. Social work alone cannot solve these
underlying problems. We as a society must recognize the very
heavy burdens we lay on those we delegate to look after nearly
100,000 children in local authority care. We need to understand the
very real difficulties they face and we need to help them to prevent
this kind of tragedy.

(The Rt. Hon. Barbara Castle, Secretary of State for Social
Services, *Response to the publication of the Maria Colwell
Inquiry Report* (1974)

Profoundly shocked by the wretched circumstances surrounding
the death of Maria Colwell, Barbara Castle (1974) promptly recognized that remedying the underlying conditions which predispose
children to die as a result of abuse and neglect requires effective
political action rather than additional social work. At the same
time, despite their limited mandate, social workers are expected
to deal with child-abuse cases which come to public attention.
However, the balance between essential intervention to protect
vulnerable children and officious interference with the rights of
parents is extremely delicate. Social workers who fail to get the
balance exactly right are likely to be publicly censured or worse.
On the other hand, having survived the ordeal of about thirty
inquiries into CAN deaths over the past decade, the social-work
profession in the UK has grown in stature and in authority.
Instead of merely responding to fierce public criticism, the British
Association of Social Workers has taken the initiative in publishing a series of authoritive reports, to be mentioned later, on the
management of child-abuse cases. Mainly addressed to social-
work practitioners, these reports are concerned with improving
the standards of professional practice. This topic is explored in
the section titled 'The framework for prevention'. The following
two sections are concerned with high-risk families and high-risk
children. The section which follows provides a brief commentary
on the role of theory.

Theory for intervention

At the jugular vein of intervention in high-risk cases is the danger of doing greater harm by removing children precipitately from their parents and severing powerful family attachments which are essential for emotional growth. But leaving a child unprotected, in a potentially lethal situation, may be equally calamitous. The decision to act or not is usually based on a mixture of administrative fiat and experience which, whether the workers are aware of it or not, is based on a set of theoretical assumptions. Einstein probably had this kind of situation in mind when he said, 'It is theory which determines what we observe', or words to this effect. However, in the absence of explicit rules or a logical framework for decision making, social workers will continue to be criticized (Goldstein, Freud, and Solnit 1979; Dingwall, Eekelaar, and Murray 1981) for being arbitrary and for the abuse of power. While social workers, like other members of the helping professions, will no doubt continue to live with uncertainty, the application of theory to practice will at least reduce the capricious elements of decision making. In relation to the exceedingly complex issues involved in family violence, theory as a guide to practice does not have to be complete or inflexible, but it must be accessible, explicit, and capable of refinement in the light of experience.

The contribution of theory to the management of high-risk cases can be considered at two levels, the general and the specific. A valuable example of the latter is illustrated by the work of Brearley (1982). Borrowing concepts from the insurance industry, he provides a rational basis for decision making in relation to risk assessment and management in social work. Brearley is, of course, concerned with the phenomenon of risk rather than its causes or its prevention. These more global concerns are best articulated by Gil (1978) who stresses the links between economics, politics, and interpersonal violence. Gil (1978: 14) writes:

> To study and treat violence in families as a discrete phenomenon with supposedly discrete dynamics and solutions, as is often done, rather than as a multi-dimensional phenomenon reflecting specific social contexts with which families interact, seems to me futile.

The next element of Gil's (1978: 15) thesis is the belief that personal violence is invariably embedded in structural violence.

> Structural violence is usually a 'normal' ongoing condition reflected in socially sanctioned practices, whereas personal violence usually involves acts which transcend formal social sanctions. Personal and structural violence should not be viewed as discrete phenomena,

however. . . . Structural violence (thus) tends to breed reactive or counterviolence on the personal level, leading to chain reactions with successive victims becoming agents of violence.

The Achilles' heel of this argument is that, faced with similar stresses and subjected to the same structural forces, only a minority of people resort to life-threatening violence. Gil (1978) avoids this dilemma by defining violence somewhat idealistically as 'acts and conditions which obstruct the unfolding of innate human potential, the inherent human drive towards development and self-actualization.' In any case, his theory fails to account for the fact that individuals do succeed, from time to time, in shaking off the succubi which breed in inequitable and stressful environments.

Between Gil's idealism and Brearley's pragmatism the paper by Williams (1982: 55) on theory as a basis for practice best meets the needs of front-line workers. Recognizing the extent to which adherence to the 'rule book' is designed to protect the reputation of child-welfare agencies, Williams' (1982: 54) warns us that the needs of clients may take a second place.

> The danger here is that administrative procedures, such as the use of 'at-risk' registers, which do have an important role in ensuring information exchange between relevant professionals, may substitute for the social work activities of assessment, planning and goal setting. Such a neglect is likely to produce intervention which is experienced by clients as rather impersonal and in which the distinctive features of particular cases may be ignored. In this way, short term protective and preventive measures may drift into unjustified, damaging or over-controlling long-term arrangements.

With rare insight into the feeling of front-line workers, Williams (1982: 44) also recognizes that encounters with family violence involve 'urgency, complexity and anxiety'.

> Over and above the specific fears the social worker may experience in such cases (e.g., fears for the safety of the victims, fear of personal injury, fear of making an error of judgement and so on) is a more generalized sense of threat or foreboding which does not attach so identifiably to specific objects. This anxiety is often pronounced in clients who may be paralysed into inactivity by it.

Noting that this tendency is likely to be exacerbated by uncertainty and confusion, Williams suggests that, in seeking clarity and explicitness, 'a goal-oriented model of intervention' is most likely to succeed.

In this otherwise valuable commentary, Williams (1982) does not, unfortunately, consider the possibility that, experiencing high anxiety, social workers may also be galvanized into needless action. A high level of unsystematic activity is, in fact, pathogno-monic of social work intervention in many high-risk cases with fatal outcomes. This difficulty is compounded by the lack of clar-ity about who the client is or, to put it another way, on whose behalf the social worker is intervening – the child, the parent(s), the family, concerned neighbours, or school teachers? Ideally, it might be said that the mutual and overriding concern is for the child's safety and best interests. In practice, however, the issues are likely to be much more complicated. For example, as often happens, parents, denying that they have harmed the child, want only to be left alone. Hostility, including threats of physical harm, as in the Maria Colwell (DHSS 1974) and Richard Fraser (Lambeth 1982) cases, is not conducive to the development of a therapeutic or any other alliance between social workers and their clients.

The framework for prevention

In the eleven years that separate the Maria Colwell tragedy in 1973 from the equally tragic death of Jasmine Beckford in 1984, a com-plex administrative system has been developed in England and Wales. Involving five main elements, this system has at its core the concept of multidisciplinary co-ordination. The five elements consist of: area review committees; multidisciplinary procedures; case conferences; key workers; child-abuse registers. According to the new draft guide published by the Department of Health and Social Security (DHSS 1986b: 28), the existing area review com-mittees will be replaced by joint child-abuse committees report-ing to a joint consultative committee in each area. The main areas of activity will be:

> a. establishment, maintenance and review of local interagency pro-cedural guidelines; b. to review significant issues arising from the handling of cases; c. to review arrangements to provide expert advice; d. to review progress on work to prevent child abuse; e. related to inquiries into the deaths of children at the hands of their parents; and f. relaned to training.

In its publication, *The Management of Child Abuse* (BASW 1985: 8), the British Association of Social Workers (BASW) admits that the British structure is not an unmixed blessing. Some workers see, 'a bureaucratic over-reaction to the highly individual needs of par-ticular children and their families designed to protect agencies and their staff.' On balance, however, the BASW accepts that the existing child-abuse structures do provide a secure framework for containing professional anxiety in which professional discretion can be wisely used. In respect to child-abuse deaths, the BASW (1985: 8) claims:

> Inquiry after inquiry into fatal child abuse cases have found little fault in local procedures but that procedures were not followed. The failure to follow such guidelines may be caused in a variety of ways ranging from poor training, to inadequate resources, poor management, low professional standards, or mistaken judgement about the meaning or, value of procedures. The failures should not be seen to imply that the procedures themselves are inadequate.

PHYSICIANS AND CHILD ABUSE

Since social workers bear the main brunt of criticism for child-abuse deaths, relatively little attention has been paid to the role of family physicians in detecting abuse and responding to it effectively. For reasons which are deeply rooted in medical history and philosophy, with rare exceptions, physicians find it difficult to function as members of interdisciplinary teams. Placing a very high value on autonomy and the maintenance of professional secrecy, they view the confidential relationship with *their* patients as the essence of good medicine. Except in the most extreme situations, the traditional doctor/patient relationship is breached with great reluctance because it diminishes the charismatic aspect of medical practice. In respect to child abuse, the situation is further complicated because the physician may also have to choose between betraying the confidence of an abusive parent and securing protection for the at-risk child. A *British Medical Journal* (*BMJ*) editorial explained this problem (BMA 1981: 170). After arguing that the child-abuse pendulum has swung too far and that the 'register' has become a fearful thing to some people, the editorial concludes: 'Certainly professional confidentiality counts for little compared with the life of an abuse child. In marginal cases, however, a large proportion turn out not to be abused children.' While one can sympathize with the physician's need to protect the confidential nature of his relationship with patients, it is naïve to believe, as does the *BJM* editorialist, that it is within the competence of physicians to determine, without reference to other professionals, whether abuse has taken place or not. To make such a decision without, for example, securing a paediatric assessment of the child, including X-ray, and a family assessment by an experienced social worker or health visitor, should be regarded as poor practice.

Apart from the obvious advantages of seeking specialist advice in diagnosing child abuse, it should also be remembered that child abuse forms only a small part of the caseload of the average GP. This was confirmed by the Royal College of General Practitioners (quoted by Hallett and Stevenson 1980: 37) which reported that 'in one practice of some nine thousand patients, twelve [child-abuse] cases were recognized in a three-year period.' This may explain why so many physicians find attending child-abuse conferences a useless activity. Since the reluctance of physicians to participate in child-abuse conferences is likely to remain a contentious issue, attempts to resolve this dilemma at the local level must be given the highest priority.

Equally problematic is the practice, illustrated by the 1985 Jasmine Beckford case, of securing consensus at case conferences by excluding dissenting voices such as medical specialists and the police. This is not intended to imply that the social workers concerned were operating in bad faith. But it is important to recognize the extent to which front-line social workers are pressured by their agency as well as by the parents to reach some kind of closure. This pressure is also related to the child's right not to be left in limbo, and the tendency of interdisciplinary conferences to 'play it safe' by postponing difficult decisions.

THE LAW AND THE COURTS

The Children and Young Persons Act (England and Wales), 1933, 1963, and 1969, and the Child Care Act (England and Wales), 1980, give the police, the National Society for the Prevention of Cruelty to Chidlren (NSPCC) and local-authority social workers, acting on the authority of a justice or a magistrate, wide powers to protect abused and neglected children as well as others who may be in danger. This includes powers to apprehend a child in an emergency as well as removing a child from his parents on a temporary or permanent basis. Once a care order is made by the court, the local authority has the same powers, duties, and responsibilities towards the child as would any natural parent. According to the Beckford Inquiry Report (Brent 1985: 19), the general principle underlying the legislation (Children and Young Persons Act, 1969), is that

> the local authority, as the parent of the child, is in total control of that child during the subsistence of the Care Order. The courts, moreover, have no general power to review or control the local authority in the proper exercise of its discretionary powers.

In addition to the Jasmine Beckford case, several other inquiries into CAN deaths have identified the need for additional legal powers to protect vulnerable children. This need is illustrated by the following cases.

Baby GWF (born 14 November 1980, died 15 January 1982)
At the age of 6 months GWF was admitted to hospital with bruises and other non-accidental injuries. An X-ray revealed a healed spiral fracture of the lower right arm. A place-of-safety order was obtained and the baby was transferred to a foster home. Charged with assault, the 19-year-old mother, with an unstable background, pleaded guilty and was conditionally discharged. Full care proceedings took place in the juvenile court. Although the social workers recommended a care order, the court made a supervision order and returned the child to his parents. Three months later he was admitted to hospital with severe brain injuries from which he died. His mother was convicted of manslaughter.

The inquiry panel (Cheshire Central Review Committee 1985) noted that the social workers, although suitably trained and experienced, failed to recognize that their understanding of child abuse was not shared by the juvenile court. Consequently the magistrates were not convinced that the baby's life would be in danger if it returned home. They also placed greater reliance on the views of the GP who had not attended any of the case conferences, and on the opinion of the consultant psychiatrist who had seen the mother twice but was not present in court to hear the evidence and to be cross-examined. The panel made two recommendations. One was that professional training be extended to include juvenile-court magistrates, court clerks, and lawyers who are likely to be involved in child-abuse cases. The second, perhaps more vital, recommendation was that 'procedures should be established whereby a decision of the Juvenile Court not to make a Care Order can be challenged if the professionals involved in the case feel strongly that the child's life is in danger.' Under the present law it seems that social services departments have no right of appeal. However, if it is believed that the magistrates have erred in law, an appeal to the High Court is possible, but there can be no stay of execution. This means that the local authority cannot protect the child against a magistrates' decision to return him to an abusive parent.

Heidi Koseda, born 16 December 1980, died November 1984
Heidi Louise Koseda died of starvation in November 1984. The exact date is uncertain because her emaciated body was not discovered until 25 January 1985. Concerned that Heidi and her

younger brother were being ill-treated, neighbours made repeated calls to the NSPCC which were not answered. And, despite frequent home visits, the health visitor also failed to see Heidi. Finally, because of concern for the welfare of a new baby, born unattended at home on 6 December 1984, the police were called. A warrant, obtained under Section 40 of the Children and Young Persons Act, 1933, enabled the police and the health visitor to enter the flat, over the parents' objection, and to see the two youngest children. 'Lisa and James were found in the lounge, both surprisingly clean and healthy, though the flat was dirty and untidy.' The parents said that Heidi was staying with a relative but refused to say where she was. The bedroom, where Heidi's body was eventually discovered, was not examined because the parents said it was damp and unsafe. However, since the warrant applied only to the baby, Lisa, who was fit and well, the police had no power to search for Heidi. Finally, because of the absence of legal powers to compel the parents to disclose the whereabouts of Heidi, and also because of concern for the welfare of the younger children, it was decided to place the names of the three Koseda children on the child-abuse register. The police then visited the home and arrested Nicholas Price, the mother's common-law partner, and charged him on the suspicion of Heidi's murder. Her body was found in the locked bedroom. Price, found guilty of murder, was sentenced to life imprisonment. Pleading guilty to manslaughter, the mother was made the subject of a hospital order under the Mental Health Act, 1983. The two surviving children were made wards of court.

Although the London Borough of Hillingdon had no legal responsibiltiy for Heidi Koseda until the day before her body was discovered, they set up a review panel to examine the involvement of the constituent members of the area review committee. Published in March 1986, the report (Hillingdon 1986), which is a model of its kind, contains a number of valuable recommendations. Those concerning the limited power of the police to search for Heidi Koseda are particularly important. Under the existing legislation, the warrant authorizing a constable to search for a child, believed to be in danger, applies only to the child named in the warrant. Having satisfied himself that the named child is not in danger, the constable has no power to inquire into the whereabouts of other children who may also be in danger. It seems that parents are not obliged by law to disclose the whereabouts of a child who is not the subject of a warrant.

Jasmine Beckford, born 2 December 1979, died 5 July 1984
Since this case is examined in the previous chapter, it is only

necessary to repeat that, in making orders committing Jasmine and Louise Beckford to the care of the local authority, the magistrates added a rider expressing the hope that the children will be reunited with their parents. Because this recommendation had such tragic results, the Beckford Inquiry Report (Brent 1985: 167) raised two main objections.

> We have already indicated our view that the rider added to the Care Orders made on 9 September 1981 by the Willesden Magistrates was at best unhelpful to the Social Services in deciding the future placement of Jasmine and Louise Beckford, and at worst was powerfully and tragically influential towards the return of the two children to their parents.

The second objection concerns the failure of the magistrates to provide reasons for their judgement in making the care orders. (Brent 1985: 171)

> We presume that magistrates do actually have reasons for all their decisions. Were it not so, it would be a blot upon our system of magisterial justice; we prefer not to contemplate the possibility that decisions are unreasoned, even if at times they appear unreasonable. The obligation to think out and articulate the reasons for a judicial decision, justifying them in a public manner, will always promote that intellectual and judicial discipline necessary to ensure sound decision making. Since care proceedings are conducted behind closed doors, and the press is rarely present to report them, the obligation to give a reasoned decision is all the greater.

Before leaving the Beckford case, child advocacy must be considered. After Jasmine's death in July 1984, care proceedings were started in respect to her sisters Louise and Chantelle. Under the authority of the Child Care (England and Wales) Act, 1980, the court appointed a guardian *ad litem* to represent the children's interests. But, when Jasmine and Louise came before the court in September 1981, their interests were represented by Ms Joan Court, a distinguished independent social worker appointed by their lawyer. Since Court was not an officer of the court, Brent Social Services were less than co-operative in providing her with the information required to complete her assessment. This would not, it is assumed, have occurred if a guardian *ad litem* had been appointed in the first place.

Once a child, particularly a very young child, has been seriously injured by a parent, or is the victim of a major 'unexplained' injury, it must be assumed that, unless removed to a safe place, his life will be in jeopardy. It is also best to assume that the home is unlikely to be a safe place for other young children, even though they may not show evidence of ill-treatment or neglect. In these circumstances, most jurisdictions provide the relevant child-protection agency with the power, on behalf of the State, to assume guardianship of the at-risk children on an emergency or temporary basis. Having obtained custody of the children, the child-protection agency, under the direction of its legal advisers, is then expected to provide a comprehensive assessment of the family in order to make further representations to the court on behalf of the children. This usually involves obtaining expert medical evidence on the nature and causes of the injuries and on the background and home situation of the suspected perpetrators. Gathering this information requires effective interdisciplinary co-operation, time, and expertise. However, because the parents are likely to be in an adversarial relationship with the child-protection agency, through their legal adviser, they may well resist releasing any kind of negative information such as might be included in a psychiatric report. For this reason, the involvement of the police in investigating serious unexplained injuries is vital.

CHILD-ABUSE REGISTER

In England and Wales, when child-abuse has been confirmed, the child's name is entered into the official child-abuse register, which it is proposed (DHSS 1986b: 20) will become a child-protection register. The purpose of the register is:

> a. to provide a record of all children in the area who are currently the subject of an interagency protection plan and to ensure that the plans are formally reviewed at least every six months; b. to provide a central point of speedy inquiry for professional staff who are worried about a child and want to know whether the child is the subject of an interagency protection plan; and c. to provide statistical information about current trends in the area.

When the abused child comes into care, except when parental rights have been formally terminated by the court, the child-protection agency is required to formulate a plan of action. This involves determining when and under what circumstances the child should be restored to his parents. Since the pressure to do so is very strong, considerable effort will be made by the social workers to improve the home environment and to reduce the family stress which, it is commonly assumed, has provoked the abuse. In order to reduce the possibility of the child's remaining in care unnecessarily and losing contact with his family, the Children and Young Persons Act (England and Wales) 1969: c.18, s.1) requires that the case be subject to statutory review every six months. In addition, if the child's name appears on the child-abuse register, his progress will also be subject to another form of review. In respect to the review and assessment process of abused children who were returned home, the report of the Social Services Inspectorate (DHSS 1985: 19–21) is alarming. Specifically the inspectors were concerned about the poor quality of statutory reviews, the absence of adequate assessments and specific goals for intervention, and the lack of measures of progress. The inspectors also noted that social workers were often confused about the purposes of child-abuse reviews within the context of the statutory review system. And, once the child was in care, 'the importance attributed to child-abuse reviews often diminished and attendance by other professionals almost ceased.' Another major concern was the fact that many child-abuse conferences were chaired by the team leader who was supervising the social worker carrying the case. The danger is that such an arrangement can lead to collusion and the exclusion of other professionals. Finally, the inspectors commented on the lack of adequate administrative/clerical support for tasks such as taking notes and preparing minutes.

High-risk families

While the expression 'high-risk family' is commonly used in the child-abuse literature, it is rarely defined. In practice, however, there is little doubt that children growing up in these hard-to-define and harder-to-serve families are liable to experience a great deal of stress, including serious physical injuries. A multiplicity of problems, including anti-social behaviour and inter-personal violence, usually brings them to public attention. But it is the propensity to violence, rather than the multiplicity of problems, which makes these families so difficult to serve It is clear, however, that the extremes of close supervision and control or non-directional supportive casework are unlikely to be helpful. Both these measures are counterproductive because they tend to contribute to the 'burn-out' of social workers and to increasing hostility on the part of the clients. Although there is a dearth of well-documented case studies, experience suggests that goal-orientated models of intervention, suggested by Williams (1982: 65), are more likely to succeed. This is because the aims and objectives of the intervention are based on mutual agreement and the client is step by step involved in the helping process. However, as Williams (1982) reminds us, it is important to recognize that since families are complex organizations, simple remedies may not work. Thus, in the context of the 'systems theory of families', he writes (1982: 56)

> what may appear to be a rather simple causal connection between factors, say between unemployment and family violence, might in practice turn out to be a very complex pattern of interacting variables. This is an example of 'non-linear' causality, one of the key ideas in systems thinking.

Thinking about high-risk families in a 'non-linear' way means becoming aware of the existence of 'complex interacting variables' rather than, say, 'one-shot' altercations between an aggressor and a victim. It makes better sense to assume that a violent and potentially lethal family situation exists when there is an actual or potential victim, an aggressor or aggressors, a motive or precipitating (trigger) factors, a time, and a place. Child abuse and other forms of family or domestic violence are almost invariably a victim-specific or situation-specific activity. By definition, the victim is a child, usually a specific child, the aggressor is a parent or caretaker, and the place is the home. Except perhaps for extended suicide, involving an overdose of prescribed drugs, the availability of a weapon is rarely an issue. But the presence in the home of an adult, usually the mother's boyfriend, who has previously abused children, does create a high-risk situation.

The risk of abuse is also influenced by time as well as place. Depressed mothers, for example, often find it more difficult to cope with children in the morning, but feel better as the day progresses. Understanding violence in this context and having access to a wide range of information about the phenomenon may be life-saving. The notion of escalation of aggression, in response to the loss of normal control, is also vital to the effective diagnosis, treatment, and follow-up of high-risk cases. Most people are able to predict, with a fair degree of accuracy, the kinds of situations or behaviours which provoke in them an aggressive response. For example, the stepfather in the Wayne Brewer case illustrated this when he said, 'Some things he [Wayne] says annoy me, and . . . I just go click and go for him and whop him' (Somerset Area Review Committee 1977). Mr Brewer's attacks on Wayne suggest that he was grossly immature and irresponsible. But even otherwise responsible and mature parents, under stress, may find themselves enraged by a child's behaviour. Most parents will recognize the feelings of anger associated with the inability to comfort a fractious child, especially at night. The transformation of these common feelings into violent action is responsible for a great deal of child abuse and a proportion of CAN deaths. Some of these deaths are caused by brain injuries due to severe shaking of very young infants. Apart from the injuries causing death, the autopsy often reveals that the infant is well developed and properly cared for. In such cases the risk of a similar injury to older siblings is negligible. If the death is associated with previous abuse and neglect, the danger to siblings is considerable.

Parents, usually mothers, who are concerned about their intensely hostile feelings toward an infant who refuses to be comforted may take the baby to the doctor with some vague complaints. Instead of reassurance that the baby is fine, the mother may be seeking an opportunity to discuss her anger and feelings of resentment or of incompetence. In particular, she may want to talk about her fear of losing control, 'going berserk', and harming the baby. Dealing effectively with this critical situation takes a great deal of time and experience which the physician may not have. But physicians should, at least, be able to recognize clinical depression with suicidal ideation. If clinical depression is diagnosed in an isolated mother with young children, then by definition a high-risk situation exists and prompt and effective action, on an emergency basis, is called for.

Since the neonaticide cases are phenomenologically quite different from the other child-abuse deaths, which usually include a history of neglect or previous violence, child-protection agencies are unlikely to be involved until after the tragedy. An alert health visitor, or public-health nurse will easily recognize 'post-partum blues'. However, the mother's initial denial may mask the seriousness of her plight. If depression and feeling inadequate or unworthy are admitted, the help-seeking message should be clearly acknowledged. Simple-minded reassurance is best avoided. Unless the family physician is known to be experienced and sensitive to the needs of mothers, advice such as 'Why not discuss this with your doctor?' may not be helpful. The physician who prescribes tranquillizers, 'to calm your nerves and pep you up', without the addition of family support for the beleaguered mother, is writing a prescription for disaster.

Neighbours are usually the first to be aware of potentially lethal family situations, yet the two most frequent errors made in assessing risk to children are ignoring the neighbours' or relatives' expressed concerns, and failing to involve neighbours and relatives as natural allies in protecting children.

High-risk children

The early literature on child abuse (Galdston 1965; Morse, Sahler, and Friedman 1970; Smith 1975; Lynch 1979; Kempe and Kempe 1978) frequently reported that abused children were often perceived by their parents as being difficult and hard to manage. This is not entirely unexpected because the population of abused children includes a high proportion of premature infants with neurological defects. It is to be expected that children who suffer brain damage as a result of abuse might well exhibit concomitant behaviour disorders (Green *et al.* 1981). In either case it is often difficult to determine if the behavioural disturbance is a cause or a consequence of abuse. There is, however, no doubt that, except for the pioneer work of Ounsted (1972) and his colleagues, the treatment of these often quite severe disturbances, commonly found in abused children, has been largely neglected.

In his now classical description of 'frozen watchfulness' in abused children, Ounsted (1972) wrote (quoted by Lynch and Roberts 1982: 98): 'They make no sounds. They keep quite still. The gaze fixates the approaching adult, but they give out no facial signs. They have learned not to ask, by word or cry; not to demand, by approach or flight; not to influence, by smile or frown.'

Aggressive behaviour is another frequently reported response to abuse. Based on a controlled study of twenty abused children, Reidy (1977: 1145) reported:

> Abused children are significantly more aggressive than nonabused, normal children in three distinct areas: fantasy, free play environment, and a school environment. Abused children expressed significantly more fantasies that contained themes of aggression and violence than did normal children.

Green (1980) found that abused children were also more likely to exhibit self-destructive behaviour than a control group of neglected but nonabused and normal children. Summarizing these findings, Jones (1982: 240) wrote: 'There is also evidence that the behaviour of abused children rarely endears them to adults and frequently provokes feelings of rejection in the caregivers.' This impression is confirmed by Lynch and Roberts (1982: 196):

> Some of the children had such strikingly disturbed, hostile and negative behaviour that not only was it impossible to assess their intellectual potential but also their lives were becoming seriously disrupted.

It is strange to discover that so many eminent clinicians and researchers in this field have neglected to consider the survival value of the behaviours exhibited by abused children. Green (1980) comes close to this when, in describing suicidal behaviour in abused children, he says: 'It seemed to be an escape from a traumatic situation, while in others it represented a "cry for help", a fantasied means of rejoining a lost love object.' Apart from this, the literature pays little or no attention to what children do or say in order to escape from potentially lethal family situations. It must be assumed that this reflects the difficulty that many otherwise competent professionals have in relating to pre-verbal infants and the low value attached to direct communications with children. For example, the physician who saw Maria Colwell shortly before her death evidently attached no significance to the fact that this almost-8-year-old child remained totally silent throughout the physical examination. Her eloquent silence was the last of a series of attempts to communicate a sense of desperation to the adults who were responsible for her protection. A description of these and other attempts will, it is hoped, illustrate that many abused children exhibit help-seeking behaviour. The fact that the child-abuse literature is virtually silent on this topic suggests that, while abused children are often seen, they are seldom heard.

Maria Colwell relied on verbal and non-verbal means of communicating her distress. Her total silence during the medical examination can be viewed as a form of protest. An even more dramatic example of non-verbal communication was her running away from the Kepple household, which she did on several occasions. Since proximity is essential to the consummation of homicide, the aggressor or victim's attempt to create a distance, by running away, should always be taken seriously and recognized as a potentially life-saving activity.

Running away was also a factor in the death of Lester Chapman, 1979. Lester, age 8.3 years, ran away from home four times before his death. On the evening of 30 December 1977 Lester ran away after being beaten by his mother. He was picked up and taken to a police station. The police surgeon examined him and recorded: 'Lester, a personable and extroverted boy, had obviously won the hearts of all the policemen that night. Lester seemed to enjoy being the centre of attention.' The doctor observed 'about eight weals on the right buttock and three on the left, with the skin broken within some of the lesions. There were no other marks on the body. It was the doctor's opinion that the physical injury . . . was of a trivial nature only but perhaps a more severe punishment than one would expect to be given a child of his age.' After some discussion with the police officers, it was agreed that a social worker should be called to take Lester home. There was no record of any conversation between the police surgeon and Lester or the social worker. There was also no evidence to suggest that the police surgeon was familiar with the article by Hall (1974) on the diagnosis of NAI, published by the Association of Police Surgeons of Great Britain and quoted in the Lester Chapman Report (Berkshire and Hampshire 1979: 43):

> It must not be assumed that the risk to the child is directly related to the severity of the injuries and whenever there is the slightest suspicion of a non-accidental causation the situation must be investigated immediately, after steps have been taken to protect the child.

Perhaps if he had been better informed, the police surgeon might have noticed that Lester was extremely thin and small for his age. If this child had been referred to someone with experience of child abuse, the diagnosis of failure to thrive or of 'psycho-social dwarfism' might have been made and Lester's sad life saved.[1]

Three days later, 2 January 1978, Lester ran away for the second time. Found by a neighbour near a canal, Lester said that he was thinking about jumping in. The social worker was called and after some discussion Lester and his mother went home together – 'apparently quite happy'. On 10 January Lester and his sister, who were absent from school, were found selling books door to door. Lester told a householder that his father had died in the war and his mother had died in a fire. The children were returned home to their parents who promptly sent them to bed. Lester ran away for the third time. When picked up by the police at 11 p.m., Lester explained that he had run away from home again because he was sent to bed without any supper. After a discussion with the duty social worker, who had no knowledge of the case, the police took Lester home to his mother. On 12 January 1978 Lester ran away for the fourth and last time. Earlier that morning it had been noticed that Lester had left the school. When questioned about his disappearance, some school children reported that Lester had said, 'I am going to the railway to get killed by a train' or 'If I can't do that, I want to run away' or 'I am going to run away and jump in the river.' On 26 February 1978 Lester's body was found fifty yards from a river in an area of old sewage sludge. The body was lying almost prone, face downwards, in soft mud. The legs from the hips downward were buried in sludge. The cause of death was exposure to cold.

Although Lester Chapman had been abused by his parents over

a long period, he failed to exhibit signs of 'frozen watchfulness' or undue aggression. On the contrary, the police surgeon described him as a 'personable and extroverted boy'. Lester Chapman also provided vivid examples of the use of fantasy as a means of communicating his plight. After being cautioned about the dangers involved in running away, Lester told a social worker about a TV programme in which a boy had run away, lived in a tree, and used matches to keep himself warm, and said that he would like to do that.

Because she was only 19 months old when she died, it might be assumed that Kim Anne Popen was far too young to exhibit help-seeking behaviour. This did not prevent the social workers from observing that, although Kim was very comfortable with her aunt, she became extremely upset when her mother tried to feed her. Later, following a feeding battle when Kim received a cut lip and tongue, Mrs Popen reported that Kim was very difficult to manage. After complaining about her temper tantrums, Mrs Popen told the social worker that Kim was much better at weekends when Mr Popen was at home. About two months before Kim was killed, Mrs Popen finally reported that Kim was aggressive towards animals and children. The social worker was also told that, when mad, Kim would hurt herself and destroy things. In these circumstances, aggressive and self-destructive behaviour in a child of this age should be regarded as pathognomonic of child abuse.

Aggressive behaviour in response to severe and persistent abuse was also noted in the Ontario case of JAD, 1983. In addition to attacking other children in the day nursery, Jeff, age 2.8 years, exhibited an unusual form of help-seeking behaviour. The worker who visited him at home recorded, 'The last two times the worker has gotten up to leave Jeff cries uncontrollably.' The significance of Jeff's crying was, unfortunately, lost on this untrained and inexperienced worker.

Not all severely abused children are depressed or aggressive. Some of them are remarkably stoical in the face of adversity. Richard Clark, age 3.6 years, for example, told his grandmother that he did not want to go home. When she asked about the bruises on his hand, his brother Bobby said, 'Ah, ah, ah! Richard, you know what you will get if you tell tales.' The grandmother reported Richard's injuries to the social worker who failed to take appropriate action until it was too late. As a result, the committee of inquiry into the Richard Clark case, 1975, criticized the social workers because they did not, at any time, talk to Richard and his brother about their feelings. Somewhat more guarded in its criticism of the physician, the committee stated (Scottish Education Department 1975: 31):

> In view of the suggestions of battering we consider that the doctor should have carried out an examination which would have disclosed all the bruises which were noticeable. Had he done so it is reasonable to assume that he would not so readily have accepted the foster-mother's explanation for the bruising which he did see and that the later sequence of events might have been very different.

The need for social workers and physicians to talk with and listen to, as well as to examine and observe, abused children is self-evident. But it is also important to recognize that, like adults, children are capable of different and sometimes paradoxical responses. One of the most frequently overlooked responses is the tendency for the victim to identify or collude with the aggressor. Examples of this appear in the Colwell case. When asked by her teacher about the bruise close to her eye, which showed signs of finger marks, Maria said that her little brother hit her with a toy. Later, in a mixed message, Maria told her teacher, 'Mummy says that I have to tell you that I did not go to the shop for coal, but honestly I did.'

Identification with the aggressor was an unexpected feature in the Wayne Brewer case, 1977. Wayne, who was killed by his stepfather at the age of 4, had a long history of abuse. The doctor who examined Wayne and confirmed his bruises reported that the child was 'thriving and happy, and not in any way afraid'. Some months later, Wayne was taken to the same doctor with a black eye which his mother said was caused by walking into the door handle. Wayne, who still appeared cheerful, told the doctor, 'Daddy did it.' The social worker who took Wayne home noted that he was very active and that within the family there appeared to be no tension or concern. This case is of particular interest because apart from the 'affectionate' relationship and lack of tension between Wayne and his stepfather, it has all the elements of a lethal family situation. The mother, who came from an abusive family, was pregnant at age 16. Wayne, a premature infant weighing 4lbs. at birth, remained in hospital for twenty days. He was then cared for by his maternal grandmother. When Wayne was 2, his 18-year-old mother married the lodger. This 20-year-old man, who was not Wayne's father, had limited ability to read and write, was frequently unemployed, inclined to heavy drinking, and experimenting with drugs. The young couple moved out of the maternal grandmother's house because she was critical of the abusive way in which Wayne was being 'disciplined' by his stepfather.

In response to sustained physical abuse and emotional neglect, it will be seen that young children manifest a remarkable spectrum of behaviours. These are by no means confined to 'frozen watchfulness', aggression, depression, or self-destructiveness, but may well include all these elements at different times and in various combinations. Unlike the aggressive and self-destructive child who is easily identified, the compliant and withdrawn child who is depressed as a result of abuse and rejection is frequently overlooked by social workers, teachers, nurses, and physicians. Cheerful, outgoing children, like Lester Chapman and Wayne Brewer, who appear to collude with the aggressor, present child-protection workers with an equally difficult challenge.

What might be termed the 'Wayne Brewer syndrome' is also overlooked in the child-abuse literature. For example, in an otherwise comprehensive and up-to-date review of the literature on the characteristics of abused children, Pearce and Walsh (1984) recognize deficiencies in intellectual skills, difficulties in relating to parents and peers, problems in forming attachments, low self-esteem, and aggression, but ignore what Oliver (1977) calls the 'false-love' phenomenon. 'Some maltreated young children', he writes, 'appear to adapt happily to controlled happy social groups, *and appear* to relate well to (and lie on behalf of) abusive parents.' Oliver (1977: 32) considers the 'false-love' phenomenon to be important for the following reasons:

1. Professional people are deceived, and fail to persevere in initiating firm action to protect the child. 2. This phenomenon also causes professional people to 'close cases' (many of which are subsequently reopened by another department), to relax supervision, or to make unjustified claims for successful casework treatment of abusive or neglectful families. 3. Abnormal and unhealthy patterns of emotional life are set up in the child, as the basis of neurosis or personality disorder when they grow up. 4. Most abusive and neglectful parents were reared with cruelty, unkindness or incompetence. They frequently present a facade of normality (including normal personal and family histories), yet have immature personalities or cruel attitudes behind this facade. The 'false love' phenomenon in one generation gives rise to episodes of otherwise inexplicable baby-battering in the next or subsequent generation.

While Oliver's hypothesis appears to be sweeping and essentially untestable, it does focus attention on the abused child's need for treatment in his own right, rather than as an appendage of his parents or caretakers. In her critical evaluation of the work of the NSPCC's Battered Child Research Department, Jones (1977: 111–18) observed: 'Only slight positive changes were noted in most aspects of parent–child relationships, leaving many doubts about the effectiveness of our treatment service in improving the quality of parenting.' Trowell and Castle (1981: 187–92) express similar concerns about the dilemma of professionals who have the dual role of protecting children against abuse and at the same time treating the family. After pointing out that the needs of the children outweigh those of the family, they conclude:

> Many of these children have survived physically, but as has been shown, have suffered severe emotional damage. Essentially, if we are to break this chain of deprivation our service should be aimed at helping the children of today, who are the potential parents of tomorrow, to be able to communicate with, and understand the needs of, their own children.

This review of the plight of high-risk children, who were killed while under the protection of the social services, confirms the wisdom of Kempe's dictum, 'If a child is not safe at home he cannot be protected by casework.' Even if they survive, without specialized treatment many of these children and their siblings appear doomed to suffer severe and lasting emotional damage. These conclusions, which have languished in the child-abuse literature for the past decade, should without delay be incorporated into child-welfare law, policy, and practice. Following the inquiry into the death of Jasmine Beckford, the British government has promised to introduce a comprehensive bill on childcare law. According to Norman Fowler, Secretary of State for Social Services (Fowler 1986), the new legislation will ensure that:

> those concerned with the care of children at risk of being abused must always put the interests of the children first. Where a child is in the care of a local authority they have a clear obligation to safeguard and promote the welfare of the child and in any conflict of interests between parents and child, those of the child must always come first.

Practice and conclusions

In normal circumstances, the stresses and strains of coping with young children are reduced when the extended family provides respite for overwrought parents and fractious infants. Friends and neighbours may also serve this purpose. When the informal supports are unavailable, baby-sitters, home helps, day-care and nursery-school programmes may be employed to give children, as well as their frazzled parents, a rest from each other. In the absence of such supports, the risk of child abuse and neglect is usually increased. This is particularly true when young parents, isolated from their relatives, lack the means or the social skills to use the available network of supportive services. This problem is exacerbated by the increasing number of single-parent families, usually headed by mothers with poverty-level incomes. The tendency to segregate these welfare-dependent families in large public housing estates creates additional problems by raising the overall level of social and psychological distress. This is revealed by a high incidence of mental illness, child abuse and neglect, vandalism, and juvenile delinquency which may reach epidemic proportions in certain neighbourhoods. The clustering of high-risk child abuse cases in these areas tends to overwhelm the child-protection agencies, erode staff morale, and increase the likelihood of punitive responses to these often desperate families.

The association between child abuse and neglect and problems such as chronic unemployment, poverty, poor housing, underfunded, poorly staffed and overworked social-service agencies, should not be ignored. Unless these structural problems are remedied, the child-protection agencies, however well motivated, can do little more than provide 'Band-Aid' relief. The danger is that they may unwittingly play an essentially punitive role in which they become identified with the other social-control agencies which serve to perpetuate, if not increase, the social inequalities. To be effective, the helping process must include an awareness of the context in which child abuse is manifested and a commitment to work in partnership with the child and, if possible, the parents in order to reduce the harm caused by poverty and alienation. Subject to this caution, strategies for intervention in high-risk cases will be considered under the following headings: identification; assessment; intervention and evaluation; summary and conclusions.

IDENTIFICATION

At the heart of this study is the inescapable conclusion that many parents at the end of their tether, fearful that they may lose control and harm their children, seek outside help. The manifestation of help-seeking behaviour in such situations may not always be explicit and persistent but it is almost invariably present. When the cry for help is successful and order is restored, the impending tragedy may be averted or at least delayed until the next crisis. Although a great deal is known about the well-publicized tragedies, very little is known about the high-risk situations which have been successfully resolved with or without professional help. Much less is known about the multitude of isolated and desperate parents, usually mothers, who manage to avoid disaster without the help of strangers.

Although help-seeking takes on a variety of forms, there are some common patterns in high-risk cases. The most obvious and frequent ones involve parents' asking for the child to be removed. This is confirmed by the DHSS *Child Abuse: A Study of Inquiry Reports* (1985: 33).

> We were also struck by the number of cases in which parents or parent figures asked for children to be removed in one way or another. Mrs Godfrey[2] kept asking for a holiday for Lisa, or for full-time nursery place, and would not be put off by offers of child guidance (LG 22, 45). . . . Similar warnings were given to the general practitioner by Mr Aukland[3] (JA 50) and to the health visitor by Mrs Piazzani[4] (MP 19(f)) and Mrs Howlett.[5]
>
> (NH: 3, 18 April, 1976)

Desperate parents may take their child to the doctor or to a hospital with some real or imagined complaint. This occurred in the case of Kim Anne Popen, 1982. Twenty-five days after she was discharged from hospital, having suffered from a fractured arm, Kim was readmitted at her mother's request, with a diagnosis of 'dehydration and high temperature'. Since the physicians failed to connect the two events, Kim was discharged without any inquiries being made about Mrs Popen's ability to cope.

Although they represent 'warning' rather than help-seeking behaviour, three equally common events associated with high-risk cases will be mentioned. While in practice they may overlap, they are best described separately.

Children being left alone
Leaving young children alone and unattended may be due to ignorance or lack of concern. It may also be an attempt to reduce the possibility of violence by increasing the distance between the aggressor and the victim. This concept is important because the feeling of being trapped by having to cope with children, virtually unaided, produces a high degree of resentment and anger which, in the absence of a more appropriate target, may be directed towards the children.

Evidence of this intense hostility is sometimes seen when children are left alone with an open fire, lighted candles, and access to matches. As if they were aware of the impending tragedy, children often scream loud and long enough to attract the attention and help of the neighbours. When the parents are sufficiently desperate or determined to escape, the volume of the TV or radio may be turned up to muffle the cries of the frightened children.

It is obviously important for the police and child-protection workers to respond immediately to calls from neighbours who complain that children are being left alone. The threat of fines or the removal of the children, if this behaviour persists, may force the parents to stay at home or, if they can afford it, to get a baby-sitter. But this, as in the Maria Colwell case, may not reduce the risk to the child. Leaving young children alone and unattended is best regarded as a sign of the family's distress. Child-protection agencies should recognize the urgent need for parents, especially single parents, to be relieved of the responsibility of caring for children twenty-four hours a day. Providing competent baby-sitters who might also serve as role models for inexperienced, depressed, or hostile mothers should be an essential part of an effective child-protection service. Co-operative baby-sitting services, organized by the mothers themselves, may be even more effective.

Falling off in attendance at school

Frequent and improperly explained absences from school were critically important in the cases of Maria Colwell, 1974, and Jasmine Beckford, 1985. Examining this situation in a broader context, two common scenarios can be described. In the first, the child is kept at home because, due to depression, lack of energy, or apathy, the parent, usually the mother, oversleeps and fails to provide clean clothing and a packed lunch. Responding to the mother's depression, the child's anxiety increases so that s/he demands more attention and reassurance. Being confined to the home makes the child restless, possibly aggressive, and certainly more difficult to manage. This desperate situation reaches a breaking point when the mother, feeling guilty and angry, lashes out at the child.

The second scenario is an extension of the first. Here the child, who has already been severely abused, is kept at home to conceal his/her cuts and bruises from the eyes of the day-care staff or school teachers. Keeping the child at home for as long as possible also prevents people from asking the child about the cause of the injuries. This may also explain the undue delay in seeking medical attention for abused children.

Failure by professionals to gain access to the child

Failure to gain access to a previously abused child should be regarded as one of the most critical danger signals. In the 1980 Carly Taylor case,[6] for example, over a period of eleven months, the health visitor made twenty-three home visits, but on no less than fourteen occasions she was unable to obtain access. Shirley (the mother) admitted that on many of these occasions she was in but did not open the door. Since the lack of access was also a feature of the Paul Brown case in 1980,[7] the Committee of Inquiry recommended that repeated failure to gain access 'should prompt the caseworker to check whether other agencies are experiencing the same problem and where necessary, initiate the appropriate action.' The death of Heidi Koseda, in 1986, illustrates that after the child has been seriously injured or killed, it is not unuusal to discover that the refusal to allow access was used by the parents to delay or avoid discovery of the child's condition. Since delay in getting medical attention may be a matter of life or death, it is obviously essential for the social worker to treat the refusal as an emergency situation. Since the GP may lack experience, it is vital for a child to be seen by a specialist or in a hospital emergency room where the staff are properly trained to examine abused children.

Even when the child is cut and bruised, the parent's explanation that it was an accident may well be accepted by physicians who prefer not to identify abuse. Social workers and public-health nurses must also learn to accept the possibility of unconscious collusion with the parents in denying or ignoring evidence of abuse and neglect. An extreme example of this situation occurred in the Ontario case 23 M.[8] Here an experienced public-health nurse, who gained access to the home and 'played' with the child four days before his death, failed to recognize that, due to multiple fractures, he was dying. Suffering from severe malnutrition, this child was 7 lbs. underweight for his age. This sad case illustrates the extent to which it is possible for professionals to become inured to poverty, pathology, and chronic suffering.

Neighbours

Next to the parents and relatives, friends and neighbours are, by far, the most frequent reporters of child abuse and neglect. Unfortunately, in many of the child-abuse deaths, typically in the case of Maria Colwell, the concerns of the neighbours were virtually ignored by the responsible professionals. Neighbours have the right as well as a moral duty to be concerned about the welfare of children and to protect them from harm. Since it is the neighbours and not the social workers who hear the screams of abused and neglected children, it makes sense to involve them formally in child-protection planning. Bearing in mind the difficulty of balancing the parents' right to privacy and autonomy with the duty of neighbours to be caring, one can consider two possible solutions. The first involves the purchase of service, on a contract basis, from a willing neighbour. In such a plan, while the parent would still maintain control over the child, the neighbour would agree to be available to cope with any crisis and to intervene under certain predetermined conditions. This would include calling in the police if the children were in any danger. Another, but not mutually exclusive, approach would be to establish in each community a volunteer self-help group based, for example, on the Parents Anonymous model. A 'hot-line' would then be available twenty-four hours a day, to respond to concerned neighbours as well as to desperate parents.

ASSESSMENT

It is striking to note that assessments, the subject of many excellent textbooks on child abuse, were absent in many of the high-risk cases which ended in tragedy. The DHSS study of inquiry reports (DHSS 1985: 35) also observed: 'The most common picture to emerge from the reports is one of information scattered between a number of agencies, and never systematically collated to form a more complete view than individual workers could achieve separately.' The information provided by the DHSS Social Services Inspectorate (1986a: 3.3.1) reveals that this unfortunate situation has not improved. After noting that 'comprehensive assessments for the purpose of long-term planning were conspicuous by their absence in seven out of the nine authorities', the report concludes that 'information useful for assessment purposes was on file but it was not co-ordinated . . . Plans made on the basis of incomplete, unco-ordinated or unrecorded information can be dangerous.'

Considering its importance, a strong case could be made for regarding the absence of a comprehensive psychosocial assessment in high-risk cases as a form of incompetence or professional negligence. As a minimum, the information contained in such an assessment should include the following elements recommended in the inquiry report into the death of Malcolm Page (Essex 1981: 7.1):

> The developmental history of the parents; the attitudes of the parents to each other and the children; the attitudes of the parents towards receiving help; the emotional needs of the children; the capability of the parents to meet the children's emotional and

physical needs; the need for medical examination of the children or
at least a consultation with a general practitioner.

The last element is somewhat contentious because, as previously indicated, it must be assumed that, with rare exceptions,
the average GP may be insufficiently experienced in child abuse
to assess the child's emotional and developmental status. To be
effective, the assessment of the abused child should involve more
than an examination of cuts, bruises, and X-rays for healing fractures. In addition to a total developmental assessment, if the child
is old enough, it is important to engage him/her in an exploration
of his/her feelings and thoughts about the abusive incident. Particular attention should be paid to signs of self-destructive and
aggressive behaviour. Since the presence of these symptoms
increases the risk of repeated injury, the provision of some child-
centred therapy may be vital. The child, in this situation, may also
need an advocate to help him/her cope with the anxiety of the
school teachers, social workers, and nurses who are likely to be
disturbed by the reported abuse. Depending on the age and
understanding of the child, s/he should also be informed of, and
feel comfortable with, the emergency procedures to be deployed
if the situation at home deteriorates. Giving abused children some
feeling of control over their lives may avoid the common tendency to blame themselves for the assault. The growing experience of autonomy may also reduce the high level of anxiety
which many of them experience.

Serious attention must also be paid to the ability of child-
protection agencies to provide professionally adequate standards
of service to meet the needs of abused children and their parents.
Since, on the basis of the inquiry report, there is considerable evidence of incompetence, it would be irresponsible not to suggest
the need for some kind of external review process, modelled, perhaps, on the hospital accreditation programmes which serve to
assure patients of acceptable levels of physical resources and professional competence.

High-risk check list

While not designed as a predictive instrument, the high-risk
check list is part of the assessment process and can play a useful
part in the identification and management of high-risk families. It
provides a relatively simple means of securing a consensus among
the involved professionals, including the court. Also, in order to
complete the check list, the key worker is required to gather information from a variety of sources including the police, physicians,

other social agencies, the parents, the extended family, and, if possible, the neighbours. Collecting and evaluating this kind of information is an essential part of the assessment process. Consultation with the various agencies provides the foundation for future interdisciplinary communication and collaboration which is vital in high-risk cases. Securing the co-operation of the parents and, if possible, the extended family, also sets the scene for their participation in the treatment programme, should this be indicated. Resistance to providing this information and refusal to co-operate should be regarded with alarm.

Enthusiasm for completing the check list should, however, be tempered with an appreciation of the various obstacles to be faced in using it. At the outset, the parents' lawyer may forbid them to talk to the social worker, although they may be willing to do so. Since this situation is most likely to arise when criminal charges are pending, the co-operation of the police is imperative. The use of the check list may also be challenged in court on the grounds that it has not been scientifically validated, which is true. The check list was devised in an earlier study of lethal family situations (Greenland 1980a). This relatively crude instrument is remarkable effective in identifying, at least in retrospect, high-risk cases. Because of the continuing need for such an instrument, it is hoped that some of the local area review committees will be encouraged to validate it. In doing so, attention should be paid to two tasks. The first involves providing formal definitions for terms such as 'socially isolated', 'abuses alcohol and/or drugs', 'prolonged separation from mother', and 'cries frequently'. The second task involves improving the scoring system. The present method of giving equal weight to all the items is obviously unsatisfactory. In the absence of a more effective instrument, it seems reasonable to assume that a high-risk situation exists when an infant has suffered a serious non-accidental injury and more than half of the check-list items, in any order, are checked.

The check list may also serve a useful function in case management because it provides an opportunity to involve the parents in setting goals for intervention. Items on the check list refer to the past ('age 20 years or less at birth of first child') which cannot be changed or to the present ('socially isolated – frequent moves – poor housing') which are modifiable. Preparing the check list provides an opportunity for parents and the professionals to develop a mutual trust and for parents, especially young women, to regain a measure of control over their lives. This is done by helping them to understand how interacting variables such as social isolation, an unwanted pregnancy, and a crying child can precipitate a dangerously explosive situation. Conversely, by participating in mutually supportive networks, beleaguered mothers can, for example, avoid becoming involved in self-defeating, exploitive relationships which increase the risk of harm to children.

No claims are made for the efficacy of the check list as a predictive instrument. If it has any merit, the check list may provide an opportunity for those concerned to understand that, within limits, they may increase or reduce the risk of violence against children. This can be done by accepting that the potential for violence is embedded in a situation rather than implanted within an individual. Recognizing the not uncommon potential for violence in stressful conditions enables the participants, who have some control over the situation, to act in rational and predetermined ways in order to reduce the risk of harm to children.

INTERVENTION AND EVALUATION

Following the report of the inquiry into the death of Jasmine Beckford, 1985, there appears to be a growing consensus about the need to treat the abused child as the 'primary client' within the family. This is confirmed in the BASW publication, *The Management of Child Abuse* (1985: 33). As a result, social workers in child-protection agencies will be required to develop professional relationships with children and to communicate with them effectively. Intervention in child-abuse cases, while not ignoring the needs of the parents, must be securely focused on the best interests of the child. Although this change will have far-reaching effects on social-work training and practice, which may take years to achieve, the benefits will by far outweigh the costs. One benefit will be to resolve public confusion about what social workers are trying to do in child-abuse cases. It is obviously very difficult for most people to understand why abusive parents should be rewarded with a new house, the services of a home-maker, and a place for the child in a day-care programme. This is hard to accept when parents who cope very well, while living in similarly poor conditions, may never be rehoused or offered a place in day care. Difficult though it is, social workers must be prepared to justify such decisions. If the neighbours are going to be involved, as they must be, in preventing child abuse and sharing responsibility for caring for abused children, they will need to understand the goals of social-work intervention.

Focusing on the abused child as the primary client will, no doubt, tend to polarize the issues to be faced in the judicial process. However, with the best interests of the child in mind, the

social worker will be required to present the court with a professional opinion on questions of risk. The relevant literature leaves
no doubt that once a child has been seriously injured by a parent,
unless the home situation is radically improved as far as the child's
safety is concerned, the risk of repeated abuse is very high. The
risk of injury or death is even greater when the child is under the
age of 2 and the initial injury involves fractures or brain damage.
The highest degree of caution must be exercised in returning very
young children to their parents when injuries of this kind are
improperly explained. Signs of deliberate torture such as cigarette
or stove burns, scalding, whipping, or unusual genital or anal
injuries, usually indicate the presence of a serious psychiatric
disorder in the caretakers which renders them unfit to care for
children. The child's life may well depend on the child-abuse
specialist's ability to convey this information unequivocally to the
court. In any event, the child-protection agency is advised to
inform the court when it is beyond its power to protect a child in
such a home. Since these extreme cases frequently involve neglect as well as brutality, the court is unlikely to resist placing the
child permanently in the care of the local authority. The marginal
cases, where the parents deny abusing the child or they admit the
abuse and express contrition, are more difficult for the court to
assess. But even in these cases it is unwise to return the child until
the psycho-social assessment is completed and a 'treatment' plan,
with explicit goals, has been agreed upon.

Paradoxically, following an attack on the child, the parents,
experiencing remorse, may well be motivated to seek help. Taking the child to a physician serves this purpose. But the seriousness of the situation may not be immediately apparent. The shock
of losing control and the feeling of relief that the child was not
killed may temporarily lift the mother's depression and improve
her morale. Unless there has been a major improvement in the
family situation, the physician should not be lulled by assurances
that, having 'learned a lesson', the loss of control will never be
repeated. Experience suggests that the next time may be the last.
This is because the lifting of the depression may give distressed
parents, fathers as well as mothers, sufficient energy to kill themselves as well as the children. In addition to bringing the possible
suicidal thoughts into the open, the parent must be encouraged to
reconstruct the exact train of events and circumstances which
precipitated the attack on the child. This should include information about the influence of pre-menstrual tension, pregnancy, disturbances of sleep, appetite, variations in mood and energy levels,
and what the child did to provoke the attack. Particular attention

should be paid to the use of alcohol and drugs, especially the benzodiazepines. Access to psychiatric consultation should be a first rather than a last resort. And, whether the child is seriously injured or not, referral to a child-protection agency is essential.

The fact that comprehensive psycho-social assessments and treatment plans were rarely available in the child-abuse cases examined by the Social Services Inspectorate (DHSS 1986a) needs explaining. The common excuse that social workers are far too busy to write up assessments is rarely true. But, if it is true, the supervisor must be at fault for not controlling the case load or for failing to provide adequate clerical support. A more likely explanation is that neither the key worker nor the supervisor is fully aware of the value of an assessment and treatment plan in the day-to-day management of high-risk cases. This was clearly so in the Jasmine Beckford case which illustrates the futility of providing a wider scatter of ill-conceived services. This practice was not, unfortunately, confined to the Beckford case. The Social Services Inspectorate Report (DHSS 1986a: 6.6) noted:

> It was obvious to inspectors that these cases receive a lot of attention from social workers and other professionals. There was concern amongst inspectors that in some case families were receiving so much service that it was difficult to assess the quality of their parenting and whether any significant changes had taken place in the family. It is also possible that when services are used in this way they inhibit rather than encourage growth of parents, especially when the emphasis of work is on watching for recurrent injuries. If the use of these resources could be planned and co-ordinated as part of an overall plan for the family there would be considerable benefits for the children.

Consciously or not, social workers involved in child-abuse cases tend to favour 'crisis intervention'. This strategy often fails in high-risk cases because it transforms complex and chronic family situations into technical problems requiring various forms of intervention on an *ad hoc* basis. This reduces, if not inhibits, the possibility of developing a continuing and shared responsibility between family members, the community, and professional helpers. Another disadvantage of the crisis-management approach is that it virtually compels child-welfare specialists to make binary or 'yes/no' decisions about whether or not the children should be taken into protective care or returned home. The alternative, of actively involving the family in decisions about the kind and duration of support required to cope with a period of particular stress, seems to be much more difficult to provide within existing child-welfare systems. The failure to share power with the distressed family often means that the decision to remove a child from home to a place of safety is interpreted as a punitive rather than as a compassionate act. This may explain why parents, who are experiencing great difficulty in managing their lives, resist having their children taken from them. Their diminishing sense of self-esteem often compels them, paradoxically, to fight for the return of a child who will only add to their grievous burdens.

Unlike the crisis-intervention model, which focuses on resolving the 'current' problem, the social-systems model, favoured by Williams (1982: 61), is holistic and rational.

> Its use can help to avoid oversimplified explanations and approaches and enable us to move away from notions of fault, individual pathology and character defects towards a broader understanding based on the relationships between the many factors involved and the interactions between family members.

Used in conjunction with the social-systems approach, sequential case recording and analysis (illustrated in chapter 5) has several advantages. Properly used it can indicate the onset of critical situations which demand immediate attention as well as of periods of relative stability and progress. As a form of case management, sequential anlaysis has the additional advantage of keeping track of all, or at least most, of the social agencies which tend to become indiscriminately involved with trouble-prone families. Since the unplanned intervention of competing social agencies is, characteristically, part of the burden carried by 'problem' families, careful monitoring of the situation is essential.

An equally important function of sequential recording is to keep track of treatment decisions and to monitor progress. Since allowing the child to remain in a chronically unrewarding, if not an abusive, environment does irreparable harm by stunting emotional and perhaps physical growth, measurement of individual progress is an essential part of the case management. Regular recording should be made of the child's height and weight, attendance at day-care programmes or school, frequency of illnesses, and reports of accidental injuries. For older children, attempts should be made to involve them in keeping records of positive events such as the acquisition of self-care skills, participation in sport and recreational activities, as well as school progress. Developing a relationship around such events enables the social worker to befriend the child without appearing to the parents to be constantly looking for signs of trouble. When this situation is well handled, the parents too will feel a measure of pride in the child's progress. However an increase in negative feelings, or evidence of hostility towards the child's growing independence, should be recognized and promptly dealt with.

It has so far been assumed that, supported by expert medical testimony and subject to the court's authority, the child-protection agency is responsible for determining how best to protect an abused child. But due to the adversarial nature of the court proceedings, the child-protection agency is likely to be challenged by the lawyer employed to represent the parents' interests. This compels the court to base its decision on the merits of the rival arguments according to the prevailing child-welfare statutes. Since the result often frustrates the best efforts of the child-protection agency, it is obviously important to understand the social significance of the judicial process.

In promoting the parents' rights in opposition to the child-protection agency, the lawyer is concerned with asserting the primacy of the parents' right to care for and control their children, within the limits allowed by law and with a minimum of state intervention. As Goldstein, Freud, and Solnit (1979) put it, 'So long as the child is part of a viable family, his interests are merged with those of the other members.' Within this concept, arbitrary interference by the state, however well intentioned, is regarded as damaging to the child, the family, and to society. Except perhaps in the most extreme cases, the judicial process is not ultimately concerned with the fate of a particular child.

The normal level of anxiety associated with child-protection work is greatly increased when, against the advice of the agency, an at-risk child is returned by the court to the parents' custody. Since the court is unable to do so itself, the child-protection agency may be directed to 'supervise the child if necessary on a daily basis'. Apart from the impracticability of this injunction, due to the hostility provoked by the judicial process, the protection of children in a hostile environment cannot be guaranteed even by daily visits. For this reason, it is suggested that six minimum conditions should be established for the return of abused children to parental care.

1   The court should order that an expert assessment be made of the cause and the circumstances in which the injuries were sustained. This should include objective social histories of the parents or caretakers and the family-support system. If relevant, evidence of abuse or neglect provided by neighbours should be presented to the court. Until the cause of the injuries is determined, if necessary with the assistance of the police, the return of the child should be regarded as hazardous. If, for legal reasons, the

child has to be returned before the completion of the investigation, the court must be formally advised that since, under its direction, the child is being returned to a potentially hazardous environment, its protection cannot be guaranteed by supervision.

2 Assuming that the abusive incident was due to a loss of control, precipitated by an abnormal level of frustration and stress, and not a reflection of the perpetrator's pathology, intervention strategies should include pre-arranged and practised plans for the protection of the children in emergency situations. Plans for coping with such emergencies should include techniques for recognizing and helping parents to cope more effectively with periodic variations in stress and impulse control.

3 Parents must be prepared for the fact that abused children, especially those over the age of 1 year, will, when returned home, respond in negative or rejecting ways. Older children may also be hostile and aggressive. Even in the best of circumstances, parents may find it difficult to avoid rejecting the child or responding in punitive ways. The infant's hostile behaviour, which is often selective and divisive, may place great strain on the marital relationship. Since this difficult situation is virtually unavoidable during the initial period of reintegration and adjustment, access to experienced professional help or grandmotherly support may be life-saving.

4 A programme of assistance, with both long- and short-term goals, should be devised by the helping agencies in co-operation with the parents and, if possible, the extended family and immediate neighbours. This should include regular 'well-baby' assessments and parent-relief-and-support programmes.

5 Since pregnancy may subconsciously be used by the mother as a means of asserting control and to re-establish self-worth, access to effective contraception is essential. An unplanned pregnancy should always be regarded as increasing the risk of abuse when children have been previously abused.

6 Where the mother's 'boyfriend' or a non-biological parent was solely responsible for the abuse, his return to the family home puts the children in jeopardy. Arrangements must be made for the police and the child-protection agency to be informed of the return, perhaps from prison, of a person who has previously abused the children.

It would be irresponsible to deny that, even with the most enterprising interventions, the outcome in child-abuse cases is disheartening. Study after study confirms that, once a child has been seriously abused and returned home following a short period in care, there is a very high risk of fresh injury. But taking the child into care, after several abusive incidents, does not guarantee a better outcome. Unless the abused child can be provided with a secure and nurturing environment, preferably before the age of 3 years, symptoms of emotional disturbance are likely to persist. This conclusion is supported by Hensey, Williams, and Rosenbloom (1983: 610) from Liverpool, who state: 'The children who best survived their experience after being taken into care were those for whom an early decision was made to sever parental contact and to place the child permanently with a substitute family.' It is extremely important for social workers with abused children as their clients to appreciate the significance of this vitally important conclusion. But, if additional evidence is required, the follow-up study by Lynch and Roberts (1982: 196) should be consulted. Their conclusions are worth incorporating into child-abuse policy and practice manuals.

Once the abuse has been detected and presumably stopped, the child's development still needs to be monitored; specific help will be required for any defect detected and will take far more time and skill than simply keeping the child safe from physical injury. One thing is certain: we cannot rely on social work services alone to fulfil this function. Even intensive, highly skilled social work help from the NSPCC Special Unit found that progress was seriously limited in some cases until follow-up individual therapy for the child was incorporated into their treatment plans.

CONCLUSIONS

The findings presented here are tentative and to some extent speculative. This is so because, for the most part, the study relied on retrospective data collected for purposes other than research. The research is also flawed by the fact that very little is known about high-risk cases that did not result in death. Even less is known about the child-abuse deaths that were successfully concealed. It is also possible that the child-protection agencies studied are by now much more effective than they once were. Subject to this caveat, the three questions posed in the preface can now be answered.

Question 1: 'Can high-risk situations be identified in advance in order to prevent the tragedy of child-abuse deaths?' The answer is a cautious yes, in many cases. Since over 80 per cent of the UK and over 60 per cent of the Ontario victims had been previously injured, it seems prudent to classify all cases of non-accidental injuries to young children as high-risk cases.

In addition to the high porportion of CAN-death victims who were previously injured, almost half of them were also stunted in growth. This suggests that concerned and experienced health-care professionals should be able to recognize these vulnerable infants. While it may not be possible to protect them all, it is reasonable to expect that with the prompt involvement of an effective child-protection agency, the lives of a high proportion of these infants can be saved.

In considering strategies for preventing CAN deaths, attention is necessarily focused on identifying the perpetrators. But they are not the only source of danger. Dangerously inept professionals, employed in inefficient child-protection agencies, hospitals, and clinics, are another source of danger. Concealing their incompetence renders all health-care workers morally, if not legally, culpable.

Question 2: 'Is it possible to identify concepts or strategies which might enable social workers, nurses, and physicians to protect vulnerable children without increasing the risk of disrupting the lives of families and children who are unlikely to suffer severe injury or death?' In the absence of experimental data, it is impossible to answer this question objectively. Yet it will have been observed that evidence of help-seeking and warning behaviour, present in a large number of cases, was frequently overlooked by social workers. Without stretching this finding too far, it is suggested that, instead of responding to the crisis of child abuse in a frozen moment of time, it might be more constructive for the intervenors to consider the violent interaction within its situational context. The advantage of this approach is that it promotes the involvement of the parents and significant others in plans to protect vulnerable children more effectively. The refusal of the parents to co-operate in this life-saving strategy should be promptly brought to the attention of the court.

Question 3: 'Do existing guidelines, regulations, or legislation enable the relevant professionals to intervene effectively and selectively in order to protect high-risk children?' The answer to this is also a guarded yes. While in theory the child-protection agencies in England and Wales and in Ontario have appropriate statutory powers to intervene effectively, they were not well used in practice. In summary it can be stated that the effective management of high-risk cases involves the following main elements:

- The assignment of a professionally competent and experienced social worker to protect the child and to help the family.

- After the initial crisis has been contained, a comprehensive assessment of the total family situation must be completed and used as a guide to intervention.

- The development by the child-protection agency, in co-operation with the parents, concerned relatives, and neighbours, if possible, of manageable goals for protecting the child, supporting the family, and reducing stress.

- Since high-risk cases almost invariably involve a host of social agencies, including the police, the child-protection agency must take the initiative in establishing interdisciplinary case conferences to monitor progress and to share concerns.

- The abused child, whether s/he remains at home or not, will probably benefit from specialized developmental assessment and treatment.

- The courts, if involved, must be reminded of the dictum that, 'if children are not safe at home, casework, however well intentioned, will not protect them.'

- Since the outcome in high-risk cases is never entirely satisfactory, a major investment in prevention makes good sense.

While much can be done within the existing framework to reduce the incidence of CAN deaths, it must be recognized that some tragedies are virtually unavoidable. How we, as a society, respond to these deaths is a measure of our humanity. In connection with the Colwell and Beckford cases in England and the Popen case in Ontario, the social workers involved were subjected to unprecendented criticism, abuse, and vilification. Thus social workers, who have not been charged with any offence, have been condemned and ignominiously punished without the opportunity to defend themselves. In order to avoid the repetition of such scandalous situations, it is necessary to develop alternative procedures for inquiring into deaths of children who were subject to supervision. This is necessary not only for the protection of social workers who are involved in high-risk cases: high-risk children must also be protected from becoming victims of defensive social work. Since the large public inquiries into CAN deaths are enormously expensive and, often, lacking in procedural fairness, it is hoped that the review-panel model (endorsed by the British Association of Social Workers in June 1982 and by the Department of Health and Social Security in June 1985) will be the widely accepted one. Failure to initiate such an inquiry promptly, as in the Tyra Henry case in Lambeth (*Social Work Today* 1986: 9) can only have disastrous consequences.

Attention must also be paid to the anguish experienced by social workers who are responsible for protecting children in situations of high anxiety where the power to act decisively is constrained by the lack of medical support. This dilemma is illustrated by two cases, one from Ontario, Canada (Ontario 1983) and the other from Perth, Scotland (Scottish Education Department 1975). Jeffery, age 3 years and Richard, age 3 ½, who had been previously abused and neglected, were severely injured, one by his mother, the other by his foster-mother. Concerned about the bruises on Jeff's eye and forehead and the discoloration of his buttocks and penis, 'which was bright red and sore looking', the social worker insisted that they should take Jeff to see a doctor. After listening to the social worker's concerns and the mother's explanation, the doctor examined Jeff and promptly diagnosed 'worms'. Medication, including anti-anxiety drugs (for Jeff), was prescribed. Two weeks later, following an attack by his mother, Jeff's stomach was ruptured.

Convinced that Richard was ill because 'his hands moved in an odd way, he didn't speak or appear to be frightened, he didn't cry but seemed to be on the verge of tears', the social worker called in the doctor who knew that battering was suspected. During the medical examination, which lasted between five and ten minutes, Richard was dressed in vest and pants. Asked to explain the bruises on Richard's arms and shoulders, the foster-mother said that 'he fell a lot'. Accepting this explanation, the doctor found nothing to suggest that Richard was being maltreated. But recognizing that the child was unwell, he recommended an investigation by a medical consultant. Five days later, on 2 May 1974, Richard was admitted to hospital suffering from a cerebral haemorrhage due to trauma sustained that day. The neuro-surgeon expressed the opinion that the symptoms observed by the social worker were due to less serious brain damage occurring two weeks earlier. Due to the severity of his injury, Richard is completely disabled, with severe retardation and hemiplegia. Jeffery, however, made a good recovery from his surgery, but his emotional wounds will take much longer to heal. His foster-mother reported (Ontario 1983: 23),

Jeff was placed in our custody. He would fall asleep and wake up screaming, 'No, mommy, no.' He seemed to be fighting sleep. He did that for two nights but is getting better now. . . . Jeffery hits me, pulls my hair and spits in my face, then he 'gives' and says 'Kiss and hug' and says 'Poor baby' and pats you on the back. . . . When somebody comes in, he pulls up his shirt and says, 'Jeffy hit'. . . . Jeffery is really disturbed and violent.

While considerable progress has been made in the past decade, in the USA, UK, and Canada, in protecting abused children once they have been identified, disturbing questions about the efficacy and wisdom of this approach remain unanswered. For example, it is obvious that the abused children currently identified under the present system, in three of the economically most powerful nations in the world, are only a fraction of the total number of brutalized and neglected children who are failing to thrive because of inadequate nourishment, environmental impoverishment, stress, and despair. Why child neglect is tolerated with a degree of indifference not accorded sexual abuse is most perplexing. The danger is that, while concentrating attention on a select group of cases, which brings relief to some traumatized children, a much larger group of chronic cases is being overlooked. The illusion is sustained that, now that the authorities are doing *something* about child abuse, there is no need for anyone else to be concerned. Perhaps this explains the sense of public outrage which follows from reports of a child-abuse death.

In considering the wider and more crucial issues, attention must be paid to the need for overhauling the present fragmented and inefficient system of caring for the health and welfare of young children, especially those living in socially and economically deprived areas. Under the present system, operating in Canada as well as in the UK, responsibility for health care of young children is divided between a hotchpotch of competing statutory and voluntary agencies. In this way a child may be attended to, or not, by a health visitor or public-health nurse, a GP, a well-baby clinic (where they exist), and the paediatric department of a general hospital. While the GP may have professional responsibility for co-ordinating these agencies, very few will claim that this is being done well. The problem becomes even more complex when, due to abuse or neglect, the child's health may also become the concern of the child-protection agency, including the NSPCC in some parts of England. Except in relation to infectious diseases, there is unlikely to be any overall monitoring of morbidity and mortality in geographically defined areas based on census tracts. As a result it is virtually impossible to make the connection between, say, social class, environmental factors, and morbidity and mortality. In any event, as far as children are concerned, the absence of disease is not the same as being healthy. For this reason a good case can be made, at least on an experimental basis, for examining the city, village, or neighbourhood in terms of the parameters which promote or demote the health and welfare of children. In this way it should be possible to identify communities which are, as it were, 'good places' for children to grow up in and those which are much less so. The benefits which follow from this *Healthy Cities* approach (Hancock and Duhl 1986) might be the reintegration of agencies concerned with the health, welfare, education, and recreation, and the involvement of residents as well as the professionals in making neighbourhoods fit for kids to live in.

This change of emphasis does not mean turning our backs on the desperate needs of abused and neglected children any more than providing clean drinking water and sewage-treatment plants obviates the need for medical specialists and hospitals. But it does result in the more effective use of a health- rather than a sickness-orientated model of children's services. However, due to the folk belief that good health depends on the availability of doctors, diagnosis, drugs, and hospital beds, resistance to alternative models of child health and welfare must be anticipated. For this reason it is impossible to contemplate any revolutionary changes in the organization and delivery of health and welfare services which threaten the interests and dominance of the health-care and social-work professionals. But a start could be made, at least in some areas, by reorganizing the health and social services for pre-school children. This should involve a variety of well-designed and generously funded long-term demonstration projects, supported by the relevant agencies, professionals, local residents, school children, and, of course, the young people who have the most to gain.

Finally, it must be emphasized that, while lives can be saved by improved techniques, life saving is not enough. Preventing child abuse and neglect and promoting child health involves nothing less than a total commitment to world peace and social justice with equal opportunity for all. Only then will children everywhere have access to food, shelter, love, security, opportunity, and the courage to grow up as caring, creative, and peace-loving adults. Living as we do in the shadow of a nuclear holocaust, it becomes increasingly obvious that no child will be secure until the well-being of children all over the world is assured.

Appendix

High-risk check lists

Maria Colwell, Kim Anne Popen, Jasmine Beckford

CHILD ABUSE AND NEGLECT			
High-risk check list			
Parents		**Child**	
Previously abused/neglected as a child	X	Was previously abused or neglected	X
Age 20 years or less at birth of first child	X	Under 5 years of age at the time of abuse or neglect	X
Single-parent/separated; partner not biological parent	X	Premature or low birth-weight	X
History of abuse/neglect or deprivation		Now underweight	X
Socially isolated – frequent moves – poor housing	X	Birth defect – chronic illness – developmental lag	
Poverty – unemployed/ unskilled worker; inadequate education	X	Prolonged separation from mother	X
Abuses alcohol and/or drugs	X	Cries frequently – difficult to comfort	
History of criminal assaultive behaviour and/or suicide attempts	X	Difficulties in feeding and elimination	
Pregnant – post partum – or chronic illness	X	Adopted, foster- or step-child	X
Name: *Maria Colwell* (25.2.65 – 7.1.73)		© Cyril Greenland, Toronto, 1978	

CHILD ABUSE AND NEGLECT				
High-risk check list				
Parents		Child		
Previously abused/neglected a child	X	Was previously abused or neglected		X
Age 20 years or less at birth of first child	X	Under 5 years of age at the time of abuse or neglect		X
Single-parent/separated; partner not biological parent		Premature or low birth-weight		
History of abuse/neglect or deprivation	X	Now underweight		
Socially isolated – frequent moves – poor housing	X	Birth defect – chronic illness – developmental lag		
Poverty – unemployed/ unskilled worker; inadequate education	X	Prolonged separation from mother		X
Abuses alcohol and/or drugs	X	Cries frequently – difficult to comfort		X
History of criminal assaultive behaviour and/or suicide attempts		Difficulties in feeding and elimination		X
Pregnant – post partum – or chronic illness	X	Adopted, foster- or step-child		
Name: *K.A. Popen* *(11.1.75–11.8.76)*		© Cyril Greenland, Toronto, 1978		

CHILD ABUSE AND NEGLECT				
High-risk check list				
Parents		Child		
Previously abused/neglected as a child	X	Was previously abused or neglected		X
Age *20* years or less at birth of first child	X	Under 5 years of age at the time of abuse or neglect		X
Single-parent/separated; partner not biological parent	X	Premature or low birth-weight		
History of abuse/neglect or deprivation	X	Now underweight		X
Socially isolated – frequent moves – poor housing	X	Birth defect – chronic illness – developmental lag		X
Poverty – unemployed/ unskilled worker; inadequate education	X	Prolonged separation from mother		X
Abuses alcohol and/or drugs		Cries frequently – difficult to comfort		
History of criminal assaultive behaviour and/or suicide attempts		Difficulties in feeding and elimination		
Pregnant – post partum – or chronic illness	X	Adopted, foster- or step-child		
Name: *Jasmine Beckford* *(2.12.79–5.7.84)*		© Cyril Greenland, Toronto, 1978		

Notes

Chapter 1

1 Total fertility rates: in the thirty years from 1952 to 1982, the fertility rates in the following countries declined as follows:

Country	1952	1982
United States	3.36	1.81
England and Wales	2.16	1.76
Scotland	2.43	1.73
Canada	3.64	1.79 (1980)

Teitelbaum and Winter 1985: 158–9

2 The perinatal mortality rates (still births plus deaths under 1 week per 1,000 live and still births), for low birthweight infants in England and Wales, declined between 1977 and 1984, as follows:

	Under 1,001 g	All under 2,501 g
1977	811	154
1984	570	89

DHSS 1984: 20

3 Quoted from McKeown (1980: 184).
4 This important finding is confirmed by Hampton and Newberger (1985).
5 Formerly the American Humane Association.
6 *Social Work Today* (1985) 17 (15): 3.
7 *Social Work Today* (1985) 16 (32): 3
8 *Social Work Today* (1986) 17 (46): 2.

Chapter 2

1 Handicaps include 'developmental delays', 'mental retardation', 'cerebral palsy', 'seizure disorders', 'galactosemia', 'failure to thrive', 'autism', 'asthma', 'multiple chronic infections', etc.

Chapter 3

1   This age group has been chosen for the sake of convenience since it represents well over 90 per cent of children on the register.

2   In subsequent years the total number of cases on the register, including the deaths, were; 1983, 1083 (nine deaths); 1984, 1584 (eight deaths); 1985, 2043 (eleven deaths). In the same period the proportion of sex-abuse cases increased as follows: 1983, 617; 1984, 1064; 1985, 1547.

3   The age distribution of the CAN death victims shown in Table 3.4 confirms that 95 per cent were age 5 or less; 59 per cent were age 0–12 months. One of the victims was age 12.

4   Semi-skilled, unskilled, or unemployed (Pharoah and Macfarlane 1982).

5   Table 3.12a shows that these differences do not reach the required level of statistical significance.

6   To avoid the onerous task of averaging all the relevant vital statistics for the ten-year period (1973–1982), 1978 was selected as the most representative year.

7   A very characteristic history in the Brixton cases is for a young man of unstable personality to emerge from a penal sentence and cohabit with an equally unstable woman who has been deserted by her husband and left with one or more children. The man is not in any way prepared for the responsibility of parenthood and, if left with dependent and apprehensive babies, as is the case when the mother goes out to work, the stage is set for trouble.' (Scott 1973b: 198)

Chapter 4

1   Although Dr Hall's study was not published until 1975, his data were evidently released to the press in 1973 in connection with the Tunbridge Wells Study Group (1973)

2   Since these tables were completed before the five additional cases, including Beckford (1985), became available, the totals have not been changed.

3   This opinion was not supported by the comparable Scottish study (Arncil *et al.* 1985: 743) which concluded:

> The recommendations from Sheffield for more breastfeeding, less smoking by parents, more health education, and better care from family doctors are desirable but, as pointed out by the *Lancet* (1985: i.322), their study does not establish causal relationships. It will be most unfortunate if parents bereaved by a cot death believe on this inconclusive evidence that parental smoking or lack of breastfeeding has led to the death of their child.

Chapter 6

1   The police surgeon who examined Lester Chapman on 30 December
    1977 refused to testify at the official inquiry. The committee may
    have had him in mind when it concluded (Berkshire and Hampshire
    1979: 66), 'Little or no special training in child abuse has been given
    to many of those involved. We emphasize the need for such training
    with all the professions. Since medical evidence is of the essence in
    non-accidental injury the training of doctors in this subject is of par-
    ticular importance. Without qualified medical support, a social
    worker is highly vulnerable in court.'

2   Lisa Godfrey, age 3.6 years, was killed by her mother in 1973. Mrs
    Godfrey was pregnant and her request for termination was refused.
    Instead the doctor put her on medication for nerves.

3   Susan Aukland, age 1.294 years, who was very small for her age, was
    killed by her father in 1974. He had previously murdered his first-
    born child.

4   Max Piazzani, age 4.194 years, was killed by his father in 1973. At the
    post mortem, the infant weighed 15½ lbs. which is the same weight
    as a normal 7-month-old infant.

5   Neil Howlett, age 2.079 years, who was grossly underweight, was
    killed by his 22-year-old mother in 1975. She had a history of emo-
    tional deprivation and had previously injured Neil.

6   Carly Taylor, age 1.042 years, was one of twins. Since both of them
    were premature, they were kept in hospital for a month after their
    birth. Up to the time of Carly's death, there were frequent reports of
    abuse and neglect. The mother, age 26, who had a history of violence,
    was on 'slimming' drugs prescribed by her physician. At death Carly
    was found to have a fractured skull, bite marks, bruising, and anal
    injuries. Mrs Taylor was convicted of manslaughter.

7   Paul Brown, age 4.411 years, was admitted to hospital on 11 August
    1976, 'deeply unconscious and in an appalling state of neglect. He
    had extensive bruising, was highly emaciated and in a filthy condi-
    tion. On the following day his younger half-brother, Liam, age 3
    years, was admitted to the same hospital for investigation. Liam was
    found to be filthy, verminous and ravenously hungry. On 19 November
    1976 Paul died from his injuries. The stepgrandparents were sentenced
    to imprisonment for ill-treating and neglecting the boys.'
        The children's mother, age 25, who had a mental age of ten, and the
    boys who had been previously abused and neglected, were well
    known to a variety of social and health agencies. This case is replete
    with examples of warning signals and help-seeking behaviour. For
    example, 'January–March, 1975, had seen a crescendo of activity on
    the part of Pauline [the mother] with requests for a move, requests for
    money, a claim that her husband might move the children, failure to
    feed the children, a claim that she was on drugs and not responsible
    for what she would do next, and a claim that she had bruised Paul's
    face.'

8 This male infant, age 1.208 years, who had been negleted by his parents, was under the supervision of the children's aid society and public-health nurse. His death was due to multiple fractures to his head, arms, and back. These injuries, occurring seven to ten days before his death, were caused by the mother who had a long history of manic-depressive illness. The child, who weighed 15 lbs. at death, was clearly suffering from failure to thrive. His emaciated body was described by the pathologist as 'putrid with vomit and excrement'.

References

AAPC see American Association for Protecting Children, Inc.

Adelstein, A.M., Goldblatt, P.O., Stracey, S.C., and Weatherall, J.A.C. (1982) 'Non-accidental injury', in Office of Population Censuses and Surveys/London School of Hygiene and Tropical Medicine *Studies of Sudden Infant Deaths*, London: HMSO.

Allen, H.D., Kosciolek, E.J., ten Bensel, R.W., *et al.* (1969) 'The battered child syndrome. Part II – social and psychiatric aspects', *Minnesota Medicine* 52 (1): 155–6.

Allen, H.W. (1982) *Judicial Inquiry into the Care of Kim Anne Popen by the Children's Aid Society of the City of Sarnia and the County of Lambton* (4 vols), Toronto: Queen's Printer for Ontario.

American Association for Protecting Children, Inc. (The American Humane Association) (1986) *Highlights of Official Child Neglect and Abuse Reporting, 1984*, Denver, Colorado.

American Humane Association (1983) 'Highlights of official child neglect and abuse reporting, in *Annual Report, 1981*, Denver, Colorado.

American Medical Association Council on Scientific Affairs (1985) 'Diagnostic and treatment guidelines concerning child abuse and neglect', *Journal of the American Medical Association*, 254 (6) 796.

Antler, S. (1981) 'The rediscovery of child abuse', in L.H. Pelton (ed.) *The Social Context of Child Abuse and Neglect*, New York: Human Sciences Press.

Arneil, G.C., Brooke, H., Gibson, A.A.M., Harvie, A., McIntosh, H., and Patrick, W.J.A. (1985) 'National post-perinatal infant mortality and cot death study, Scotland, 1981–82, *The Lancet* 843 (i): 740–3.

Asch, S.S. and Rubin, L.J. (1974) 'Postpartum reactions: some unrecognized variations', *American Journal of Psychiatry*, 131 (8): 870–3.

Baher, E., Hyman, C., Jones, C., Kerr, A., and Mitchell, R. (1976) *At Risk: An Account of the Work of the Battered Child Research Department*, London: Routledge & Kegan Paul.

Bakan, D. (1971) *Slaughter of the Innocents: A Study of the Battered Child Phenomenon*, Toronto: CBC Learning Systems.
Baldwin, J.A. and Oliver, J.E. (1975) 'Epidemiology and family characteristics of severely abused children', *British Journal of Preventative Social Medicine*, 29 (4): 205–21.
BASW see British Association of Social Workers.
Bates, R.P., Bennett, R.C., and Greenland, C. (1983) 'Evidence of failure to thrive in infants who were severely abused or whose deaths were due to abuse or neglect' (unpublished).
Bennie, E.H. and Sclare, A.B. (1969) 'The Battered Child Syndrome', *American Journal of Psychiatry* 125 (7): 975–9.
Berger, D. (1978) 'Child abuse and neglect in Orleans Parish: an overview', *Journal of the Louisiana State Medical Society* 130 (11): 221–4.
Berkshire and Hampshire County Councils and Area Health Authorities (1979) *Report of the Committee of Inquiry into the Case of Lester Chapman*, Berkshire and Hampshire County Councils.
Black, D. (Chairman) (1980) *Report of a Research Working Group on Inequalities in Health Care*, London: Department of Health and Social Security.
Blacker, C.P. (ed.) (1952) *Problem Families: Five Inquiries*, London: Eugenics Society.
Brearley, C.P. (1982) *Risk and Social Work*, London: Routledge & Kegan Paul.
Brent (1985) *A Child in Trust: The Report of the Panel of Inquiry into the Circumstances surrounding the Death of Jasmine Beckford*, London: London Borough of Brent.
Brewer, C. and Lait, J. (1980) *Can Social Work Survive?*, London: Temple Smith.
British Association of Social Workers (1975) 'Code of practice for social workers with children at risk', *Social Work Today* 6 (11): 345–50.
——(1981) *Social Work in Child Care: Children at Risk – BASW's Code of Practice*, Birmingham: BASW Publications.
——(1985) *The Management of Child Abuse*, Birmingham: BASW Publications.
British Medical Journal (1981) 'Child abuse: the swing of the pendulum', 18 July, 283: 170.
Buchanan, A. and Oliver, J.E. (1977) 'Abuse and neglect as a cause of mental retardation: a study of 140 children admitted to subnormality hospitals in Wiltshire', *British Journal of Psychiatry* (131): 485–67.
Castle, B. (1974) *Response to the Publication of the Maria Colwell Inquiry Report*, London: DHSS.

Castle, R.L. and Kerr, A.M. (1972) 'A study of suspected child abuse, London: NSPCC.

Cheshire Central Review Committee on Child Abuse (1982) *Report of an Enquiry Panel into the Examination of the Implications of the Death of a Child, G.W.F.* Chester.

Christoffel, K.K., Kiang, L., and Stamler, J. (1981) 'Epidemiology of fatal child abuse: international mortality data', *Journal of Chronic Diseases* 34: 57–64.

Cooper, C. (1975) 'The doctor's dilemma – a pediatrician's view', in A.W. Franklin (ed.) *Concerning Child Abuse*, Edinburgh: Livingston.

Cooperstock, R. (1976) 'Psychotropic drug use among women', *Canadian Medical Association Journal* 115: 760–3.

Cooperstock, R. and Hill, J. (1982) *The Effects of Tranquillization: Benzodiazapine Use in Canada*, Ottawa: Health and Welfare, Canada.

Cooperstock, R. and Lennard, H.L. (1979) 'Some social meanings of tranquillizer use, *Sociology of Health and Illness* 1 (3).

Court, S.D.M. (1980) Foreword in R.G. Mitchell (ed.) *Child Health in the Community*, Edinburgh: Churchill Livingstone.

Creighton, S.J. (1979) 'An epidemiological study of child abuse', *Child Abuse and Neglect* 3(2): 601–5.

—— (1980a) 'Deaths from non-accidental injury in children' (letter), *British Medical Journal* 281 (6233): 147.

—— (1980b) *Child Victims of Physical Abuse, 1976: The Third Report on the Findings of NSPCC Special Units Registers*, London: National Society for the Prevention of Cruelty to Children.

—— (1984) *Trends in Child Abuse*, London: National Society for the Prevention of Cruelty to Children.

—— (1985) 'An epidemiological study of abused children and their families in the UK between 1977–1982', *Child Abuse and Neglect* 9 (4): 441–8.

Creighton, S.J. and Owtram, P.J. (1977) *Child Victims of Physical Abuse: A Report on the Findings of NSPCC Special Units Registers*, London: National Society for the Prevention of Cruelty to Children.

Davies, M. (1977) *Support Systems in Social Work*, London: Routledge & Kegan Paul, quoted from Williams 1982.

DHSS (Department of Health and Social Security) (1974) *Report of the Committee of Inquiry into the Care and Supervision Provided in Relation to Maria Colwell*, London: HMSO.

—— (1982) *Child Abuse: A Study of Inquiry Reports 1973–1981*, London: HMSO.

—— (1984) *On the State of Public Health: The Annual Report of the Chief MOH of the DHSS*, London: HMSO.

—— (1985) Child Abuse Inquiries. A Consultative Paper (U.K.), London: HMSO.

—— (1986a) Social Services Inspectorate *Inspection of the Supervision of Social Workers in the Assessment and Monitoring of Cases of Child Abuse when Children, Subject to a Court Order, have been returned Home*, London: HMSO.

—— (1986b) *Child Abuse – Working Together: A Draft Guide to Arrangements for Interagency Cooperation for the Protection of Children*, London: HMSO.

Diamond, L.J. and Jaudes, P.K. (1983) 'Child abuse in a cerebral-palsied population', *Developmental Medicine and Child Neurology* 25: 169–74.

Dingwall, R., Eekelaar, J., and Murray T. (1981) *Care or Control?*, Oxford: Centre for Socio-Legal Studies, Working Papers, Wolfson College.

—— (1983) *The Protection of Children: State Intervention and Family Life*, Oxford: Blackwell.

Dobash, R.E. and Dobash, R.P. (1979) *Violence Against Wives: A Case Study against Patriarchy*, New York: Free Press.

Donzelot, J. (1979) *The Policing of Families*, New York: Pantheon Books.

Downing, D. (1978) 'A selective study of child mortality', *Child Abuse and Neglect* 2 (2) 101–8.

Ebbin, A.J., Gollub, M.H., Stein, A.M., and Wilson, M.G. (1969) 'Battered child syndrome at the Los Angeles County General Hospital', *American Journal of Diseases of Children* 118: 660–7.

Elmer, E. (1967) *Children in Jeopardy: A Study of Abused Minors and their Families*, Pittsburgh: University of Pittsburgh Press.

Elmer, E. and Gregg, S.G. (1967) 'Developmental characteristics of abused children', *Pediatrics* 40 (4): 596–602.

Essex (1981) Essex County Council, Area Review Committee *Report on the Death of Malcolm Page*, Chelmsford.

Fagan, J.A., Stewart, D.K., and Hansen, K.V. (1983) 'Violent men or violent husbands? Background facts and situational correlates', in David Finkelhor *et al.* (eds) *The Dark Side of Families: Current Family Violence Research*, Beverly Hills: Sage Publications.

Fontana, V.J. (1970) 'Physical abuse of children', *Pediatrics* 45 (3) Pt 1: 509–10.

Fowler, N. (1986) Government action on child abuse in response to the Beckford Report', DHSS Press Release, London 6 May.

Franklin, A.W. (1973) 'Non-accidental injury to children: reports and resolutions: the meeting of the Tunbridge Wells Study Group sponsored by the Medical Education and Information Unit of the Spastics Society' (unpublished).

—— (1975) 'Statistics of child abuse' (letter), *British Medical Journal* 98–9, 12 July 1975.

Friedrich, W.N. (1976) 'Epidemiological survey of physical child abuse', *Texas Medicine* 72: 81–84.

Galdston, R. (1965) 'Observations on children who have been physically abused by their parents', *American Journal of Psychiatry* 122: 440–3, quoted in George and Main 1980.

Garbarino, J. (1982) *Children and Families in the Social Environment*, New York: Aldine Publishing Company.

—— (1983) 'What we know about child abuse' (unpublished MS) quoted in Newberger, Newberger, and Hampton 1983.

Gelles, R.J. (1975) 'The social construction of child abuse', *American Journal of Orthopsychiatry* 43: 611–21.

Gelles, R.J. and Strauss, M.A. (1986) *Is Violence Towards Children Increasing? A Comparison of 1975–1986 National Survey Rates*, Durham, New Hampshire: Family Violence Research Program.

George, C. and Main, M. (1980) *Abused Children: Their Rejection of Peers and Caregivers*, in Tiffany Martini Field (ed.) *High-risk Infants and Children*, New York: Academic Press.

Gil, D.G. (1970) *Violence Against Children: Physical Child Abuse in the United States*, Cambridge, Mass.: Harvard University Press.

—— (1978) 'Societal violence and violence in families', in J.M. Eekelaar and S.N. Katz (eds.) *Family Violence*, Toronto: Butterworth.

Goldson, E., Cadol, R.V., Fitch, M.J. and Umlauf, H.J. (1976) 'Non-accidental trauma and failure to thrive: a sociomedical profile in Denver', *American Journal of Diseases of Children* 130 (5): 490–3.

Goldstein, J., Freud, A., and Solnit, A.J. (1979) *Before the Best Interests of the Child*, New York: Free Press.

Gonzales-Pardo, L. and Thomas, M. (1977) 'Child abuse and neglect, *Journal of the Kansas Medical Society* 78 (2): 65–9.

Gray, J., Cutler, C., Dean, J., and Kempe, C.H. (1976) 'Perinatal assessment of mother–baby interaction', in R.E. Helfer and C.H. Kempe (eds) *Child Abuse and Neglect: The Family and the Community*, Cambridge, Mass.: Ballinger.

Green, A.H. (1980) 'Self-destructive behavior in battered children', *American Journal of Psychiatry* 135 (5): 579–82.

Green, A.H., Voeller, K., Gaines, R., and Kubie, J. (1981) 'Neurological impairment in maltreated children', *Child Abuse and Neglect* 5 (2): 129–34.

Greenland, C. (1971a) 'Prodromal signs of dangerous behaviour', *La Prensa Medica Mexicana*: 323–4 (presented to the V. Congresso Mundial de Psychiatria Mexico, 1971).

—— (1971b) 'Evaluation of violence and dangerous behaviour associated with mental illness', *Seminars in Psychiatry* 3: 345–56.

—— (1973) *Child Abuse in Ontario*, Toronto: Ministry of Community and Social Services, Research and Planning Branch.

—— (1978) *Child Abuse Deaths in Ontario: Research Report for the Task Force on Child Abuse*, Toronto: Ministry of Community and Social Services.

—— (1980a) 'Lethal family situations: an international comparison of deaths from child abuse', in E.J. Anthony and C. Chiland (eds) *The Child and His Family: Preventive Child Psychiatry in an Age of Transition*, New York: John Wiley.

—— (1980b) 'Psychiatry and the prediction of dangerousness', *Journal of Psychiatric Treatment and Evaluation* 2: 97–103.

—— (1984) 'Deaths due to child abuse and neglect in the UK, USA and Canada', PhD thesis, University of Birmingham.

—— (1986) 'Inquiries into child abuse deaths', *British Journal of Criminology* 26 (2): 164–73.

Greenland, C. and Rosenblatt, E. (1975) 'Early identification of child abuse', *Dimensions in Health Services*, 52 (5): 10–12.

Gregg, G.S. and Elmer, E. (1969) 'Infant injuries: accident or abuse?', *Pediatrics* 44 (3): 434–9.

Guthkelch, A.N. (1971) 'Infantile subdural haematoma and its relationship to whiplash injuries', *British Medical Journal* 2: 430–1.

Hall, M.H. (1974) 'The police surgeon', Association of Police Surgeons of Great Britain, quoted in Berkshire and Hampshire 1979.

—— (1975) 'A view from the emergency and accident department', in A.W. Franklin (ed.) *Tunbridge Wells Study Group Concerning Child Abuse*, Edinburgh: Churchill Livingstone.

Hallett, C. and Stevenson, O. (1980) *Child Abuse: Aspects of Interprofessional Co-operation*, London: Allen and Unwin.

Hampton, R.L. and Newberger, E.H. (1985) 'Child abuse incidence and reporting by hospitals: significance of severity, class and race', *American Journal of Public Health* 75 (1): 56–9.

Hancock, T. and Duhl, L.J. (1986) *Healthy Cities: Promoting Health in the Urban Context*, a background working paper for the 'Healthy Cities Symposium', Lisbon, Portugal, 7–11 April 1986.

Helfer, R.E. (1970) 'Physical abuse of children', *Pediatrics* 46 (4): 651–2.

Helfer, R.E. and Kempe, C.H. (1976) *Child Abuse and Neglect: The Family and the Community*, Cambridge, Mass.: Ballinger.

Hensey, O.J., Williams, J.K., and Rosenbloom, L. (1983) 'Intervention in child abuse: experience in Liverpool', *Developmental Medicine and Child Neurology* 25: 606–11.

Hillingdon (1986) London Borough of Hillingdon Area Review Committee, *Report of the Review Panel into the Death of Heidi Koseda*, London.

Howells, J.G. (1975) 'Deaths from non-accidental injuries in childhood' (letter), *British Medical Journal* 3 (5984): 651–2.

Hunter, R.S. and Kilstrom, N. (1979) 'Breaking the life cycle in abusive families', *American Journal of Psychiatry* 136 (10): 1320–2.

Hunter, R.S., Kilstrom, N., Kraybill, E.N., and Loda, F. (1978) 'Antecedents of child abuse and neglect in infants: a prospective study in a newborn intensive care unit', *Pediatrics* 61 (4): 629–35.

Hyman, C.A. (1978) 'Some characteristics of abusing families referred to the NSPCC', *British Journal of Social Work* 8 (2): 171–9.

Jackson, G. (1972) 'Child abuse syndrome: the cases we miss', *British Medical Journal* 2: 756–7.

Jason, J., Andereck, N.D., Marks, J., and Tyler, C.W. (1982) 'Child abuse in Georgia: a method to evaluate risk factors and reporting bias', *American Journal of Public Health*, 72 (12): 1353–8.

Jones, C.O. (1977) 'A critical evaluation of the work of the NSPCC's battered child research department', *Child Abuse and Neglect* 1 (1): 111–18.

Jones, D.N. (ed.) (1982) *Understanding Child Abuse*, Sevenoaks, Kent: Hodder & Stoughton Educational.

Kadushin, A. and Martin, J.A. (1981) *Child Abuse – An Interactional Event*, New York: Columbia University Press.

Kaplan, D. (1962) 'A concept of acute situational disorder', *Social Work* 7, quoted in Williams 1982.

Kaplun, D. and Reich, R. (1976) 'The murdered child and his killers', *American Journal of Psychiatry* 133 (7): 809–13.

Kempe, C.H. (1968) 'Some problems encountered by welfare departments in the management of the battered child syndrome', in R.E. Helfer and C.H. Kempe (eds) (1968) *The Battered Child*, Chicago: University of Chicago Press.

——— (1978) 'Sexual abuse, another hidden problem', *Pediatrics* 62 (3): 382–9.

Kempe, C.H. and Helfer, R.E. (1972) *Helping the Battered Child and his Family*, Philadelphia: Lippincott.

Kempe, C.H., Silverman, F.N., Steele, B.F., Droegmueller, W., and Silver, H.K. (1962) 'The battered child syndrome', *Journal of the American Medical Association* 181 (1): 17–24.

Kempe, R.S. and Kempe, C.H. (1978) *Child Abuse*, Cambridge, Mass.: Harvard University Press.

Klaus, M.H. and Kennel, J.H. (1970) 'Mothers separated from their newborn infants', *Pediatric Clinics of North America* 17: 1015–37.

Knowelden, J., Keeling, J., and Nicholl, J.P. (1984) *A Multicentre Study of Post-Neonatal Mortality*, University of Sheffield Medical Care Research Unit.

Koel, B.S. (1969) 'Failure to thrive as a continuum', *American Journal of Diseases of Children* 118: 565–7.

Kotelchuck, M. (1984) 'Infant mortality vital statistics data: new uses for an old measure', in D.K. Walker and J.B. Richmond (eds) *Monitoring Child Health in the US: Selected Issues and Policies*, Cambridge, Mass.: Harvard University Press.

Kotelchuck, M., and Newberger, E.H. (1983) 'Failure to thrive: a controlled study of familial characteristics', *Journal of the American Academy of Child Psychiatry* 22 (4): 322–8.

Lambeth (1982) *Report of an Independent Inquiry. Richard Fraser, 1972–1977.*

The Lancet, 'Postneonatal mortality in the UK', 2 (8424): 322.

Lasch, C. (1979) *The Culture of Narcissism*, New York: Warner Books.

Lauer, B., Broeck, E.T., and Grossman, M. (1974) 'Battered child syndrome: review of 130 patients with controls', *Pediatrics* 54 (1): 67–70.

Lealman, G.T., Haigh, D., Phillips, J.M., Stone, J., and Ord-Smith, C. (1983) 'Prediction of child abuse – an empty hope?', *The Lancet* 8339 (25: 1423–3.

Leicestershire Area Health Authority (1980) *Carly Taylor, Report of an Independent Inquiry.*

Leicestershire County Council (1980) *Report of an Independent Inquiry into the Death of Malcolm Page.*

Lerner, M. (1976) 'Social differences in physical health', in J. Kosa and I.K. Zola (eds) *Poverty and Health: A Sociological Analysis*, Cambridge, Mass.: Harvard University Press.

Los Angeles County ICAN (1982) Case Review Committee *Report* (unpublished) 14 July 1982.

Los Angeles County (1986) 'A profile of suspicious child deaths: a report to the ICAN Policy Committee', (unpublished).

Lynch, M.A. (1975) 'Ill-health and child abuse', *The Lancet* 2 (7929): 317–19.
—— (1979) 'Recognizing a child at increased risk of abuse', *Paediatrician* 8 (4): 188–99.
—— (1985) 'Child abuse before Kempe: an historical literature review', *Child Abuse and Neglect* 9 (1): 7–15.
Lynch, M. and Roberts, J. (1977a) 'Early alerting signs', in A.W. Franklin (ed.) *Child Abuse: Prediction, Prevention and Follow Up*, Edinburgh: Churchill Livingstone.
—— (1977b) 'Predicting child abuse: signs of bonding failure in the maternity hospital', *British Medical Journal* 624–6.
—— (1982) *Consequences of Child Abuse*, London: Academic Press.
McCarthy, B.J., Rochat, R.W., Cundiff, B., Gould, P.A., and Quave, S. (1981) 'Child abuse registry in Georgia: three years of experience', *Southern Medical Journal* 74 (1): 11–16.
McDowall, D. (1986) 'Poverty and homicide in Detroit, 1926–1978', *Victims and Violence* 1 (1): 23–4.
Macfarlane, A. (1982) 'Seasonal variation in postneonatal mortality', in *Studies in Sudden Infant Deaths*, 'Studies on Medical and Population Subjects' no. 45: 9–17, London: HMSO.
McGrath, P.G. (1982) 'The psychiatrist's view,' in J.R. Hamilton and H. Freeman (eds) *Dangerousness: Psychiatric Assessment and Management*, London: Royal College of Psychiatrists.
McKeown, T. (1980) *The Role of Medicine*, Princeton: Princeton University Press, quoted by P.B. Medawar, 'In defence of doctors', *The New York Review* 15.5.80: 29.
McLaren, D.S. and Read, W.W.C. (1975) 'Weight/length classification of nutritional status', *The Lancet* 2: 219–21.
MacLeod, L. (1980) *Wife Battering in Canada – The Vicious Circle*, Ottawa: Canadian Advisory Council on the Status of Women.
Maine Department of Human Services (1983) *Children's Deaths in Maine: 1976–1980 – Final Report*..
Mark, V.H. and Ervin, F.R. (1970) *Violence and the Brain*, New York: Harper and Row.
Ministry of Indian Affairs and Northern Development, Canada (1980) *Indian Conditions: A Survey*, Ottawa.
Mitchell, R.G. (ed.) (1980) *Child Health in the Community*, Edinburgh: Churchill Livingstone.
Mohr, J.W. and McKnight, C.K. (1971) 'Violence as a function of age and relationship with special reference to matricide', *Canadian Psychiatric Association Journal* 16: 29–32.
Montgomery, S. (1982) 'Problems in the perinatal prediction of child abuse', *British Journal of Social Work*, 12 (2): 189–96.

Morris, T. and Blom-Cooper, L.A. (1964) *A Calendar of Murder: Criminal Homicide in England since 1957,* London: Michael Joseph.

Morse, C.W., Sahler, O.J.Z., and Friedman, S.B. (1970) 'A three-year follow-up study of abused and neglected children', *American Journal of Diseases of Children* 120: 439–46.

Nadelson, C.C. (1986) , presidential address: 'Health care directions: who cares for patients', *American Journal of Psychiatry* 143 (8): 952.

National Center for Child Abuse and Neglect (NCCAN) (1981) National Study of Incidence and Severity of CAN, Washington: NCCAN.

—— (1984) National Study of Incidence and Severity of CAN, Washington: NCCAN.

Newberger, E.H. and Bourne, R. (1978) 'The medicalization and legalization of child abuse', in J.M. Eekelaar and S.N. Katz (eds.) *Family Violence, an International and Interdisciplinary Study,* Toronto: Butterworth.

Newberger, E.H., Newberger, C.M., and Hampton, R.L.. (1983) 'Child abuse: the current theory base and future research needs, *Journal of the American Academy of Child Psychiatry* 22 (3): 262–8.

New York City Mayor's Task Force on Child Abuse and Neglect (1983) *Report on the Preliminary Study of Child Fatalities in New York City.*

Nicholls, E.S. and Davies, J.W. (1980) *Accidents, Poisonings and Violence in Canada: An Overview,* Ottawa: Department of National Health and Welfare.

Nottinghamshire Area Review Committee, Standing Inquiry Panel (1985) *Report of the Inquiry into the Case of Reuben Carthy, d.o.b. 7.4.82.*

Oates, R.K. (1984) 'Personality development after physical abuse', *Archives of Disease in Childhood* 59: 147–50.

Oliver, J.E. (1977) 'Families in which children suffer maltreatment', In A. White Franklin (ed.) (1977) *The Challenge of Child Abuse,* London: Academic Press.

—— (1983) 'Dead children from problem families in NE Wiltshire', *British Medical Journal,* 286: 115–17.

Oliver, J.E. and Taylor, A. (1971) 'Five generations of ill-treated children in one family pedigree', *British Journal of Psychiatry* 119: 473–80.

O'Neill, J.A., Meacham, W.F., Griffin, P.P., and Sawyers, J.L. (1973) 'Patterns of injury in the battered child syndrome', *The Journal of Trauma* 13 (4): 332–9.

Ontario Association of Professional Social Workers, (1983)

'Report of the Children's Services Committee subcommittee on the trial of the staff of Brockville CAS in connection with the Jeffery Disotel case' (unpublished).

Ontario, Office of the Registrar General (yearly) *Vital Statistics*.

Ounsted, C. (1972) 'Biographical science: an essay on developmental medicine' in B. Mandelbrote and M.C. Gelder (eds) *Psychiatric Aspects of Medical Practice*, London: Staples Press, quoted in Lynch and Roberts 1982.

Ounsted, C. and Lynch, M.A. (1976) 'Family pathology as seen in England', in R.E. Helfer and C.H. Kempe (eds.) *Child Abuse and Neglect: The Family and the Community*, Cambridge, Mass.: Ballinger.

Ounsted, C., Roberts, J.C., Gordon, M., and Milligan, B. (1982) 'Fourth goal of perinatal medicine', *British Medical Journal* 284 (6319): 879–82.

Parton, N. (1979) 'The natural history of child abuse: a study in social problem definition', *British Journal of Social Work* 9 (4): 431–51.

—— (1981) 'Child abuse, social anxiety and welfare', *British Journal of Social Work* 11: 391–414.

—— (1985) *The Politics of Child Abuse*, London: Macmillan.

Pearce, J.W., and Walsh, K.L. (1984) 'Characteristics of abused children: research findings', *Canada's Mental Health* 32 (2): 2–5.

Peckham, C.S. and Jobling, M. (1975) 'Deaths from non-accidental injuries in childhood' (letter) *British Medical Journal* 2 (21): 686.

Pelton, L.H. (1978) 'Child abuse and neglect: the myth of classlessness', *American Journal of Orthopsychiatry* 48 (4): 608–17.

Pennsylvania Medicine (1978) 'Child abuse report proves value of Act 124', *Pennsylvania Medicine* 81 (7).

Pfohl, S. (1977) 'The discovery of child abuse', in J.V. Cook and R.T. Bowles (eds) *Child Abuse Commission and Omission*, Toronto: Butterworth.

Pharoah, P.O.D. and Macfarlane, A. (1982) 'Recent trends in postneonatal mortality' , in *Studies in Sudden Infant Deaths*, no. 45, Office of Population Censuses and Surveys, London School of Hygiene and Tropical Medicine, London: HMSO.

Philp, A.F. and Timms, N. (1957) *The Problem of the Problem Family*, London: Family Service Units.

Pizzey, E. and Shapiro, J. (1982) *Prone to Violence*, Feltham, Middlesex: Hamlyn Paperbacks.

Reed, R.B. (1984) 'Height and weight measures' , in D.K. Walker and J.B. Richmond (eds) *Monitoring Child Health in the US:*

Selected Issues and Policies, Cambridge, Mass.: Harvard University Press.

Reidy, T.J. (1977) 'The aggressive characteristics of abused and neglected children', *Journal of Clinical Psychology* 33 (4): 1140–5.

Resnick, P.J. (1969) 'Child murder by parents: a psychiatric review of filicide', *American Journal of Psychiatry* 126 (3): 325–34.

Roberts, J., Lynch M.A., and Goulding, J. (1980) 'Post-neonatal mortality in children from abusing families', *British Medical Journal*, 281 (6233), 102–4.

Robertshaw, C. (1981) *Child Protection in Canada*, Ottawa: Health and Welfare Canada.

(Rodenburg, M. (1971a) 'Child murder by a depressed mother: a case report', *Canadian Psychiatric Association Journal* 16 (1): 49–53.

—— (1971b) 'Child murder by depressed parents', *Canadian Psychiatric Association Journal* 16 (1): 1–47.

Rose, N. (1976) *Register of Suspected NAI. A Report on Registers Maintained in Leeds and Manchester by NSPCC Special Units*, London: NSPCC.

Rosenbloom, L. (1985) 'The outcome of abuse for children: adoption and fostering', *The Quarterly Journal of British Agencies for Adoption and Fostering* 9 (2): 36–8.

Rowe, D.S., Leonard, M.F., Seashore, M.R., Lewiston, N.J., and Anderson, F.P. (1970) 'A hospital program for the detection and registration of abused and neglected children', *New England Journal of Medicine* 282 (17): 950–2.

Royal College of General Practitioners (HC.329.11, 1977: 149), quoted by Hallett and Stevenson 1980: 37.

Rutstein, D.D., Berenberg, W., Chalmers, T.C., Child, C.G., Fishman, A.P., and Perrin, E.B. (1976) 'Measuring the quality of medical care', *New England Journal of Medicine* 294: 582–8.

Ryan, W. (1976) *Blaming the Victim*, New York: Random House.

Samaroff, A.J. and Chandler, M.J. (1975) 'Reproductive risk and the continuum of caretaking casualty', in F.D. Horowitz (ed.) *Review of Child Development Research*, vol. 4, Chicago: University of Chicago Press.

Schloesser, P.T. (1964) 'The abused child', *Bulletin of the Menniger Clinic* 28 (5): 260–8.

Schur, E.M. (1973) *Radical Nonintervention: Re-thinking the Juvenile Delinquency Problem*, New Jersey: Prentice-Hall.

Scott, P.D. (1973a) 'Parents who kill their children', *Medicine, Science and the Law* 13 (2): 120–6.

—— (1973b) 'Fatal battered baby cases', *Medicine, Science and the Law* 13 (3): 197–210.

Scottish Education Department (1975) Social Work Services Group *Report of the Committee of Inquiry into the consideration given in the steps taken toward securing the welfare of Richard Clark by Perth Town Council and other bodies or persons concerned*, Edinburgh: HMSO.

The Select Committee on Violence in Marriage (1975) *Report from the Select Committee on Violence in Marriage together with the proceedings of the committee, Session 1974–5*, vol 1, London: HMSO.

Shaheen, E., Husain, S.A., and Hays, J. (1975) 'Child abuse – a medical emergency', *Missouri Medicine* 72 (9): 532–50.

Simons, B., Downs, E.F., Hurster, M.M., and Archer, M. (1966) 'Child abuse: epidemiological study of medically reported cases', *New York State Journal of Medicine* 66: 2783–8.

Skinner, A.E. and Castle, R.L. (1969) *78 Battered Children: A Retrospective Study*, London: NSPCC.

Smith, S.M. (1975) *The Battered Child Syndrome*, London: Butterworth.

—— and Hanson, R. (1975) 'Interpersonal relationships and child-rearing practice in 214 parents of battered children', *British Journal of Psychiatry* 127 (6): 513–25.

Social Work Today (1986) Tyra Henry Investivation 'Delay will fuel criticism', *Social Work Today* 17 (35): 9.

Somerset Area Review Committee for Non-accidental Injury to Children (1977) *Report of the Panel Review on Wayne Brewer*.

Speight, A.N.P., Bridson, J.M., and Cooper, C. (1979) 'Follow-up survey of cases of child abuse seen in Newcastle General Hospital 1974–5', *Child Abuse and Neglect*, 3 (2) 555.

Steele, B.F. and Pollock, C.B. (1968) 'A psychiatric study of parents who abuse infants and small children', in R.E. Helfer and C.H. Kempe (eds) *The Battered Child*, Chicago: University of Chicago Press.

Stevenson, O. (1974) 'Minority reports on events up to 22 November, 1971', in *DHSS Report of the Committee of Inquiry into the Care and Supervision Provided in Relation to Maria Colwell*, London: HMSO.

—— (1979) 'Comment: tragedies revisited', *Social Work Today* 10 (21): 1–3.

Straus, M.A., Gelles, R.J., and Steinmetz, S.K. (1980) *Behind Closed Doors: Violence in the American Family*, New York: Doubleday/Anchor.

Sunday Times (1973) 'Two babies are battered to death each day', 11 November 1973: 1. London.

Tanner, J.M., Whitehouse, R.H., and Takaishi, M. (1966) 'Standards from birth to maturity for height weight, height velocity, and weight velocity, "British Children" (1965) Part 1', *Archives of Diseases in Childhood* 41 (219): 454–71.

Teitelbaum, M.S. and Winter, J.M. (1985) *The Fear of Population Decline*, Orlando, Florida: Academic Press.

Texas Department of Human Resources (1981) *A Study of Child Deaths Attributed to Abuse and Neglect*, Austin, Texas: Child Abuse and Neglect Resource Center.

Titmuss, R.M. (1943) *Birth, Poverty and Wealth*, London: Hamish Hamilton.

Trowell, J. and Castle, R.L. (1981) 'Treating abused children', *Child Abuse and Neglect* 5 (2): 187–92.

US Department of Health and Human Services (1981a) *National Study of the Incidence and Severity of Child Abuse and Neglect*, Washington, DC: DHSS (Pub. No. (OHDS) 81–30325).

—— (1981b) *Better Health for our Children: A National Strategy: The Report of the Select Panel for the Promotion of Child Health 1*: 109–10, Washington: US Government Printing Office.

—— (1981c) *Better Health for our Children: A National Strategy: The Report of the Select Panel for the Promotion of Child Health*, IV, Background Papers: 27, Washington: US Government Printing Office.

Vietze, P.M., Falsey, S., O'Connor, S., Sandler, H., Sherrod, K., and Altmeir, W.A. (1980) 'Newborn behavioural and interactional characteristics of non-organic failure-to-thrive infants', in T.M. Field (ed.) *High Risk Infants and Children, Adult and Peer Interactions*, London: Academic Press.

Whitten, C.F. (1981) 'Growth failure', in N.S. Ellerstein (ed.) *Child Abuse and Neglect: A Medical Reference*, New York: John Wiley.

Williams, B. (1982) 'Theory as a basis for practice', in Social Work Services Group, Scottish Education Department (ed.) *Violence in the Family: Theory and Practice in Social Work*, Edinburgh: HMSO.

World Health Organisation (1977–8) *Manual of the International Statistical Classification of Disease, Injuries and Causes of Death*, 2nd vol., Geneva.

—— (1985) *World Health Statistics Annual*, Geneva.

Name Index

Subject Index